Contemplation
in a World
of Action

Gethsemani Studies

*in Psychological and
Religious Anthropology*

Ernest Daniel Carrere, o.c.s.o.
Series Editor

Funded by a generous grant from
Richard C. Colton, Jr.

Thomas Merton

Contemplation in a World of Action

Foreword by Robert Coles, M.D.

University of Notre Dame Press
NOTRE DAME, INDIANA

Designed by Wendy McMillen
Set in 10.5/14 Galliard by The Book Page, Inc.

Library of Congress Cataloging-in-Publication Data
Merton, Thomas, 1915–1968.
    Contemplation in a world of action / Thomas Merton.
        p.   cm. — (Gethsemani studies in psychological and religious
anthropology)
    ISBN 0-268-00834-5 (pbk. : alk. paper)
    1. Monastic and religious life.   2. Spiritual life—Catholic
Church.   I. Title.   II. Series.
    BX2435.M46   1999
    248.8'94—dc21   98-46482

∞ *The paper used in this publication meets the minimum requirements*
of the American National Standard for Information Sciences—Permanence of
Paper for Printed Library Materials, ANSI Z39.48-1984

Contents

Foreword

The pages that follow give us a great gift: Thomas Merton, the well-known storyteller who wrote with an engaging, sometimes captivating lyrical intensity, as well as essayist who dared contemplate in the middle years of this past century an America gone awry, both at home and in its actions abroad, now addresses us in quite another way.

This very Thomas Merton, so known to many of us for his life's moral and spiritual drama, for his courageous, compelling, often special and idiosyncratic voice (his manner of being!) turns his attention (and with it, ours) to the world he called his own for so long, that of the monastery and, beside it, the secular world we take for granted in our daily lives. Ironically, Merton does so with fear of irony. He who took sharp and pointed aim at many secularists and the occasional emptiness and sadness of their lives now reaches out with a telling gratitude and humility to those whose thoughts and theories, whose ways of seeing and understanding, have something (so he feels) to offer the "monastic milieu." A whole tradition of psychological introspection and social observation is daringly embraced, welcomed, given close scrutiny for all it can mean to monks who are, after all, fellow human beings of us who live in colleges and universities, in hospitals, law firms, and places of business.

In a sense, it is no surprise that Merton here so vigorously and knowingly turns to Freud and his intellectual descendants. Again and again the word "identity" or the phrase "identity crisis" gets summoned, although nowhere mentioned is the name of child psychoanalyst Erik H. Erikson, who first used this language. His immensely important writing and research constantly emphasize the struggle so many of us wage, in adolescence and beyond, as we try to find a personal destiny for ourselves and try also to make commitments to others. We give ourselves over to others, both individuals and institutions and, more broadly, to places where we work and to neighborhoods in which we live, while reserving for ourselves a certain distance: the right, it can be said, to be appreciative and responsive and loyal, with the obligation to find a proper respect for our own personal or private ideas and ideals.

Indeed, as I read through Merton's comments on the monastic life as it has developed and changed over the centuries (and not least here in America), I kept remembering Erik H. Erikson's words as I read them in his various writings and as I was privileged to hear them as a member of a seminar he taught and, eventually, as someone who interviewed him many times, often with the help of a tape recorder—in the end, writing his biography.

No wonder, then, I remembered a particular conversation with Erikson when I read a chapter titled "The Identity Crisis" in Merton's book. In fact, throughout the book, in chapter after chapter, the child psychiatrist and psychoanalyst in me was stirred, as was the student of Erikson and of his teacher Anna Freud (she almost single-handedly got her father to pay close heed to young people and their tensions as they tried to find a life for themselves).

Erikson never allowed himself to forget his own situation. He could be a bemused, even worried observer of America's youth, its young men and women at times lost in their fads, crushes, kicks, but not rarely lost in themselves, in preoccupations, worries, fears that were all too unnerving. Nevertheless, like Merton, he could readily turn his gaze inward and thereby take stock of the profession that meant a lot to him, the people he knew as colleagues, the places they assembled. Thus, in his Harvard Library study during the summer of 1967 amidst the struggles of the civil rights era, many of them instigated and kept going by young people in the midst of "adolescence," this response after I had given him some descriptions of my work in the South with those youths: "As I listen to you I realize how much they have to say to people like you and me: *we* have some rules and regulations, some outmoded customs and ideas and principles to examine and outgrow, *both!* I look at our [psychoanalytic] institutions, and I see plenty of the conformity and smugness some of our 'rebellious' adolescents denounce. It's so easy for *us* to use our psychological language to put down others—and all the while we fail to notice our own shortcomings, and worse! That's the big question, once you start being really honest with yourself (never mind honest about what you see in others!)—how do you keep your eyes and ears open, and hold on to what you've been given in your profession? I mean, how do you accept what you really do value— and take that acceptance seriously enough so that you see where mistakes have been made, wrong directions pursued?"

He had himself stressed "fidelity" as a proper and salutary out-come of the "identity crisis"—the way one caught up in such confusion, turmoil, uncertainty, and perplexity can at the same time explore new ideas and new ways of seeing, being, and learn as well what really matters in this or that world, what is worth respecting on the one hand or setting aside, leaving behind on the other. "Erik walks a tightrope often with ease and grace," Anna Freud told me in London as she, very much like him, was distinguishing between what of a particular tradition she held close to her heart but also found worthy of criticism, in need of vigorous disagreement, refu-tation. In her amplifying words: "Sometimes we become all too sure of ourselves, all too willing to denounce others, renounce what they said—a measure of our passion to control things and, I regret to say, hear only the echoes of our own voices!"

I know Thomas Merton would have shared with Miss Freud and with Erik Erikson, were they somehow brought together, the expe-riences he shares here with us. He would have heard from them, in return, their assents, seen from them nods, widened eyes of interest and of awakened memory and reflection.

Here is a book that very much belongs to any of us who want to consider young people as they seek their vocations, and to older people who need to stop and think not only what they believe and want to see happening in others, but what has happened in themselves, to them and their co-workers, trusted colleagues.

Always the honest, open-minded witness, the bold explorer, Thomas Merton is always, too, the knight of faith, anxious to prove the resiliency, the breadth and depth of his beloved religious and spiritual legacy, anxious to affirm his obvious adherence to its teachings, its centuries-old tenets that are still handed down, but anxious to do so with candor and a thoroughgoing intellectual tenacity, a psychological acuity, all rendered with the narrative skill and brilliance we have come to expect of him. True, he has left us for his maker—but this book, like others of his, keeps him very much where we want him, need him, right in our (thinking) midst.

Robert Coles, M.D.

Preface

Gethsemani Studies in Psychological and Religious Anthropology is a long name for a series of books about a very elemental reality: being human. One does not have to agree with Kierkegaard that being human is becoming human, but we all recognize that to some measure we must deepen the person we are and that the task is a challenging and never-ending concern. Focusing on this imperative, Gethsemani Studies explores, through the twin perspectives of psychology and religion, the dynamics and depths of being fully human.

An integrated or dialogical perspective is always anticipated in the works; nevertheless, a title favoring the religious standpoint may appear if it bears psychological ramifications, while a title devoted to psychological issues may appear if it is foundational or contributes to the integrated and humanizing dialogue.

This dialogue embraces the entire range of dynamic psychology, from Freud and Jung to Kohut and Lacan, with special predilection, perhaps, for the insights of psychoanalytic object relations theory, while the work of Kernberg, Spotnitz, and Searles, to name only three, offers the promise of equal enrichment.

Affirming that one's "first task is to be fully human," Thomas Merton's *Contemplation in a World of Action,* reissued here in a restored, corrected edition, is the first work of our series. The spiritual and psychological insights of these essays were nurtured in the milieu of monastic renewal, but their issues are universal, as Merton lays a foundation for personal growth and transformation. Above all, this classic underscores that there is no dichotomy or dualism between being spiritual and being human.

Those familiar with the 1971 edition will note that five chapters on the eremitical life do not appear in this volume. While thriving incidentally in some of our monasteries, the hermit life is no longer a burning issue in the order, and the vast majority of Merton's readership does not have the opportunity to enjoy the demands of eremitical solitude. More to the point, these chapters were not part of the book that Merton prepared; they were added after his death in an effort to collect a portion of his unpublished papers. Readers who still wish access will be pleased to know that these essays are being published by another press.

The 1971 edition proved to have a number of typesetting errors. Several obscured the author's meaning, and in one instance the omission reversed Merton's point completely.

Several paragraphs from Merton's original essay have been restored to chapter two because their absence in the published version produced a glitch in the chapter's logic. In addition, Merton's prose has been restored in a handful of places where the editorial pen had attempted to improve a transition, with results that were clearly from an alien hand. Other restorations clarify incidentally.

Many people are responsible for Gethsemani Studies and for the publication of its first volume.

Above all, the series would have remained an impossibility without the presence of Dick Colton. Dick recognized in the earliest, most speculative discussions that the series represented a worthy project. His dedicated interest cut through the hesitation that impedes new endeavors, jump-starting the involvement of all, while his generous grant underwriting the series enabled Notre Dame and the Abbey of Gethsemani to work concretely toward its realization.

Jeff Gainey of the University of Notre Dame Press immediately perceived the potential of such a series and has labored as a wonderful colleague to realize its possibilities. Jim Langford, press director, has been an indispensable collaborator, sagely contributing insights from his rich publishing experience. The superb staff he and Jeff have assembled has been an absolute delight throughout our preparations. Father Timothy Kelly, Abbot of Gethsemani, has made it possible for me to assume the full-time burdens and joys that being editor imparts.

Jennifer Mick of the Merton Studies Center in Louisville has always been of great and generous assistance whenever I appeared for research. Edward Bauer helped me check the initial computer scan of the *CWA* manuscript, while preliminary cover graphics were evaluated by Jeannette Cantrell of the Bardstown Art Gallery. Bill and Mary Lou McCaa, Kim, Ann, and Grant Hutton have all contributed to the project. Brother Patrick Hart, keystone of the Merton community, has been a marvelous colleague and a great help. Dr. Robert Coles can't be thanked enough for his wholehearted response to our invitation to contribute a foreword. His collaboration has been a blessing beyond words for all of us.

Ernest Daniel Carrere

Contemplation
in a World
of Action

ONE

Renewal of Life in the Monastic Milieu

I
Problems and Prospects

Before the Second Vatican Council the monastic orders had begun to consider the question of renewal. Some efforts at renewal were already under way. But these efforts mostly presupposed that existing institutions would continue as they already were and had been for centuries. Changes in the horarium, in the liturgical celebration offices, in the formation and recruitment of new members, in the size and character of the community, in the understanding and observance of the vows would suffice to meet the requirements of aggiornamento. After the Council, even though the decree *Perfectae Caritatis* was very general and in no sense revolutionary, religious as a whole have begun to question the basic institutional structures of the religious life. Though this is not what the Council formally enjoined upon them, it has been an inevitable result of the investigations and self-questioning which the Council demanded.

The monastic orders have hitherto proved themselves among the most conservative in the Church in the sense that they have tended more than the active institutes to preserve a traditional and somewhat archaic style of life. Before the Council, even those who were in favor of the most sweeping changes still seemed to have thought of the monastic community as permanently established on medieval foundations. The renewal of the monastic life has seemed, to many monks and to general chapters, to demand merely a modernization and adaptation of familiar medieval patterns, freeing them of all that was most obviously feudal and antique, but maintaining their structure, since that structure is conceived to be essential to the monastic way of life.

This is obviously not enough. The monks have been under fire from critics outside the monastic orders. Many have openly questioned the right of the monastic orders to continue in existence. It is a bit ironic to see that when Protestants themselves have begun to rediscover monastic values, the Lutheran arguments against monasticism have been adopted and turned against the monks by some Catholic publicists. Thus the very essence of the monastic life itself is attacked, as if the very nature of monasticism made all renewal and adaptation to the present needs of the Church impossible. This presupposes, however, that the monastic life is *essentially* medieval and that if the medieval formalities, ritualism, observances and conceptions of the vowed life are discarded, there will be nothing left. What complicates matters is that the conservative element in monasticism does, to a great extent, accept this challenge on their critics' terms, assuming that the medieval forms are of the essence and must therefore be preserved. This incites the younger and more radical element to side with those who demand that the monks leave the cloister, come out into the world, join in the labor of evangelization and justify their existence by active and secular lives. This sweeping attack takes for granted that "the contemplative life" is sterile, foolish, wasteful, selfish and that it serves no purpose but to keep monks immature, walled off from contemporary reality, in a state of self-delusion, dedicated to childish formalities.

Some monks are quite willing to accept this diagnosis, and they also maintain that the only remedy is active work in the world. In effect, however, this extreme solution does not differ from the anti-monastic view in any way. It amounts to an abandonment of the monastic vocation—a capitulation to the arguments of those who deny that there is any place left for a life which "leaves the world." Indeed, the vagaries of a theology and spirituality which overemphasized "contempt for the world" have all been blamed on the monks. Some critics even seem to think that all the aberrations in the theology and devotionalism of an entrenched and defensive Christianity, suspicious of the world and excessively clerical in its outlook, are to be traced to monasticism. It is true that medieval monasticism did exercise an enormous influence on postmedieval spirituality but, once again, must we assume that medieval monasticism is the *only* possible form?

Medieval monasticism was feudal, aristocratic, highly ritualized, thoroughly organized. The medieval monk might indeed lead a personally austere life, and the atmosphere of the monasteries was often not only highly cultured and spiritual but often genuinely mystical. Contemplative *otium* (leisure) was paid for by hard sacrifice, but the monk (while no doubt seriously concerning himself with the Benedictine ladder of humility) found himself at the top of society in a privileged kind of existence. This air of aristocratic leisure, of privilege and of lordly isolation from the common run of men became more frankly questionable when monasteries were, in fact, places of easy and comfortable retirement from the responsibilities of secular existence. There is, then, plenty of historical warrant for the suspicion that the monastic life can become merely a refuge for the inadequate. On the other hand, the struggle to restore monasticism after the French Revolution had almost swept it out of existence certainly modified this. There are, it is true, a few highly aristocratic communities still in existence. No one seriously considers them ready for renewal. Everyone recognizes that these do indeed belong to the feudal past. Nevertheless this suspicion has caused many to question all large and manifestly prosperous monasteries as if they were as feudal as twelfth-century Cluny. This is by no means true. Nevertheless, it must be admitted that the nineteenth-century restorers of monasticism were not only traditionalists in theology and spirituality but even at times royalists and feudalists in politics. They deliberately attempted to restore the medieval structures of monasticism in Europe as models for a reformation of medieval society. Those who came from Europe to make new foundations in America were seldom tempted to question this concept until very recent years.

The fact that this "triumphalist" monasticism is seriously undermined today means that all the arguments which it advanced to justify its existence are now questionable.

Is it enough to wall the monk off in a little contemplative enclave and there allow him to ignore the problems and crises of the
world, should he forget the way other men have to struggle for
a living and simply let his existence be justified by the fact that
he punctually recites the hours in choir, attends conventual Mass,
strives for interior perfection and makes an honest effort to "live a
life of prayer"? Do these innocuous occupations make him a "contemplative"? Or do they make of the monastery a dynamo which
"generates spiritual power" for those who are too busy to pray?
The famous argument of Pius XI in *Umbratilem* (praising the
Carthusians) has been twisted out of shape by decades of routine
monastic self-justification, and the sound, traditional theology of
that document has been gradually distorted into a quaint superstition, a kind of magic prayer-wheel concept which has lost all power
to convince anyone.

On the other hand, no one who is familiar with authentic monastic theology will be seriously disturbed by these arguments, which
are all based on the false premise that monasticism is and can only
be the sham gothic stereotype re-created a hundred and fifty years
ago. The monastic community does not have to be a museum or a
liturgical showplace with a college or brewery attached. There are
other possibilities, and the monk can justify his existence without
rushing back to join in the apostolic life which is, in fact, just as seriously questioned as the monastic life itself.

The essence of the monastic vocation is positive, not negative. It
is more than a matter of turning one's back on the world and then
doing something or other that can be effectively carried on behind
walls—saying prayers, painting pictures, brewing beer, navel-gazing,
or what have you.

The monk is (at least ideally) a man who has responded to an
authentic call of God to a life of freedom and detachment, a "desert
life" outside normal social structures. He is liberated from certain
particular concerns in order that he may belong entirely to God. His
life is one dedicated completely to love, the love of God and man,
but a love that is not determined by the requirements of a special
task. The monk is, or should be, a Christian who is mature enough

and decided enough to live without the support and consolation of family, job, ambition, social position or even active mission in the apostolate. He is also mature enough and determined enough to use this freedom for one thing only: the love and praise of God and the love of other men. He is mature and free enough to exercise a love of other men that is not confined to this or that apostolic routine, this or that particular form of work.

The monk is not defined by his task, his usefulness. In a certain sense he is supposed to be "useless" because his mission is not to *do* this or that job but to *be* a man of God. He does not live in order to exercise a specific function: his business is life itself. This means that monasticism aims at the cultivation of a certain *quality* of life, a level of awareness, a depth of consciousness, an area of transcendence and of adoration which are not usually possible in an active secular existence. This does not imply that the secular level is entirely godless and reprobate, or that there can be no real awareness of God in the world. Nor does it mean that worldly life is to be considered wicked or even inferior. But it does mean that more immersion and total absorption in worldly business end by robbing one of a certain necessary perspective. The monk seeks to be free from what William Faulkner called "the same frantic steeplechase toward nothing" which is the essence of "worldliness" everywhere.

Teilhard de Chardin has developed a remarkable mystique of secularity which is certainly necessary for our time when the vast majority of men have no choice but to seek and find God in the busy world. But where did Teilhard acquire this perspective? In the deserts of Asia, in vast solitudes which were in many ways more "monastic" than the cloisters of our monastic institutions. So too Bonhoeffer, regarded as an opponent of all that monasticism stands for, himself realized the need for certain "monastic" conditions in order to maintain a true perspective in and on the world. He developed these ideas when he was awaiting his execution in a Nazi prison.

What the monastic life should provide, then, is a special awareness and perspective, an authentic understanding of God's presence in the world and his intentions for man. A merely fictitious and abstract isolation does not provide this awareness. The symbol of medieval monasticism is the wall and the cloister. Instead of merely being self-enclosed, the modern monk might perhaps emulate Teilhard in the desert of Mongolia or Bonhoeffer in prison. These are more primitive and more authentic examples of what a charismatic solitude can mean!

The need for a certain *distance* from the world does not make the monk love the world less. Nor does it imply that he never has any contact with the outside world. Certainly the monastic community has the right and duty to create a certain solitude for the monks: it is no sin to live a silent life. But at the same time the monastic community owes other men a share in that quiet and that solitude. Obviously the balance must be very delicate, for quiet and solitude are destroyed by the movement of crowds. But the fact remains all the more true: the monk has a quiet, relatively isolated existence in which it is possible to concentrate more on the *quality* of life and its mystery and, thus, to escape in some measure from the senseless tyranny of quantity.

It is certainly true, then, that this special perspective necessarily implies that the monk will be in some sense critical of the world, of its routines, its confusions, and its sometimes tragic failures to provide other men with lives that are fully sane and human. The monk can and must be open to the world, but at the same time he must be able to get along without a naive and uncritical "secularity" which blandly assumes that everything in the world is at every moment getting better and better for everybody. This critical balance is no doubt difficult to achieve. But it is something which the monk *owes to the world*. For the monastic life has a certain prophetic character about it: not that the monk should be able to tell what is about to happen in the Kingdom of God, but in the sense that he is a living witness to the freedom of the sons of God and to the essential difference between that freedom and the spirit of the world. While admitting that God "so loved the world that he gave his only begotten Son" (John 3:16), the monk does not forget that when the Son of God came into the world it did not receive him because it *could* not. It was bound to oppose and reject him (John 1:10–11, 7:7, 15:18, 14:17, etc.).

The monastic life then must maintain this prophetic seriousness, this wilderness perspective, this mistrust of any shallow optimism which overlooks the ambiguity and the potential tragedy of "the world" in its response to the Word. And there is only one way for the monk to do this: to live as a man of God who has been manifestly "called out of the world" to an existence that differs radically from that of other men, however sincere, however Christian, however holy, who have remained "in the world."

In other words, the problem of monastic renewal is this: though it must obviously involve a radical reshaping of institutional structures, the renewal is by no means merely an institutional concern. It would be a great mistake to assume that renewal is nothing but reorganization or even juridical reform. What is needed is not only new rules but new structures and new life. The new life stirs, but faintly, incoherently. It does not know if it can exist without the old structures. What is also needed is a new outlook and a new faith in the capacities of modern men to be monks in a new way. Then the organization of monastic life can perhaps become less cramped, less obsessive, less narcissistic, and new life can develop with creative spontaneity. This spontaneity should be rooted in living tradition. But living tradition must not be confused with dead conventionalism and futile routine, as it so often has been. The situation of monasticism in America is now such that a genuine renewal, and not merely a few new rules, is imperative if American monasticism is to continue a fruitful existence.

Authentic renewal is going to demand a great deal of variety and originality in experimentation. Obviously, the mere issuing of decrees and ordinances from the top down, carried out mechanically on a massive scale, will simply stifle what life is left in monasticism. On the other hand the danger of irresponsibility and levity in ill-considered innovation remains real. But renewal must be bought at the price of risk. Undoubtedly a juncture obsession with novelty for its own sake will cause the ruin of some monastic communities. The winds are blowing and a lot of dead wood is going to fall. The true strength of monasticism is to be sought in its capacity for renunciation, silence, prayer, faith, and its realization of the cross in our life.

All genuine renewal must seek life at the source of life: the cross and resurrection of Jesus.

Fortunately there are signs that such a renewal, though perhaps still tentative and painful, is trying to get under way.

The monastic orders came to America in the nineteenth century. On one hand the Cistercians (Trappists) brought with them a strictly enclosed penitential form of common life which disconcerted Americans more than it inspired them. The Benedictines brought missionary and apostolic abbeys which maintained schools, colleges, parishes, and seminaries on the frontier, thus fulfilling an urgent need, but tending to depart from the ancient contemplative tradition of monasticism.

One of the most curious phenomena in the life of the American Church after World War II was the sudden interest in the strict contemplative life of the Cistercians and the rush of vocations to the three Cistercian abbeys, which rapidly made foundations in all parts of North America and even in the Southern Hemisphere. Those of us who lived through this minor explosion took it more or less as it came, but now we look back on it aghast, realizing that we cannot really account for it and soberly aware that it was not an unequivocal success. On the contrary, most of those who entered Cistercian monasteries by the scores and even by the hundreds (there were in all about two thousand postulants received into the Gethsemani community over a period of some ten years in the forties and fifties) later took their departure. Most of those who left went during their novitiate. Others were dispensed from simple and even solemn vows.

It is perhaps too soon to decide what this commotion signified. But this much can certainly be said: there was a sincere interest in monastic ideals and a genuinely experienced *need* for what the monastic life offered. There were many authentic monastic vocations and they were *lost*. Men who clearly demonstrated their ability to live as excellent monks found themselves defeated and confused by a system that apparently frustrated their development. They discovered two things: first, that they wanted what the monastic life had to offer; second, that the monastic life was now built in such a way that what it offered remained, for many monks, a dream or an impossibility. In effect, one could live fruitfully enough as a novice, but after that one became caught in a complex and fatal machinery in which one was finally exhorted to renounce even what he had come to the monastery to find. This does not mean that the values of monasticism no longer existed, but that they were present in a form that made them morally, psychologically or spiritually inaccessible to many modern men and women. The Cistercians themselves recognized this, and already in the early fifties considerable changes began to be made in the daily schedule and in the various observances. These changes have continued to be made, and the whole shape of the life has been significantly altered in the last fifteen years. But the problem of renewal remains just as real and just as perplexing as before, since changes in schedule and in details of observance do not seem to have gotten down to the root of the matter. Nor will they ever do so as long as medieval or baroque attitudes prevail.

Meanwhile monastic foundations of a new type began to be made, in the fifties, more than ten years before the Council. Already the "Primitive Benedictine" monasteries like Mount Saviour and Weston felt that monasticism had to get off to a new start. Pioneering efforts were attempted, especially in the vernacular liturgy. The community structure of two classes, lay brothers and priests, was modified to create a community of simple monks in one class, only a few of whom were priests. At the same time the Primitive Benedictines applied themselves to a more serious study of monastic tradition and of the Bible, while experimenting in more flexible and simple formulas of monastic observance than those which had been imported from Europe by the big monasteries a century before. The keynote of the new monasticism was a simple, natural, more or less hard life in contact with nature, nourished by the Bible, the monastic fathers and the liturgy, and faithful to the ancient ideal of prayer, silence, and that "holy leisure" *(otium sanctum)* necessary for a pure and tranquil heart in which God could be experienced, tasted, in the silence and freedom of the monk's inner peace. It can be said that though the Primitive Benedictines were at first criticized (doubtless because they were envied), the older monasteries soon began in various ways to imitate them and attempt changes along lines which the Primitive Benedictine experiments had suggested. Thus even before the Council decree *Perfectae Caritatis,* all the monks were working more or less at renewal.

The ferment produced by the Council resulted in increased and unexpected activity among the Cistercians. Monks of the larger abbeys or even of their small foundations began to question the existing formula as such and to seek opportunities to make a new beginning of their own. Several small experimental foundations have therefore been made by Cistercians in various parts of the United States. These have generally not managed to get a high degree of official backing. Their state is still, at the time of writing,* too uncertain for any kind of comment, particularly since detailed information has not been readily available.

Finally, the question of a completely solitary life in hermitages has been admitted back into the full light of the monastic consciousness after centuries of burial in the darkness of suppressed fantasies. This was made possible and even necessary by the fact that Dom Jacques Winandy, a retired Benedictine abbot from Luxembourg who had lived as a hermit in Switzerland and then Martinique, formed a colony of hermits in British Columbia. This colony was recruited largely from Cistercian and Benedictine abbeys in the United States, where there have always been a few monks attracted to complete solitude. Taking stock of the situation, the Cistercians realized that a place might be made for hermit vocations within the order itself. It is now possible for Cistercians to obtain permission to live as hermits in the woods near their monasteries—a solution which had also been arrived at ten years before by the Primitive Benedictines. This in fact is nothing radically new: there exists a long tradition of Benedictine hermits going back to the time of Benedict himself. It is admittedly a good solution but it affects only a few individuals. These have the advantage of a solitary life and of freedom to develop according to their own needs and personal vocation. They have a minimum of

*[1967]

concern about temporalities, and they are able to continue their monastic life as members of the community where they made profession. Normally, however, monks have neither the desire nor the grace to live this particular kind of life, and the real problems remain to be solved in the context of common living.

All that has been attempted so far is a provisional beginning, and we cannot yet safely predict what will happen to the monastic movement in this country. One thing is certain: the destinies of the big monasteries are not what they were thought to be a decade ago, and the large new buildings put up to accommodate the many who are no longer there may one day seem a bit bleak and void. But things are certainly a lot quieter—and more peaceful. Life in a big Cistercian monastery may be far from the perfect ideal, but monastically there is still a lot to be said for it, and many of the monks may grudgingly admit that they never had it so good. The admission is, however, no sign of complete satisfaction, because all eyes are on the future, and the present state of affairs is not accepted by anyone as final. How good do they expect to have it?

Speaking as one who has more or less retired to a marginal existence, I am inclined to think they are not yet quite sure themselves. Nor is anyone quite sure just what direction the monastic renewal will take. It may go in different directions in different places: one monastery may be concerned with more openness to the world, another with a return to the desert wilderness and solitude. There is room for variety and for original solutions, provided always that the essence of the monastic vocation is respected. But there is uncertainty because, even to the monks themselves, that essence has seemingly never been quite clear.

In order to understand monasticism, it is important to concentrate on the *charism of the monastic vocation* rather than on the *structure of monastic institutions or the patterns of monastic observance.*

Most of the ambiguities and distresses of the current renewal seem to come from the fact that there is too much concern with changing the observances or adapting the institution and not enough awareness of the charism which the institution is meant to serve and protect. Indeed, one sometimes feels that too many monks have the cart before the horse and assume that the vocation or charism exists for the sake of the institution, that men who are called by God to the peace and inner freedom of the monastic life can be regarded as material to be exploited for the good of the monastic institution, its prestige, its money-making projects and so on.

Obviously, in a community life each monk will want to do an honest job of work and earn his share of the bread that is placed on the common table. But we must be fully aware of the fact that men do not come to a monastery today in order to live the routine busy life of an employee in a big business corporation. The mere fact that a busy life is lived in a monastic enclosure does not make it "contemplative." There are certain forms of exhausting and meaningless servitude which are characteristic of "the world." It is of the very essence of the monastic life to protest, by its simplicity and its liberty, against these servitudes. Of course there is obedience in the monastic life: it is the very heart of that life. Obedience is, paradoxically, the one guarantee of the monk's charismatic inner liberty. But obedience must always be consciously oriented to the fulfillment of the monastic vocation in the monk's own person and not *merely* to the impersonal success of some business project. Not only is there serious danger of monastic obedience being used today to frustrate the true purpose of monastic life, but the renewal may be carried out in such a way that this deformity is carefully protected and preserved. Indeed, one sometimes feels that all sorts of token changes are made on a superficial level, with care being taken to see that in no case the priority of the institution over the person will ever be threatened. In such conditions, "renewal" can never be anything but futile.

The whole question of monastic work, and of the support of the monastic community, is today an extremely vexed one. On the one hand there are monks who are claiming that the only honest way for a monk to earn his living is to go out and be a wage earner and then return at night to his community (in this case a small group) and his life of contemplation. Others are for a more complete return to nature and to primitive forms of farm work and handicrafts, etc. Still others think that a highly mechanized monastic "plant" will guarantee enough leisure for reading and contemplation. All these solutions have clear disadvantages, and they all seem to suffer from distorted perspectives and even from a kind of pragmatism that is concerned not with the essence of monasticism but with one or another aspect of it. The ones who want to go and work in factories are concerned with being and appearing poor and also with sharing the lot of the workman in the modern world. Poverty and work are, it is true, essential to the monastic life: but so too is a certain authentic solitude and isolation from the world, a certain protest against the organized and dehumanizing routines of a worldly life built around gain for its own sake. The danger is that the witness of monastic poverty will simply get lost in the mammoth machinery geared for one thing only: profit. The same thing happens when the monastery itself becomes a prosperous industrial unit with the monks working in offices and living on a comfortable income. As to the primitive and ideally agrarian setup: this tends to become a self-consciously arty-and-crafty venture in archaism which, in practice, has to be supported by benefactions from the mammon of iniquity.

When the concern for institutional adjustment is uppermost, then all monastic problems tend to fall into this kind of pattern. It becomes a struggle to adjust the institution in order to emphasize some one aspect, *some particular value,* which an individual or a group appreciates over all the others. When everything is centered on liturgy and on the harmonious, aesthetic decorum of traditional monasticity, then poverty and work may suffer. When everything is centered on poverty and labor, then the community may be overworked and lose interest in reading, prayer and contemplation. When everything is centered on "openness to the world" the monks may become agitated and self-complacent gossips and under the pretext of "charity" forget that love which originally drew them to the monastery. In the past an excessive Trappist rigorism produced communities of well-meaning and devout men who sometimes bordered on the boorish or the fanatical.

Actually, the renewal of monasticism cannot have any real meaning until it is seen as a renewal of the *wholeness* of monasticism in its *charismatic* authenticity. Instead of concentrating on this or that means, we need first of all to look more attentively at the end. And here, while we must certainly focus accurately on the traditional ideal, a little realism and common sense will not be out of place. These were, after all, characteristic of that Benedictine Rule on which, whatever may be our time and its problems, renewal will normally be based.

The charism of the monastic life is the freedom and peace of a wilderness existence, a return to the desert that is also a recovery of (inner) paradise. This is the secret of monastic "renunciation of the world." Not a *denunciation,* not a denigration, not a precipitous flight, a resentful withdrawal, but a liberation, a kind of permanent "vacation" in the original sense of "emptying." The monk simply discards the useless and tedious baggage of vain concerns and devotes himself henceforth to the one thing really necessary—the one thing that he really wants: the quest for *meaning* and for *love,* the quest for his own identity, his secret name promised him by God (Apocalypse 2:17) and for the peace of Christ which the world cannot give (John 14:27). In other words the monk renounces a life of agitation and confusion for one of order and clarity. But the order and clarity are not his own making; nor are they, so to speak, an institutional product, an effect of exterior regularity. They are the fruit of the Spirit. The monastic life is a response to the call of the Spirit to espousals and to peace in the wilderness (Hosea 2:19–20).

The monastic charism is not, however, one of pure solitude without any community. It is also a charism of brotherhood in the wilderness: for the monk, even though he may eventually, in an exceptional case, live as a hermit, is prepared for solitude by living in close brotherly relationship with his fellow monks in the monastic community. This closeness is understood as being, at least ideally, a very human and warm relationship, and the charism of the monastic life is, and has been from the beginning, a grace of *communion* in a shared quest and a participated light. It is then a charism of special love and of mutual aid in the attainment of a difficult end, in the living of a hazardous and austere life. The monk is close to his brother insofar as he realizes him to be a fellow pilgrim in the spiritual "desert." Monastic work, obedience, poverty, chastity, are all in some way colored and tempered by the communal charism of brotherhood in pilgrimage and in hope.

Obviously the monastic life is not purely charismatic. Nothing could be more ruinous for monasticism than to turn a lot of inexperienced monks loose to live without any institutional structures and without organization—or to assume them capable of improvising new institutions overnight. Though the monastic life today is too rigidly institutionalized and too hidebound with senseless traditions, the basic lines of a monastic communal structure must be preserved and the authentic wisdom, drawn from the experience of ages in which monasticism was fully *lived,* must not be lost. The new monastic communities will need to be much more democratic than in the past. The abbot will have to be a spiritual father, not a prelate, a police chief and a corporation president rolled into one. The monks will have to have much more initiative in running their own lives, and the abbot will have to concern himself more with genuine spiritual guidance than with institutional control. The spiritual role of the superior presupposes a certain freedom and discretion in the subject. The superior can no longer arrogate to himself the right to do all his subjects' thinking for them and to make all their decisions for them. Obviously, in the period of transition, mistakes will be made. But with the grace of God these mistakes themselves will be more fruitful than the stifling inertia of overcontrol. The monks will learn for themselves some lessons that they could never learn any other way.

The charism of the monastic vocation is one of simplicity and truth. The monk, whether as hermit or as cenobite, is one who abandons the routines, the clichés, the disguised idolatries and empty formalities of "the world" in order to seek the most authentic and essential meaning of the dedicated life on earth. Ideally speaking, then, the monastery should be a place of utter sincerity, without empty and deceptive formalities, without evasions, without pretenses.

Often, the rules and disciplines of community life have merely created an atmosphere of formalism and artificiality which, instead of helping the monks to live in close rapport as true brothers, served only to estrange them from one another. It is tragic that in the name of discipline and obedience monastic silence has been exploited as a means of keeping the monks out of touch with each other, indeed fearful and suspicious of one another. Monastic enclosure has at times become nothing more than a means of keeping the monks ignorant of the outside world in the hope that they would become indifferent to its tragic conflicts and not create any bother by having problems of conscience over things like war, poverty, race and revolution.

There is no question that one of the most disturbing things about the monastic institution for most of those moderns who have come seeking to give themselves to God in solitude, prayer and love, has been the current interpretation of religious vows, especially obedience. One who dedicates himself to God by vows today finds himself committed for life to a massively organized, rigidly formalistic institutional existence. Here everything is decided for him beforehand. Everything is provided for by rule and system. Initiative is not only discouraged, it becomes useless. Questions cease to have any point, for you already know the answers by heart in advance. But the trouble is that they are not answers, since they imply a firm decision to ignore your questions. Obedience then no longer consists in dedicating one's will and love to the service of God, but almost in the renunciation of all human rights, needs and feelings in order to conform to the rigid demands of an institution. The institution is identified with God and becomes an end in itself. And the monk is given to understand from the start that there is *no alternative* for him but to regard this institutional life in all its details, however arbitrary, however archaic, however meaningless to him, as the *only way* for him to be perfect in love and sincere in his quest for God. This has been impressed upon him not only as a most solemn religious duty but almost as an article of faith: indeed, the young monk who has serious problems with a life that may seem to him increasingly fruitless and even absurd, may be forcefully told that he is failing in Christian faith and verging on apostasy!

It is here that we see how far the perversion of the "spiritual dynamo" idea can sometimes be carried. The monastic institution, with its constant prayer, its regularity, its impeccable observance, its obedient and submissive monks, is implicitly regarded as a beautiful machine which, as long as it runs smoothly, obtains infallible results from God. The object of the monastic order, of the superiors, chapters and so on, is to make sure that the machine is well oiled and keeps running exactly as it should. Faith assures us that the monastic machine is exerting an irresistible influence on God who, it is assumed, takes a mysterious pleasure in the operation of this ingenious toy. The legal clockwork of monasticism has been specially devised by the Church to enchant the Almighty and to cunningly manipulate his power. For what? For the institutional benefit of the rest of the Church—its manifold projects, the conversion of infidels, the return of heretics and apostates to humble submission, the humiliation and destruction of the Church's enemies and so on. Obviously such a valuable machine must not be tampered with in any way. "Renewal" simply means a cleaning and oiling that will make the clock run more perfectly than before!

The most tragic misunderstandings have arisen from this attitude which, in some cases, one must frankly admit it, savors of gross superstition and arrogance. In any event, it has led to the ruin of many monastic vocations which seemed to be in every respect serious and genuine. One feels that if there had been a little flexibility, a little humaneness shown—if the monk, when he began to have trouble with the life, had been allowed a change of scene or a more genuinely human relationship with his brothers—he might have adjusted to the life after all. Unfortunately, there still exists such a grave fear of the austere institutional image being tarnished by concessions that vocations are sacrificed in order to preserve a monastic facade.

As everywhere else in American life, there has been an enormous amount of neurotic anxiety in monasteries. The tendency has been, in each case, to blame the individual. Sometimes, however, one wonders if a certain neurotic pattern has not finally got built into the system itself. Indeed one might at times wonder if the system does not require and favor neurotic insecurity, both in subjects and in superiors, in order to continue functioning as it does. Certainly neurosis is not endemic in monasticism as such. But a particular concept of monastic regularity and obedience does seem to encourage

neuroses while loudly deploring them and advocating therapy—
which then becomes part of the process.

Monks are human in their needs, their frailties and also in their unconscious efforts to compensate for what they have given up by
leaving the world. The man who has renounced family life and the
love of children may, without realizing it himself, seek compensation
in some other way—for instance by dominating other people. Men
and women in the cloister have sometimes been notoriously aggressive, ambitious, given to a bitter and thoroughly worldly struggle for
political power in their community. Those who lack the forcefulness
required to exercise power themselves are content to live as monastic
Peter Pans in passive dependence on those whom they flatter and try
to manipulate. In the long run, they find that this passivity too implies a certain power, for by subservience and manipulation they can
get their own will incorporated into the system and have their ideas
imposed by a superior.

The man who loves power can, with most idealistic motives,
seek to gratify this love not only by exercising his power over his con-
temporaries, but even by building his will into the structure of the
institution so that later generations will go on being dominated by
him long after his death. In the current effort at renewal, it may
happen that this kind of underground power struggle is being carried on without the monks realizing it too clearly. Many of those
who are most enthusiastic and active in the work of "renewal" seem
to be going about it in such a way as to make sure that *their* ideas and
plans will not be seriously contested and that, in the end, it will be
their reforms that will win out. It also unfortunately happens that the
adjustment these people advocate is superficial only: and if they have
their way, they will hand on the status quo, embellished with a few
trimmings of their own, and it will be a monument to themselves.
This "monumental," "massive" and basically static concept of the
monastic life is certainly to blame for the institutional rigidities that
prevent true adjustment today. But such monasticism as this cannot
survive. It is doomed. The sense of outrage, protest and refusal is
too evident in monastic communities. Unfortunately there is also a
growing impatience, and those who allow themselves to become ob-

sessed with the problem may forget that monastic renewal is God's work and not theirs, and they too may be tempted, in a basically selfish desperation, to abandon the effort that the Church asks of them.

The monastic movement needs leaders who must come from the new generation. These must have the patience to undergo the testing and formation without which their ability cannot be proved. No one will entrust himself to the guidance of men who have never had to suffer anything and have never really faced the problems of life in all their bitter seriousness. The young must not be too ready to give up in despair. They have work to do! Fortunately there are creative forces at work. There are communities and superiors who are fully aware of the real nature of the monastic vocation, not simply as a summons to become a cog in an institutional machine, but as a charismatic breakthrough to liberation and love. It is more and more clearly realized that fidelity to monastic tradition no longer means simply dictating preformulated answers to all the questions of the young monk and forcing him to look at his life through somebody else's glasses. Tradition is not passive submission to the obsessions of former generations but a living assent to a current of uninterrupted vitality. What was once real in other times and places becomes real in us today. And its reality is not an official parade of externals. It is a living spirit marked by freedom and by a certain *originality*. Fidelity to tradition does not mean the renunciation of all initiative, but a new initiative that is faithful to a certain spirit of freedom and of vision which demands to be incarnated in a new and unique situation. True monasticism is nothing if not creative.

The creativity in monastic life springs from pure love: the natural desire of man for truth and for communion, first of all, and the supernatural gift of grace in the spirit of the Risen Lord, calling man to the highest truth and most perfect communion in the Mystery of Christ. Love is not mere emotion or sentiment. It is the lucid and ardent response of the whole man to a value that is revealed to him as perfect, appropriate and urgent in the providential context of his own life. Hence there are innumerable ways in which man can be awakened from the sleep of a mechanical existence and summoned to give himself totally in the clarity of love. To restrict vocations to this or that narrow area, as if there were only one way to love, is to stifle the spirit and fetter the freedom of the Christian heart. Why are people so intent on refusing others the right to see a special value in a life apart from the world, a life dedicated to God in prayer "on the mountain alone," when the New Testament itself repeatedly shows Christ retiring to the solitary prayer which he himself loved? Certainly one can find God "in the world" and in an active life, but this is not the only way, any more than the monastic life is the only way. There are varieties of graces and vocations in the Church and these varieties must always be respected. The specific value that draws a Christian into the "desert" and "solitude" (whether or not he remains physically "in the world") is a deep sense that *God alone suffices*. The need to win the approval of society, to find a recognized place in the world, to achieve a temporal ambition, to "be somebody" even in the Church seems to them irrelevant. They realize themselves to be called to a totally different mode of existence, outside of secular categories and *outside of the religious establishment*. This is the very heart of monasticism; hence a firmly "established" monasticism is a self-contradiction.

The creative spirit of initiative in monasticism is bound to be killed by an exaggerated emphasis on a well-established monastic "presence," an undue concern with law and ritual and with the externals of observance. The true creative spirit must be fired with love and with *an authentic desire of God*. This means, in so many words, that the monastic vocation is one which implicitly, if not explicitly, seeks *the experience of union with God*. True, the humility and obedience which are essential to the monastic life are absolutely necessary to purge this desire from all elements of self-will and of spiritual ambition. But the need for spiritual liberation, the need for vision, the hunger and thirst for that perfect "justice" which is found in total surrender to God as love to the Beloved: these are the only real justifications for the monk's wilderness life and his desert pilgrimage. If these are systematically frustrated, and if institutional formalities are everywhere substituted for the inner desire of holiness and union, monks will not remain in the monastery. If they are true to themselves and to God they will be compelled to look elsewhere. This is the real problem of monastic renewal: not a surrender to the "secu-lar city" but a recovery of the deep desire of God that draws a man to seek a *totally new way of being in the world.*

This is perhaps a better way of envisaging the monastic vocation. There is no longer any place for the idea that monasticism is mere *repudiation* of the world. It is not enough to "say no," to develop "contempt" for the world and to spend one's life in a walled-up exis-tence which simply rejects all the pleasures, interests and struggles of the world as suspect or as sinful. This negative idea of monasticism has caused it to be completely misunderstood by its critics because it has so often been misunderstood by the monks themselves. And that is why, when the young monk in quest of renewal looks for some-thing to say "yes" to, he comes up with the same "yes" as the world itself. In either case, there is no real awareness of what monasticism is all about.

The monastic life is neither worldly nor unworldly. It is not ar-tificially "otherworldly." It is merely intended to be liberated and simple. The purpose of monastic detachment—which demands gen-uine sacrifice—is simply to leave the monk unencumbered, free to move, in possession of his spiritual senses and of his right mind, ca-pable of living a charismatic life in freedom of spirit. To love, one must be free, and while the apostolic life implies one mode of free-dom in the world, the monastic life has its own freedom which is that of the wilderness. The two are not opposed or mutually exclusive. They are complementary and, on the highest level, they turn out to be one and the same: union with God in the mystery of total love, in the oneness of his Spirit.

In the solitude of the monastic life, the monk begins obscurely to sense that great depths are opened up within him and that the charism of his monastic vocation demands an obedience that is carried out in an abyss too deep for him to understand. It is an obedi-ence that permeates the very roots of his being. Such obedience is far more difficult than any compliance with the will of man, but it must be tested by rule, by discipline, and by submission to the wills of other men. Otherwise it is sheer illusion. Nevertheless, for rule and command to retain their worth in the monastic life, they must be seen in their right relation to the ultimate purpose of that life. Monastic obedience exists not to make yes-men and efficient bureaucrats who can be used in institutional politics, but to liberate the hearts and minds into the lucid and terrible darkness of a contemplation that no tongue can explain and no rationalization can account for. And it must always be remembered that this contemplative liberation is a gift of God, granted not necessarily to the perfect only, and certainly not as a prize for political collaboration with the schemes and ambitions of others.

It remains to speak one word to the monks themselves; that is, to those who now, at this time, are persevering in monasteries and hermitages. That word is: *do not be impatient and do not be afraid.* Do not imagine that everything depends on some instant magic transformation of constitutions and of laws. You already have what you need right in your hands! You have the grace of your vocation and of your love. No earthly situation has ever been ideal. God does not need an ideal situation in order to carry out his work in our hearts. If we do what we can with the means and grace at our disposal, if we sincerely take advantage of our genuine opportunities, the Spirit will be there and his love will not fail us. Our liberation, our solitude, our vision, our understanding and our salvation do not depend on anything remote from us or beyond our reach. Grace has been given us along with our good desires. What is needed is the faith to accept it and the energy to put our faith to work in situations that may not seem to us to be promising. The Holy Spirit will do the rest. There will continue to be monasteries in the mountains and the forests of this continent. And they will be good monasteries, places of silence, of peace, of austerity, of simplicity, of prayer, and of love. They will house communities of men who love one another and share with the world the light they have received, though in a silent and obscure way. They will open out onto the desert solitude in which every monk, at one time or another, whether for a short time or for life, seeks to be alone in the silence and the mystery of his God, liberated from the images of Egypt and from the Babel of tongues.

Yet there is no such thing as a purely charismatic monasticism without any institution. There will always be laws and Rules. And Christ must always be especially present in the person of an abbot, a spiritual father. Indeed spiritual fatherhood itself is a charism and one of the greatest. Not only is it a signal blessing for any monastic community, but it is essential for the work of genuine renewal. Without experienced guides who are completely open to the full dimension—the mystical and prophetic dimension—of love in Christ, renewal will mean little more than the replacement of old rules by new ones and of old traditions by novel frenzies.

II

Vocation and Modern Thought

To what extent are the vocation problems of novices and monks the result of a conflict between "modern thought" and "traditional monastic ideas"? To what extent is this inevitable conflict something we are able to understand and resolve? Obviously our novices are men (or at least "boys") of our time. This is a fact which is irreversible. Should we regard this as a misfortune? We would be very foolish if we did. Is "modern thought" an irreparable evil? Should we assume that the only way a postulant can adapt to our life is to submit to a total and ruthless process of disinfection so that he is completely cleansed of all twentieth-century ideas? This would be an insult, at once presumptuous and absurd. It would mean the extinction of the monastic life. We must on the contrary try to understand how modern ideas can become relevant and acceptable, indeed useful, in helping us to meet our monastic problems.

And yet we must preserve our detachment and our sense of proportion. In opening our minds to modern thought (and after all this means recognizing that we too are "moderns") we must also realize its limitations and its own peculiar hazards. Above all we must be aware of its complexities, its variations, its confusions, since "modern thought" is not a harmonious unity. Modern man is not in agreement with himself. He has no one voice to listen to but a thousand voices, a thousand ideologies, all competing for his attention in a Babel of tongues. Our responsibility to modern man goes far beyond playing games with him, learning some of his lingo in order to tell him what we imagine he wants to hear. Our responsibility to him begins within ourselves. We must recognize that his problems are also ours and stop imagining that we live in a totally different world. We must recognize that our common problems are not to be solved merely by logical answers, still less by official pronouncements. Yet in taking the modern temper seriously we must not accept all its myths and illusions without question, or we will end up by echoing slogans without meaning, substituting sociology, psychoanalysis, existentialism and Marxism for the message of the Gospels. We must use the insights of modern thought, but without deceiving ourselves. The satisfaction that comes from being in tune with our times is certainly not a charism, still less a sign of supernatural life.

We must concern ourselves with the failure of vocations, not the failure of poor vocations or nonvocations, but the failure of apparently good vocations. It is not the fact that novices and young professed leave the monastery and return to secular life but, rather, that some who seem very serious and well endowed, who have apparently adapted well at first, who have been good monks, undergo a vocation crisis (often after five or ten years in the monastery) and leave. The reason given is not so much an inability to accept the physical hardships of the life (no longer so great) but an incapacity to accept any longer the climate of thought and certain attitudes prevalent in the monastery. This is not primarily a failure of faith, or a deep religious crisis, but a psychological incapacity to accept as authentic the climate of thought in which they think the monks are bound to live. Many ambiguities and misunderstandings are involved here on both sides.

To begin with, though this is not generally a purely religious crisis, it may well be so. The psychological temptation can quite easily become a failure of faith. Nevertheless, we cannot understand it properly if we regard it merely as an intervention of the devil and a loss of faith. What happens is that communication tends to break down under certain pressures that arise when the young monk suddenly takes a critical and objective view of the monastery and of his fellow monks. Now, the fact that he does this relatively late in his monastic life (even after solemn profession) raises many serious questions.

These questions seem to him to invalidate his supposed vocation, while his superiors tend to take the attitude "*Si non es vocatus, fac te vocatum,*" appealing naturally to his vow. This may seem to the young monk an incomprehensible attitude, an "infidelity" on some other level which he has newly discovered—or thinks he has discovered—but which he cannot clearly discern. He thinks he has found "the truth" about himself and that he must "obey" his new insights.

The great question is this: has he simply relinquished his commitment to a way of life and to a belief which now seems threatening to the very roots of his being? Is he "discovering" himself in a secular and psychological sense and taking refuge in this discovery so as not to have to confront the severe demands of God's word spoken in mystery and apparent "absurdity"? Or is he on the contrary hearing that word clearly for the first time and obeying its demand to relinquish an inadequate and complacent security which he had embraced passively and without serious motives?

These questions should be anticipated before profession, indeed before the entrance of the postulant into the novitiate. But they cannot always be anticipated.

Hence, once the monk is professed, he must in some way learn to answer his questions in the monastery, in his vow of *conversatio morum*. The monastic commitment and consecration does remain the most deep and authentic solution. But how can he understand this? He must be formed with such a capacity to understand. The monastic ideal must consequently be presented in an understandable way, in all its depth, in its existential reality and its demands, not in formulas of words and slogans. What is called for today is not a crude modernizing of monastic tradition but a new and sharp perspective on the real values which are latent in the monastic life and tradition and which modern man can reasonably expect to find there. The values are certainly there, but they may be hidden through the lack of attention and sensitivity on the part of those who have hitherto been satisfied with old formulas and conceptions which need to be rethought and seen from a new angle, with greater and more serious concern. Need we add: the vows must no longer be regarded in a spirit of vain observance, magic or superstition?

There is no point in stressing modern moral confusion, broken homes, delinquency, alcoholism, pornography, drug addiction, teenage riots, etc., etc., which are only *symptomatic,* not the real trouble. Rather than analyze the mentality of the (American) affluent and marketing society, we will simply note two essential aspects of this climate of thought.

Alexis Carrel remarked: "Technological progress has run wild, and in doing so has ceased to take serious account of man's real needs except as an afterthought." In other words, the development of technology is not really geared to human needs. Carrel said: "The environment which science and technology have succeeded in developing for man does not suit him because it has been *constructed at random without regard for his true self."**

Also, though we still pay lip service to the old myth that what is good for the market is good for everybody, as a matter of fact the development of new products and the marketing of commodities has really little or nothing to do with man's real good and his real needs. The aim is not the good of man but higher profits. Instead of production being for the sake of man, man exists for the sake of production. Thus we live in a culture which, while proclaiming its humanism and pretending indeed to glorify man as never before, is really a systematic and almost cynical affront to man's humanity. Man is a consumer who exists in order to keep business going by consuming its products whether he wants them or not, needs them or not, likes them or not. But in order to fulfill his role he must come to believe in it. Hence his role as consumer takes the place of his identity (if any). He is then reduced to a state of permanent nonentity and tutelage in which his more or less abstract presence in society is tolerated only if he conforms, remains a smoothly functioning automaton, an uncomplaining and anonymous element in the great reality of the market.

It is characteristic of this affluent marketing society to generate at the same time unrealistic expectations and superficial optimism overlaying an undercurrent of suspicion, compounded of self-doubt,

* *From Man the Unknown*

inferiority feelings, resentment, cynicism and despair. In all our young postulants, these two conflicting forces tend to be present, even where there is great simplicity and good will and though the negative trend (doubt) may be rather thoroughly repressed. It soon comes out, however.

What is worse, since our society is one in which man is expected to sell himself and put himself across by flashing a favorable image of himself and by having high expectations of himself, this too affects the mentality of our postulants. Those who are most glib and adroit in this matter may sell themselves as very earnest vocations, while others who are simpler and less aggressive may seem to "have nothing" that recommends them for monastic life.

However, it must be said that they are conscious of all this and all more or less deliberately come to the monastery to escape this system of false values and to find here values that are at once more honest and more in the human measure.

I would say that this manifests itself particularly in a very real concern for monastic simplicity and poverty and for complete honesty in monastic observance. This may at times express itself in ways that sound fanatical and neurotic, but in the main it seems to proceed from the Holy Spirit and is one of the more authentic signs of a true vocation. Yet it is precisely those who have this ideal who also tend to develop problems and dissatisfaction.

There is no question that most of our postulants are quite conscious of the confusion and disorder of the world and honestly intend to leave that all behind them. They come to us precisely because they are aware of the chaos of life outside. But the problem arises when, after a certain time, the kind of order and peace that they find here is finally rejected by them as unsatisfactory. Why?

Here we need to survey the background of modern thought. It may be useful to remind ourselves that "modern thought" is very complex and is in rapid evolution. It is not homogeneous, but is rather made up of many conflicting trends and new developments, and very often trends tend to develop side by side without much influence on each other. It is therefore extraordinarily difficult to say precisely what is going on in "the mind of modern man." We live in a world of chaotic and revolutionary change. The development of rapid communications and of mass media has insured a certain superficial uniformity in the thinking of "the common man" all over the world. And yet can we say precisely who is this "common man"? He has an enormous variety of ideas and influences acting upon him, and often his mentality is an extraordinary mixture of mental clichés that he has picked up at random without knowing where they come from or what they imply. Yet his mind often remains shallow, dissatisfied, frustrated—unless by chance it becomes simply complacent and passive, habitually reacting to mental stimuli without real thought and without mature response.

However, we can say that the man of our time who has been "educated," say on a level corresponding to American college, has been exposed to the ideas of those thinkers who have revolutionized thought, and indeed society itself, in the last hundred and fifty years. It is necessary therefore to cast a glance at some of these thinkers.

Who are they? Marx, Darwin, Kierkegaard, Nietzsche and, later, Freud, Jung, Adler, etc., Lenin, Mao Tse-tung (rather than Stalin who was no thinker; Mao's thought has not reached us, but it is seminal in Latin America, for instance in the ideology of Castroism). We should also mention Bergson, Dewey, Croce, Ortega de Gasset; then Sartre, Heidegger, Buber and other leading existentialists. Finally, we find Teilhard de Chardin mediating much of modern thought to Catholics, with Mounier, G. Marcel and, on the evangelical side, men like Bultmann and Tillich.

Catholicism, at least on the seminary level, has tended to ignore these men or to dismiss them airily, except perhaps for Teilhard who is immensely popular. But we must frankly recognize the importance of these thinkers; they have all in one way or another concerned themselves very deeply with the predicament of modern man: with his special needs, his peculiar hopes, his chances of attaining these hopes. This concern in itself is by no means incompatible with a Christian outlook. Christianity too must be profoundly concerned with twentieth-century man, with technological man, "posthistoric" man, indeed what is sometimes called "post-Christian" man. In the Church there can be no "post-Christian" man, no mere technological pagan. There is only man redeemed by Christ.

If modern man has a peculiar outlook appropriate to his rapidly developing world, Christianity cannot and does not ignore him or his ideas. The Church seeks to understand his ideas and to share them. We in the monasteries cannot ignore them. Schema 13 of Vatican II makes it an obligation to understand contemporary man as he is, not as we want him to be.

The American bishops who discussed religious liberty in the third session of the Council all frankly accepted the "modern outlook" on the dignity of the person and the rights of conscience. We too must be concerned with this outlook as expressed in the lives of our postulants.

There is more at stake than "human dignity" and the "rights of conscience." We do not merely confront nineteenth-century liberal man and his simple belief in self-realization by freedom in a free economy governed by inherently reasonable laws. We confront twentieth-century man in his desperation and despair, his hopeless quest of an identity, perhaps his renunciation of identity: Not only may we meet him halfway in his desire that his freedom be recognized and developed, but we may even have to restore to him a basic hope in his very capacity to be a person, to have an identity and to dedicate himself fully to the service of God.

The nineteenth century declared that God was dead, and now the twentieth, in consequence, has come to discover that without God man himself doubts the validity and meaning of his own existence. When "God died" there was something in man that died also. If we do not resuscitate these dead men—our own dead selves—with the word of the gospel, we will only consecrate dead men to a "dead God." And those who come to us will ask themselves what profit there can be in seeking the living among the dead.

Hence it would be both useless and absurd simply to cry out that the atmosphere is polluted by modern errors and try to disinfect it. It is not only impossible to get rid of all the influences exercised on modern man by the thinkers we have mentioned, but also, there is no need to do so. On the contrary, we have to take these influences into account and try generously to make use of them to the extent that modern thought can serve the purposes of truth and of the monastic life.

We cannot, for instance, neglect or overlook the tremendous effect that the worldview of modern science has had. Monastic life and liturgy especially belong to the days of the Ptolemaic, earth-centered universe, with God in the empyrean perhaps not more than one hundred miles above us! The Anglican bishop John A. Robinson, in his book *Honest to God,* struggled rather naively with the problem of a religion that conceives God as being "out there." However, this is not too urgent a problem for us at the moment since in fact the universe of relativity and quantum physics is not what is upsetting our young monks. On the contrary, they find it awe inspiring, as we all should and do.

"Scientific atheism" is certainly no real problem any more, except in those who still cling to the complacently oversimplified illusions of nineteenth-century liberalism. What is more important and disquieting is the blank passivity and indifference of modern mass man, who is in a confusion in which serious concern for truth on any level may become impossible: the greatest problem is the despair and languor of a depersonalized man incapable of authenticity. But such men do not ordinarily enter monasteries. We must assume in our postulants at least a beginning of capacity for some thought of their own, some authentic religious concern. And we have supposed that this thinking and concern will inevitably be influenced at least unconsciously by "modern thought."

Who were some of the makers of modern thought and what were they saying?

We think of Marx as simply saying that capitalism must be overthrown, and as being "against private property," therefore against the natural law, but one idea that he investigated in depth was the dehumanization of man in industrial society. His remedy was not just revolution but that man must own the means of production which he uses; he must not be reduced to the level of an object or a machine to be used by someone else: he must preserve his dignity as man. He must be the master of the means of production and not their servant. He must live among machines in such a way as to acquire and preserve his full human identity and responsibility to his fellow man.

We usually think of Freud as saying that the restrictions of conventional morality are bad for man since they prevent him from carrying out his sexual desires. In point of fact, that is not what Freud is saying. Freud is deploring a social situation in which man does not learn to love in a full and mature manner insofar as his passions remain in a crude infantile state which keeps him from being fully human, fully able to give himself in love. Sexual indulgence is not for Freud a good in itself. On the contrary, it may be selfish and infantile and, hence, a source of pathology. In a word, we can see that for Freud too it is a question of man developing psychologically as well as biologically in such a way that his sexuality is in the service of his full identity as a person capable of giving himself, and not a blind force that overwhelms and smothers his identity. (Incidentally, depth psychology has certainly had a revolutionary effect on the modern concept of man and on the consequent idea of morality. Whether group analysis should be a normal practice in monasteries is a question I can only mention in passing. The question exists and has its risks.)

Freud, too, like Marx, has unsettled the monastic conscience. Even though the average postulant has not read Freud, he has grown up in a climate of thought profoundly modified by the influence of depth psychology. Just as the influence of Marx has made people question the "superstructures" of bourgeois society and see in them possibilities of hypocrisy and illusion, so the influence of Freud has made people at least confusedly aware that all that appears to be "moral" and "virtuous" is not necessarily authentic.

Kierkegaard, along with Nietzsche and then, later, Sartre and Heidegger (though they all approach it in different ways) are telling us substantially that elaborate conventional structures of thought, language, cult, etc., are all doing the exact opposite from what they originally pretended to do: instead of bringing man in contact with reality, and helping him to be true to himself, they are standing between man and reality, as veils and deceptions. They prevent him from facing "anguish." All urge man to discard the impediments of conventional thought in order to face himself directly, take upon himself the burden of anguish and contingency, face the awful reality of death, and use his freedom not as one who is enmeshed in the artificialities of social convention but as one who sees himself, with all his limitations, grounded in nothingness and yet in his true dignity, his freedom, his ability to establish his personal identity and "choose" to be himself, even though he is nothing.

The literature of the late nineteenth and early twentieth century has been deeply concerned with authenticity and the problem of finding one's "true self" in an artificial and inauthentic society. T. S. Eliot's *The Waste Land* and *The Hollow Men* state the problem. In *Four Quartets,* his greatest poem, Eliot uses traditional spiritualities and symbols to rise above identity, to achieve a personal deliverance from a commonplace and fictitious identity in the stream of historical continuity or, rather, in the "now" which stands behind all events and includes them all together. For more recent writers, the very existence of a "personal identity" has been called into question. This has resulted in a systematic and destructive questioning of all that seemed to earlier writers to offer support for an authentic identity. For novelists and dramatists of the absurd it is perhaps true to say that the only authentic identity is the recognition that identity itself is an illusion and hence the best man can do with his "freedom" is to accept, and take responsibility for, his own despair. Postulants in our monasteries have perhaps not been reading the pessimistic literature, yet can we say that they are totally unaffected by it when such ideas make themselves felt everywhere?

Meanwhile the nineteenth-century belief in progressive evolution has persisted side by side with existentialist pessimism, and one may say that in the United States as well as in the Communist countries the prevailing climate is one of official optimism. Sometimes the optimism of Christian eschatological hope takes on a coloring of evolutionist expectations, looking forward to a spiritual and religious climax at the end of the evolutionary process. Thus we have a combined Christian and evolutionist optimism opposed to the pessimism that sees the world as falling into entropy, meaninglessness and self-destruction. For some, man is only on the threshold of a glorious fulfillment which will for the first time make him really "man." For others, history is already at an end. Man is running down like an unwound clock. He is already in his posthistoric inertia.

Both Darwin and Teilhard de Chardin are concerned with the development of man toward the fulfillment of his true (historic and biological) destiny, and Teilhard, mingling Marx and Darwin with Christianity, looks forward to the recapitulation of all in Christ, the eschatological and supernatural goal to which man has been destined by God. This means, for Teilhard de Chardin, a Christianity that fully accepts "the world" and recognizes its destiny as a redemptive force fully rooted "in the world." Hence Teilhard is concerned with the Christian's identity as a Christian person and a member of Christ with a responsibility not only to his fellow man but to the whole of creation and to all the past history of creation. Man, in Teilhard as in Marx, finds himself at a point where the whole fulfillment of the world depends on his enlightened and free choice—a grandiose and noble vision.

All these thinkers, with all their different approaches, with their optimism on one hand and their pessimism on the other, agree more or less in one basic emphasis: upon the problem of authenticity, the predicament of man in technological and mass society in which, in fact, he is not reaching maturity but, on the contrary, becoming fixed in infantilism and irresponsibility, in which he passively submits to systematic stultification. Hence they all concern themselves with the need for man to discover his identity (or at least his lack of "identity") and assume mature responsibility for himself in his world and in history. All tend to look upon man, whether individually or collectively, not as a static essence fixed in a stable condition, but as a dynamism or a "project," a "freedom," a person responsible for "creating" a world and an identity proportionate to his plight. Now, though this "humanism" and "personalism" may occur in a frankly atheistic context, we must learn to distinguish, more carefully than we do, what is "godless" in Marx and Freud, for instance, and what proceeds from implicitly Christian roots. It has been said that the revolt against Christianity is a form of "judgment" pronounced in and by history upon the failure of Christians to meet the demands of God's Word in their time. Hence it is that Marxism, for one, frankly seeks to achieve the aims and promises of biblical messianism (world unity, peace, harmony, justice, love) by the formal rejection of Christianity and indeed of all religion. The Marxian idea of man postulates that religion, being essentially a mystification, actually prevents man from realizing the ideals which it proposes to him. Hence, in a way, to abandon the "mystification" and work for the proposed ideal is to fulfill the spirit and genuine claims of religion. Naturally Marxism does not look at it in this way, but Christian thinkers influenced by Marxism tend to do so. In any event, the personalist and humanist ideals of modern thought are not always radically incompatible with the Christian ideal. The rejection of God and of the Church is of course frankly anti-Christian. But the goal of human freedom, peace, and unity is not unchristian in itself. On the contrary it stems from the New Testament idea of freedom before God, the freedom of the sons of God, the dignity of man redeemed in Christ and man's vocation to work out historically, in harmony and love, the redemption of the whole world in Christ. Hence these characteristic modern aspirations should present no special difficulty to us. We should be able to "save" and "redeem" those aspirations which are authentically germane to Christianity even though buried in a matrix of atheism.

The real problem then is not that young men come to us and find the life boring, or insipid, and leave in order to go back where they can have a good time. It is not simply that they feel themselves hemmed in and suppressed and reject all forms of discipline in order to go back to the world where they have every chance to seek fulfillment of their desires and of their will, unhampered by authority and restrictions. This is not the point at all.

On the contrary, they usually come (except for those so young and callow that they have no notion what they are doing in the first place) seriously concerned with one thing above all: they want to *give their lives a religious and human meaning.*

They recognize that life in the world as it is today tends to be confused and meaningless even on a human level. Hence they come to the monastery not only to save their souls in the next world but, before that, to save their dignity and integrity as human beings in this life, to discover their true identity, so that they will be able to know themselves and give themselves fully and maturely to God.

This is perfectly in accordance with the teachings of the Fathers, especially of the first Cistercians. St. Bernard makes clear that the monastic life first of all restores man's nature in its capacity to know truth, to experience the truth in ourselves, to experience the truth in our normal, human relations with other people. St. Bernard definitely stresses the natural aspect of this restoration which must come before the supernatural elevation of man (of course he does not use Thomist terminology). When we have experienced the truth in ourselves and in others we are ready for the (mystical) experience of Truth in itself, that is in God.

Other Cistercians follow this line of thinking. For instance, Adam of Perseigne: his letters describe the monastic formation as "therapy" for people who in the world have been seriously disordered and have lost the balance and sanity proper to their nature.

Here is where the problem arises.

Young men come to the monastery seeking truth in themselves, seeking to experience themselves as real and authentic human beings. They come seeking identity, and an experience of identity which is largely denied them or frustrated in the world.

However, we must not misapprehend the nature of their quest and assume that they come to the monastery seeking a different "answer" or a different explanation of life. They themselves may be unaware of this, and they may at first seem to expect "answers" and indeed a whole new set of explanations, a systematic outlook on life in which everything "fits" and "makes sense." Thus, for instance, if we assume that modern man is simply rootless and disoriented and try to give his life direction and meaning with a logical, scholastic view of the universe and of the economy of salvation, we may at first arouse his curiosity, but we must take care not to lead him into what he considers a further and more radical disappointment. The "answers" that modern man seeks and needs are not those of the neat verbal formula or the logically constructed system. There is in his very being a profound distrust of logic and of system. His need and his hope are in a realm of paradox where strict logic cannot reach because it is the realm of the personal and the unique. The very meaning of personal identity is lost if we suppose that it conforms to precedent and to the general type. The question of identity and of meaning in our personal life can never be adequately answered by logic but only by life itself. Yet we live in a world where words, formulas, official answers and a seemingly logical system may pretend to decide everything for us in advance. If modern man, seeking his true self, seeking the existential atmosphere of an exploration that has not been determined beforehand, comes to a monastic life and discovers that all his questions are answered in advance, all his decisions are made for him, all his movements are expected to fit in with a rigid logical necessity of black and white, absolute right and wrong, he may try earnestly to accept the answers, and may seem to succeed for a few years. But in the end he will feel as frustrated in the monastery as he did in the world. He will not find himself because he will not be able to seek himself. He will simply have been told who and what he is expected to be.

We must not be too quick to think that because modern man is in a state of uncertainty what he wants is absolute certainty at any price. In an age when science has discovered the utility of an "uncertainty principle" to correct the errors and false perspectives engendered by the logical certitude of classical physics, there is also felt to be a need for a more existential spirituality in which uncertainties and hesitations are to some extent accounted for and in which everything is not immediately and forever settled by good resolutions and categorical affirmations that see all things in black and white.

It is quite true that most Americans suffer a prolonged and severe identity crisis and many never really pull through it at all. Hence we can expect postulants to come to us in the midst of this crisis. But we will not solve it for them (and indeed no one can solve it for them anyway) if we assume that "identity" means something akin to "character building" as propounded in the do-it-yourself manuals for success in developing a "strong personality" (whatever that may be). A monastic spirituality that assumes that the individual is a center of volitional force that is supposed to exert itself upon or against a world outside and around it can at best only perpetuate the illusory identity which no man in his right mind would consent to have: that of a mythical and detached "subject" existing entirely outside all "objective" reality, able to understand everything by pure reason and to dominate everything by his own will. Such an identity could not exist except as a caricature of God. And it is unfortunately true that many men have tried to solve their identity problem by this fraudulent imitation of what they imagine their Creator to be. The problem is much more subtle than that. It is resolved only by a much deeper and much more mysterious commitment that begins with the acceptance of a place and a destiny which one can never completely understand because it belongs, not simply to an ordered and natural system of laws, but to a supernatural order of grace and love, an order of freedom in which nothing is scientifically predictable and everything has to be taken as a wager, with daring and with unbounded trust.

To decide everything beforehand and to say just what precise form the challenge of grace will necessarily take is to empty grace of its meaning and reduce the gospel of love to a system of legalistic security. We must take care not to reduce the monastic life to a purely commonsense machinery of rules and official decisions in which there are only token sacrifices and formal worship, and in which there is no longer anything unpredictable except the day-to-day detail of trivial and absolutely necessary frustration.

The monastic life attracts people who look for meaning and identity precisely because it is a life of solitude. But if it is too completely and minutely organized, it will in actual fact prevent the monk from ever entering into the authentic solitude of heart in which alone he can find himself in finding God.

A Jesuit author, writing of the prevalence of the identity crisis in America and of the American fear of solitude, says:

> Critics have also noted the American fear of loneliness. Individual identity is sacrificed in an effort to stay close to the herd, to be no different from others in thought, feeling, or action. To stand aside, to be alone, is to assert a personal identity which

refuses to be submerged. Society will not tolerate this. Innumerable social features are designed to prevent it: stadiums to accommodate thousands at sport events, open doors of private rooms and offices, club cars on trains, shared room in colleges and boarding houses, countless clubs, organizations, associations, societies, canned music (for silence is unbearable) piped into hospitals, railway cars, and supermarkets.

Yet one of the surest signs of the resolution of the identity crisis is an increased capacity for being alone, for being responsible for oneself. The gradual process that will end in perfect identity involves an awareness of the fact that there are decisions in life and aspects of life's struggle that a person must face alone.

For as a young person becomes clearer in his own mind of his role in society and of his personal identity, he is likely also to become more aware of how he differs from others. Gradually he becomes conscious of his isolation from others, not because others are pulling away, but because the fullness of personal identity cannot be achieved without some degree of aloneness. Here there is a paradox: the more richly a person lives, the more lonely, in a sense, he becomes. And as a person, in this formative isolation, becomes more able to appreciate the moods and feelings of others, he also becomes more able to have meaningful relationships with them.

But the unwritten code of our national culture prohibits aloneness, and this is the second causative factor for a prolonged identity crisis: the obstacles our society imposes to prevent personal reflection.*

One of the most characteristic American ways of evading the identity problem is conformism, running with the herd, the refusal of solitude, the flight from loneliness. This exists even in monasteries and can create a serious problem if, for renunciation and inner solitude, it tries to substitute a false atmosphere of collective euphoria

*Barry McLaughlin, S.J., *Nature, Grace and Religious Development*, pp. 46–47.

and corrupt our cenobitic life with a vapid "togetherness." Togetherness is not "community." To love our brother we must first respect him in his own authentic reality, and we cannot do this if we have not attained to a basic self-respect and mature identity ourselves.

Are our efforts to be more "communal" and to be more of a "family" really genuine or are they only new ways to be intolerant of the solitude and integrity of the individual person? Are we simply trying to submerge and absorb him and keep him from finding an identity that might express itself in dissent and in a desire for greater solitude? Are we simply trying to guard against his entering a "desert" of questioning and paradox that will disturb our own complacencies?

We are likely to meet postulants in two kinds of identity crisis: those whose adolescent identity problem has not been solved and practically cannot be solved because they are too neurotic; and those with an identity crisis on a deeper spiritual level. The former do not really want an identity. They do not want to be mature and we can do nothing with them.

Unfortunately, since they generally appear to be docile and obedient, and even seem quite "spiritual" sometimes, they are too often accepted, with bad consequences.

The latter people are capable of maturing spiritually. They have excellent qualities, and they are handicapped only by the deep self-doubt and inner confusion that come from not experiencing themselves as really having a mind and a will of their own, as being fully persons with true personal convictions and the ability to love, to give themselves, to surrender to God.

They may perhaps be slightly neurotic, but they can be helped and they can make a good adjustment. These are the ones we are concerned with. They come to the monastery hoping to find a real meaning for their life. They come with some of the critical ideas and some of the hopes sown by Marx, Freud, etc., in the air of our times, and they have some of the demands and expectations which have been created by modern thought. They bring with them the confusions and contradictions of modern thought. They do not usually have the "unchristian" presuppositions of secular thought, and so we ought to accept them as they are, face their needs as reasonable and valid. We ought to try to do something for them.

At the same time we must, while respecting their personal integrity, recognize that they may be strongly impregnated with the romantic sense of need and longing. The "self" they seek to "realize" is perhaps an unreal, an impossibly "pure," consciousness (which they may momentarily confuse with Cassian's *puritas cordis*). They may, on the basis of this quest for romantically pure feeling, justify every rebellion against whatever disturbs them and divests them from that quest of narcissistic peace. In this case they need to know that what they seek is inauthentic and that its inauthenticity cannot be excused by appeals to modern writers whom the "monks do not understand."

But suppose the young monk wakes up to the fact that he came to the monastery with romantic illusions, that he is being kept there by suggestions and directions which point to an impossible goal of "pure contemplation," a narcissistic or Platonic beatitude of pure self-consciousness masking as consciousness of God? Surely this awakening is serious and requires to be understood.

In any event, these distinctly modern young men are going to come to us with certain modern questions and difficulties. Their questions and difficulties are going to focus a spotlight of criticism on some features of our monastic life. In point of fact these difficulties will call in question the very meaning of the monastic life of "contemplation" and indeed of religion itself. Basic ideas such as that of obedience to religious authority, of liturgical worship, of interior prayer, of poverty, may be called into question. If these concepts are found in fact to be somewhat formalistic and arbitrary, if they have lost their value as signs, if they are reduced to a pious routine substituting for true love of God and genuine worship, their "mystery" will be reduced to "mystification." The modern young man will be wounded with a profound resentment and will begin to think that all these things have been imposed on him by a religious system which does not really have his true interest at heart, but only requires that he become a submissive cog in a religious machine.

This of course may and often does imply a failure of faith, a movement of withdrawal and doubt, a refusal to encounter the demands of God's Word and to make the fundamental sacrifice of one's own will without which no monasticism is possible. Nevertheless, there may also be an element of genuine scandal in the way monastic observance is understood and carried out by a given community.

What can we do about this?

It is usually at the point when we realize that there is definite criticism and challenge implied by these problems that we run into difficulties with these young monks.

First, insofar as their problems themselves imply criticism of the life (they could not have the problem in that form unless they experienced the life as "wrong" for them), we may tend to deny the existence of the problem or even the reality of their subjective experience.

Here we must be careful of manipulating the word "neurotic" with too much abandon. Maybe the problem is not pathological at all. On the contrary, it may very often happen that the awakening of the problem, the ability to experience it as a problem after several years in the monastery, is the sign of an awakening of identity. It is precisely the reality and importance of the experience that ought to engage our attention. This is a sign of growth and, hence, a sign that the monk is reaching out for a truth, a good that ought to become his. He is now at a point of critical confrontation, not only with his own human condition, but with the Word of God addressed directly and in mystery to his own human freedom, asking his free adherence to the law and love of Christ, inviting him to follow Christ in sacrifice.

But if we refuse to accept his problem as valid, if we simply try to dismiss it, and even to question his sanity or his sincerity, we immediately aggravate the crisis. One thing the young monk knows and experiences is the human reality and urgency of his problem. At the same time he profoundly and earnestly doubts that our observances and our obedience have any further relevance to his problem. This doubt is, in fact, at the heart of the problem. Hence we only intensify his ambivalence and his torment if we implicitly say, "Renounce your doubt, accept obedience and monastic observance on our terms, and you will have peace." This will almost fatally drive him out of the monastery if, in fact, what he needs is precisely to see and understand the monastic life not in our terms but in his, that is to say, in terms of his own capacity to find it meaningful. In a word, if we simply reduce the choice to the acceptance of monastic life because we say it is meaningful, if we insist that he must take our word for this or else stand convicted of faithlessness and cowardice, he will finally decide that our monastic observance is nothing but a mystification. And he will leave. His departure will perhaps be more our fault than his. He will almost have to leave in order to be true to himself. Our refusal to listen to his problem, our demand that he should simply cease to have this problem, is in effect a confession of our own inadequacy, our own incapacity to meet him on a fully personal level.

Secondly, we treat this critical awakening as the beginning of rebellion that has to be firmly put down. And in order to do so we demand not understanding but unconditional submission. We do not see that what the monk is asking of us is not so much a magic and official solution to all problems but the recognition of his new identity (as a person who experiences this thing about the monastic life, who sees the monastic life in this new and difficult light) and the loyal effort to cooperate with him in trying to clarify something that is as yet clear neither to him nor to ourselves. We refuse him this recognition and demand that he cease to question "the system" and our official interpretation of it. We demand that he simply accept our answer even though to him it seems to have nothing to do with his question.

Then when the young monk begins to raise questions that we ourselves do not want to face, we not only try to impose an answer but we even try to change the question. Our answer consists in reformulating his question in a way that seems acceptable to us because then we can give it an answer that we approve of—and that requires no new adjustment!

What then should we do? If we recognize that in questioning his vocation the young monk is also seriously questioning us and our vocation, should we then enter into his doubt and share his own perplexities? Should we too call everything into question, reexamine everything, and wonder what we are doing in the monastery ourselves?

It seems to me that what is called in question is not our monastic life but rather some of the presuppositions which we, as slightly dated moderns, have read into it. And the most questionable of these is our persistent conviction that life consists of questions and answers, and that "problems" and "decisions" and "choices" are of overwhelming importance, so that at every moment we have to be thinking of right and wrong, commitment or evasion, sincerity or insincerity, maturity or immaturity. We keep all these questions going full blast every waking hour of the day and even during the hours when we ought to be asleep, and we drive the young monk to torment himself with these questions even more than we torment ourselves. Perhaps our problem consists in wanting to have problems and consequently creating them out of nothing in order to seek solutions!

Certainly our life is full of real problems, some of them perhaps without solution. It would be an impertinence to suggest that all our problems are fabricated. And yet we are so obsessed with the idea that we are supposed to possess "answers" and "solutions" for everything that we evade the difficult problems, which are all too real, by raising other less real problems to which we think we have the answer.

The naked faith that enables us to bear the apparent futilities and failures of ordinary life is not made stronger or more pure when it is clothed in facile explanations. Pious rationalizations which pretend to justify "the ways of God to men" often generate more doubt than courage and distract our hearts from the difficult labor of freely accepting what we actually are.

The monk is a man *like* other men, and his problems are basically those of other men and other Christians. He is "present to the world" insofar as he is able truly to experience and share the anguish of his fellow man in the face of suffering, time, evil and death. What he does "more" than others is simply that he tries to face this anguish, not with more subtle rationalizations, but with greater humility and deeper awareness of his own poverty, not in a purer climate of "inner beauty" (whatever that might be) but with a more intransigent and lucid honesty, not with more stoicism or resignation, but with a conscience more determined because more firmly rooted in the sense of God and in abandonment to him.

If we are too much concerned with ideal monastic projects, questions of pure worship and exquisite inner fervor, questions of perfect regularity and more angelic renunciation, we evade the more basic human problems and find ourselves in unreality.

Thus we begin earnestly to reconsider the young monk's questioning of our life. Sincere efforts to understand the "problem" are made. We try to answer the objections of the young monk but, usually, on a level where our attempt tends to be meaningless. We strive to meet him halfway in his difficulty with our life and to try to work out some way of changing the pattern of the life so that it will make more sense to him. Our changes in observance, liturgy, horarium, work and so on are generally our well-intentioned response to the "difficulties" of young monks. We intend thereby to help him answer his questions and find happiness in a "meaningful" dedicated life.

Without being a prophet of gloom, I must say that legislated changes in the externals of our life are not going to solve this problem as long as our mentality itself is not deepened and clarified. The restlessness of the new generation has finally awakened a response, but is it the response of Christian and monastic wisdom or is it simply a protective reflex of our own insecurity? It seems to me that we are now becoming self-consciously and naively "modern," hastily and uncritically adjusting any and every formula that seems to fit the new situation, without "changing our minds" in any deeper sense.

Basically our trouble remains the same: an obsession with questions and answers, with problems and solutions, with momentous decisions, and even with "identity" raised to the level of a kind of absolute. The traditional wisdom of monasticism and of the gospel ought to help us see through this mystification and bring us back into contact with reality. Our life does not consist in magic answers to impossible questions but in the acceptance of ordinary realities which are, for the most part, beyond analysis and therefore do not need to be analyzed.

We will help the monk through his "identity crisis" only if we refrain from making him too conscious of his identity, or his lack of identity, and of his crisis. And we will prove ourselves wise and discreet monks if instead of making a problem out of everything in the monastic life, we are first content with living it in the spirit of the gospel, with a sincere and healthy realism, refraining, as far as possible, from judging everything and everyone at all hours of the day and night.

The act of judging is an act by which we set ourselves apart as unique, as "outside" the common run of beings, as something totally special and apart, taking a godlike view (*eritis sicut dii*) of men and events. We ask questions, we "have problems," we seek to make "authentic decisions" because we believe in this mystification, this spurious and romantic "identity" of the self that stands apart and affirms itself by judging others. As long as man thinks that the solution of his "identity crisis" consists in achieving this capacity for self-assertion, we can have no peace in our monasteries. "Judge not, that you be not judged."

Nevertheless, the monk does judge, and before he can learn to stop judging he must realize that this is what he is up to. He must become able to get along without it.

All explanations and "definitive answers" on a religious level will remain meaningless and inadequate to the monk as long as in his heart he experiences an "existential doubt" of the value of the monastic life *for him.* Many of those who are tempted to leave can easily articulate their problem in these terms: "What is the use of my undergoing all this suffering and hardship (in my mind, struggling with the apparent meaninglessness of this life) if in the end it will not be worth anything anyway?" They are seriously confronted with what they feel to be the problem of useless suffering. The answer of "dark faith" and "believe what you cannot see" fails to convince them because it seems to them to be little more than verbalization. On the contrary, they are deeply affected by what seems to be the failure and inauthenticity of others who have, in all docility, contented themselves with this advice.

What do they see? Too often they see men who have abdicated their human identity and reality (in good faith) and are leading lives without human authenticity, simply passive, evading responsibility, and humanly impoverished, often to a serious degree. For example, they may sometimes see men who have been in the monastery for years and whose simplicity is not that of spiritual childhood but, frankly, that of neurotic infantilism.

They may see men who seem to be obeying and who, in fact, are simply the products of a life of overcontrol. (The idea that every slightest move of the monk and even his inmost thoughts are not supernatural and monastic except when subject to complete control is disastrous for modern man. This proceeds from a false supernaturalism.) These people cannot be entrusted with the simplest job without expecting instructions and commands at every step. They lack sound judgment and even common sense. They are often eccentric and their spirituality tends to be both naive and bizarre. Yet because they maintain a servile attitude they are praised and rewarded. In point of fact the emptiness and futility of their lives are a real scandal to the young monk. How often do we not hear novices and young monks saying: "If I remain in the monastery will I become like Father so-and-so?"

If all these things are true, should they not be admitted and faced? Certainly the solution is not simply to tell the young monk to close his eyes and act as if these realities were not real. But if we want to get to the root of the problem we have to ask why these inevitable human failures attain to so great an importance and become so great a problem. After all, if you have failings I may notice them and be sorry for you, but do they have to upset my whole life?

It is the conviction that we have to confront all problems and definitely settle them that leaves young monks disturbed and unhappy about the failures of others. But a true and mature identity does not consist in the ability to give a final solution to everything—as if the "mature person" were one for whom there were no longer any mysteries or any scandals. We discover our identity when we accept our place and our way in the midst of persons and things, in a historical situation, that we do not have to completely understand. We simply see that it is our own place and decide to live in it, for better or for worse. In the light of this simple and primordial acceptance, a natural consent, an obedience to reality that is already analogous to the obedience of faith, we can finally "be ourselves." Our mind is "made up" and so we do not have to keep unmaking it and putting it together again with new judgments, many of which are irresponsible and rash.

Of course when a monk is making up his mind to leave his monastery he easily finds all kinds of bad examples to persuade him that he is right. He may tend to ignore the really mature and well-adjusted monks, the serious and solid ones who are living an authentic monastic life. Yet a further problem arises: for practical reasons, the ones who are solid and mature are usually officers or have some important job. Hence the others argue that in fact one has to have a job to "become mature" and that activity is the solution. This may even become a generalized response to the problem, and a whole monastery may get the idea that all the monks will benefit if all are more active, more outgoing, more in contact with outsiders, perhaps even engaged in parish work.

But in any event, it is a sign of immaturity and lack of identity to remain so dependent on the good and bad examples of others that we allow their lives to influence our own lives in a decisive manner. The fact that some other monks are unhappy or lead fruitless lives has nothing to do with my staying in a monastery or leaving it, if I am a mature person capable of assuming responsibility for my own life and my own response to the call of God.

Another point of great importance is the question of monastic priesthood in the light of the identity problem. Because of the background of the postulants and the very important part formerly played by the priest in immigrant communities in America, the ideal of "being a priest" is deeply rooted in the psychology of the American Catholic—for religious as well as for social and personal reasons. Often the idea of "becoming a priest" is one and the same as the idea of fully becoming a person, of being someone who really counts, whose life has a full meaning. This ingrained presupposition has a great deal to do with psychological conflicts in the community.

It seems that we ought to examine some of the main features of our monastic life, liturgy, study, formation, silence, enclosure, conversion of manners, and especially monastic work in order to see how these can all be rethought in such a way as to meet the problem of identity and authenticity.

As matters stand, I can say that of the observances which most young monks feel to be artificial and inauthentic, the chapter of faults easily takes first place. Then we must run the whole gamut of monastic community relations, affected by silence, by artificial and archaic customs, etc. The choir, too, is the scene of much depersonalization and anguish. Much trouble is had with distorted and conventional notions of asceticism. A wrong use of superficial mystical ideas can play havoc with some who are suffering from the "emptiness and angst" of depersonalization and neurosis.

After merely touching upon these points as topics for further thought, I would like to suggest one area where we can hope for good results, and that is monastic work. Work that is productive, properly organized, and remains in contact with nature, work that is truly physical and manual, outdoor work, work that is properly learned and well done, work that is managed and taught on a human and monastic level and not carried out like factory-type drudgery or office routines—such work can do much to help the young monk find his identity and grow in Christ, by teaching him to accept himself, work in harmony with others, and feel himself fully part of a world, made by a loving Father, in which his own work has a redemptive and sanctifying quality because it is united with the labor and sacrifice of the Incarnate Son of God.

Looking back over these pages we everywhere find expressions like "identity crisis," "authentic personal existence" and "meaningful choice." These are common currency in the realm where psychoanalysis and existentialist thought work together to explain some of modern man's confusions and render them more tractable. Whether or not the postulant who enters our monastic life is himself using these concepts, or even aware of them, he is at any rate one who is prepared to think in such terms. He is perhaps, in actual fact, still in the midst of an identity crisis himself, and his vocation may be due in part to such a crisis. He has come to the monastery in the hope that here he can be true to himself or at least discover whether or not he is anybody at all. In other words, he has a soul to save, a life to be endowed with meaning not only on the supernatural level but even in terms of nature, "the world" and this present life. In other words, whether or not we want to take this phraseology with complete seriousness, we might as well face the realities which it attempts to describe, even if we ourselves want to see them somewhat differently ourselves.

After all, the traditional and popular language of the Gospels speaks of "losing" one's inmost self, one's soul, one's personal and spiritual reality. To "find" and to "save" this inmost and secret reality, one must hear the word of the gospel, the word of the cross, the message of salvation and grace. To become aware of oneself as a Christian is to discover one's full identity as one who has been sought and found by the inscrutable mercy of God. The discovery of this "true self" is also a discovery of one's responsibility to other such selves, one's brothers in Christ, one's fellowmen, including those who are still lost, who have still not entered the light of this saving and supernatural recognition.

There are some men who cannot sufficiently deepen and clarify this discovery of themselves in Christ until they enter a monastery and devote their whole life to an existential realization, a living out in deed and in fact, of this mysterious relationship to God and to other men. Such persons desire to express their identity in a paradoxical recognition that they are a "nothing" that has been called to a life of pure love and praise, so that their very identity, like the identity of the angels, is that of beings who praise and thank the Source of all Life for being just that: the Source of all Life.

Thus in the highest sense the monastic and contemplative life seems to be a sacrifice of identity, a "loss of the self," in order that

there may be no self but that of God who is the object of our contemplation and of our praise. And this, paradoxically, is not self-
alienation but the highest and most perfect "self-realization."

Unfortunately when this dimension of the spiritual life is grasped
only verbally, as a proposed ideal which is "conceived" and "imagined" but not actually experienced, it may be grossly misunderstood,
and the misunderstanding may lead to grave distortions of the personality. The mystique of humility and contemplation is good only
for those who have an identity which they are capable of surrendering as though it were a nothing, in exchange for the "all" of
God in which they too are found and recovered, with all the world
besides. To the immature man for whom the accession to full identity is too difficult a step, a role of passivity and anonymity, a laud-
able and highly respectable "nothingness" can become a very convenient evasion. In these pages we have not paid much attention to
those who have succeeded in playing this role in a monastic habit.
They exist, and they are at times a scandal to others who are more
seriously concerned with not keeping the talent of identity and
personal being buried in the routines of a trivial and forfeited existence.

This chapter has concerned itself chiefly with monks who have
a known capacity to live the monastic life tolerably well but who,
coming face to face with what can be called the "crisis of identity"
after they have been for some years professed, come to believe that
the only honest solution, the only "authentic" way of confronting
the problem, is to admit frankly that they were mistaken when they
entered the monastery and return to the world to begin life again
outside as mature and sober beings who have sloughed off their
illusions.

This is a formula that is quite modern and becoming very familiar. In some cases we cannot doubt that in order to be fully honest
and true to himself, as well as to God, the young professed may as
well frankly admit his mistake and leave. But in many other cases it
seems probable that the conclusion, ringing with earnest appeals to
authenticity and identity, has been arrived at by pure rationalization.

In other words, it is fraudulent. It is "inauthentic." And it constitutes an infidelity to the Word of God and to grace.

There will always be evasions. There will always be reasons why
we can never be competent to judge these evasions. But it remains
for us to recognize that a climate of questions and answers, problems
and solutions, a climate of seemingly infallible logic, order, efficiency
and clarity, may be quite deceptive. It may tempt men to rationalize.
It may corrupt in them a capacity for humility and sincere obedience
to God's truth and God's will as it is encountered in the existential
mystery of daily life.

It is natural that a younger generation should respond to rationalizations about authority with other rationalizations about authenticity. In such cases, there is not only a problem of the younger
generation but a problem of all generations. It is the problem of
substituting verbal questions and answers for the reality of life itself
in which questions will often answer themselves if we let them alone.

It is our habit of treating everything as a question—in other
words, of always tugging at things for an "answer" instead of letting
them be themselves—that quite often provokes vocation crises in the
monastery. After one has become sufficiently frustrated by a useless
search for answers and solutions where there are really few problems
or none at all, it is easy to conceive that the biggest and most authentic answer is to question one's original commitment and to go
back on it.

The primitive simplicity and authenticity of the monastic life itself should eventually calm the enraged hunger for "answers" and
allay the itch to be having and solving problems. Unfortunately
the very hope of "primitive monastic simplicity" seems to present itself only as a problem and as a decisive question to end all questions.
The only answer is not a new formula or a new program but simply
life itself in peace, humility, simplicity and silence. There are some
problems in life which are not to be solved except by being *lived* with
all the honesty, humility and courage that grace and nature can provide for us.

In the end, while admitting the reality of the "identity crisis" and
of the "need for authenticity," and while adjusting our own view of

the monastic life by a sage consideration of these concepts, we will
relax our rather obsessive grip on some of the more obdurate myths
of authoritarian logic and return to the basic respect for life, for faith,
for truth, for experience and for man himself which is implied in the
teachings of primitive monastic tradition. The monastic life itself has
retained its primitive validity or can easily recover it where the basic
principles of the life are respected. Where there is a genuine life of
solitude, poverty, prayer, silence, penance, work, charity, obedience:
where the law of the gospel, which is a law of love and grace, is fully
and fervently kept and not obscured by legalism and sermonizing,
it will be easy to see that here is a way of authenticity and truth
in which man does not merely discover and assert a private identity, a
"personality" in the sense of a successful role, but learns that the
truest way to find himself is to lose the self he has found in Christ.

III

The Identity Crisis

The crisis of religious vocations is no secret. It is everywhere the same. The departure of professed, including very many who have proved themselves capable of living a good religious life and apparently of successful adaptation, constitutes a vexing problem in all orders, not excluding our own.

If we try to study this problem in terms of the thinking, the mentality, the outlook, the psychology of the postulant, which all play an important part in his vocation and adaptation, perhaps we can evaluate the problem in some depth and not be content with superficial analysis. Naturally we will have to be content with only one or two aspects of the question.

It would be a mistake to presuppose that it is important to pinpoint the "fault," for instance, by "blaming" all the trouble on "modern youth," or blaming it on a retarded form of spirituality in the monasteries. It is rather a question of finding out the genuine and new needs of a new generation and of discovering how God asks the monastic life to meet these needs.

It is not enough to point to the moral disintegration of an affluent society, to broken homes, alcoholism, irresponsibility, delinquency and other widely prevalent evils, and then simply say that the modern postulant, even when he has the best kind of good will, is really deprived of the moral fiber and courage which the life requires.

Nor is it adequate to assume that in "the world" everybody is abandoned to strong and lusty passions and all are carried away with animal spirits, seeking unrestrained pleasure and infallibly getting what they seek. This is a totally misleading picture of the modern world in America, where in point of fact, though pleasure is presented and marketed under the most glowing colors, it eludes even those who can afford everything they desire. What is wrong with the world is not the satisfaction of carnal desires but universal confusion and frustration, leading to a collapse of real interest in life, the danger of despair, and the search for an outlet in various forms of extremism, fanaticism, or nihilism: or else, more commonly, a mindless and routine conformity to the demands of a highly organized social machine. These are symptoms. They are not the problem itself.

One might also be tempted to point to modern thought in all its various manifestations and to see in it nothing but so many incitements to revolt, to the assertion of self-will and lust, the love of anarchy and rebellion against all authority and all morality. All the most influential thinkers of modern times are thus regarded as disciples of demons and prophets of evil. Though we are not acquainted with them, we feel we "know" enough about them to reject them without further investigation. We feel we can say, without even a second thought, that they are in great part responsible for the mystery of evil, restlessness, dissatisfaction, doubt and rebellion in modern youth. They have "poisoned the mind of man." And there is nothing for us to do but counteract the poison of anarchy and self-will by the medicine of obedience, authority, control, etc.

Is it really that simple?

Who are these thinkers? Let us just name a few, going back a hundred years. Marx, Darwin, Kierkegaard were flourishing then. Nietzsche came soon after. Then Freud, Jung and Adler along with Lenin, then Sartre, the existentialists (Christian and otherwise). There is no question whatever that these thinkers have completely revolutionized the thought of modern man. They have created a whole new climate of thinking, and the chief reason for the impact of Teilhard de Chardin on modern thinking both in and out of the Church is due to the fact that he knows his Marx and Darwin.

But let us ask: Are all these men simply madmen or villains? Is it true that they are simply trying, out of malice, passion or envy, to undermine a beautiful and well-ordered world? Is not their concern for man something very genuine and are not their insights extremely valuable on occasion, even for us? Whatever may have been the remedies they prescribed, we ought to attend to their diagnosis of modern man. All of these thinkers are deeply concerned with the problem of man since the industrial revolution. They are trying to understand and explain the progressive dehumanization of man in the world of the machine, and trying to tell him some way to get control of himself and of his world so that he can be himself again.

Right or wrong, these prophets are all concerned with the main problem that faces us: Man is not himself. He has lost himself in the falsities and illusions of a massive organization. How can he recover his authenticity and his true identity? All these thinkers, even the Christians, tend to regard conventional forms of religion as being in league with the forces which have diminished and depersonalized man.

Whether we like it or not, their thought applies to us, and it is bound to affect us, even if only by the fact that they have created a climate of questioning, criticism and doubt in which the best of our postulants are going to come to us asking for authentic values and demanding not that we meet the requirements of an ancient written code, but that we be genuinely and spontaneously human first of all. This is a challenge rather than a problem.

Most postulants who come to our monasteries (with the possible exception of teenagers who have spent several years in a minor seminary) are deeply conscious of their need to give their lives a meaning which they cannot seem to find in the world outside. More and more postulants come to the monastery with the vague sense that they have not yet fully confronted the problem of identity. They are hoping that in the monastery they can finally work through their identity crisis. But it must be said at once that the monastery is not the place for that. Monastic life presupposes that one has found his identity and has profound personal convictions and personal standards to go on. Many postulants who have this problem are only vaguely aware of it. Others are more conscious of it, but cannot explain it. Obviously, few are able to be articulate about it. If they were, it would mean that the problem was already half solved. Yet even then, does their experience in the monastery help them to develop a deeper insight?

The crisis of identity which is everywhere normal in adolescence has become a grave problem in America extending far beyond adolescence and through young adulthood. Possibly there are many who never really resolve this problem in our society. One of the characteristics of "mass society" is precisely that it tends to keep man from fully achieving his identity, from operating fully as an autonomous person, from growing up and becoming spiritually and emotionally adult.

What is meant by identity? Many facets of the concept could be considered. For practical purposes here we are talking about one's own authentic and personal beliefs and convictions, based on experience of oneself as a person, experience of one's ability to choose and reject even good things which are not relevant to one's own life.

One does not receive "identity" in this sense along with life and vegetative existence. To have identity is not merely to have a face and a name, a recognizable physical presence. Identity in this deep sense is something that one must create for oneself by choices that are significant and that require a courageous commitment in the face of anguish and risk. This means much more than just having an address and a name in the telephone book. It means having a belief one stands by; it means having certain definite ways of responding to life, of meeting its demands, of loving other people and, in the last analysis, of serving God. In this sense, identity is one's witness to truth in one's life.

This does not mean merely the capacity to cling with conviction to official or external standards, to values which one does not personally experience as good but which one accepts in order to experience security, in order to please authority and so on.

The monk or novice who thinks he strongly feels certain values in our life and apparently embraces them simply because he experiences the security of "belonging" and of pleasing someone else, or pleasing the community, or the superior, etc., is perhaps evading the identity crisis. He is not in a position to make a serious choice of his vocation. Yet many have gone on to vows in this state of mind, urged by superiors to do so.

On the other hand, the problem of opposition raises an identity crisis for many. They confront things in the life that raise serious questions. These questions are perfectly reasonable and legitimate questions. But a person who has not really matured thinks that the mere presence of such questions is a problem, an infidelity. He may choose to question the values of the monastic life, but in doing so he imagines that he is automatically rejecting them, and then the life becomes unbearable because, though he cannot apparently accept the monastic life, he also feels he cannot commit himself to anything else. Since he has no definite ideas or standards of his own he has nothing to "stand by" and, hence, in that sense feels himself to be "unreal" and without identity. He is not able to question, to doubt, and to make a choice. The fact of questioning seems to him to dictate a negative choice, especially if he is surrounded by others who communicate the same insecurity and doubt to him. Of course there is no real solution to the identity crisis simply in opposing authority. This is an adolescent trait. In a supposed "adult" who simply wastes time pitting himself against authority in trivialities there is a real lack of identity, or a false identity which maintains itself by provoking resistance (attention) rather than by flattering or cajoling authority. In either case, the "center" of identity is experienced to some extent not in oneself but in the other. This is "alienation" in a psychological sense.

In the Middle Ages, the mentality of the monastic postulant was much less confused than it is today. Society was homogeneous. There was a great deal of violence and disorder, but one moral and religious standard was accepted as relevant. The meaning of the monastic life was hardly questioned, though an individual might conceivably doubt its relevance for him. Today everything is in question: monasticism, Christianity, reason, all values, humanity itself. Hence it is no longer easy for a person to discover his identity by choosing and embracing certain well-established traditional standards that no one doubts and simply experiencing these as his own.

To choose a value that is questioned and doubted is to place one-self in the position of being doubted. The mature person is able to assume this risk. He can embrace an unpopular idea, commit himself to it and to its consequences, and accept the fact that it means be-coming a problem and even in some way a "scandal" to others. It is in this way that most people today have to establish and affirm their identity. But it takes courage to do this. Hence *all* values are ques-tioned, or can be; to embrace any of them is to become an object of questioning and doubt. Those who shrink from personal respon-sibility shrink from this also. They seek to rest on an infallible au-thority or else take refuge in an area where questions are not asked.

What we are now about to say is in no sense an attack on "regu-larity" and exact observance of rules and customs. We are taking for granted that a mature and responsible man accepts the obligations of his state of life objectively and seriously fulfills them. A good monk keeps his rule and has mature and serious spiritual motives for doing so.

But there are others who in actual fact welcome the passivity and irresponsibility that are possible in a strictly controlled and organized life. For these the monastery offers opportunities for a false solution to the identity problem. Their obedience may be an evasion. These persons fear insecurity and seek security from a well-established and approved system that nobody questions. Rules clearly say what is right and wrong. The monk can turn his back on the world with its problems and forget it. He can simply follow the rules, do what he is told, and have security because everyone around him holds that this is "right" and that to do anything else is "wrong." He no longer has to think. Choices are made for him. Others are responsible. He need not care.

Furthermore, this conduct on his part is rewarded. He causes no trouble. He is therefore approved. His "rightness" is confirmed by the approval of superiors, and he feels he is "a good religious." His one source of insecurity is the apparent questioning of rules and standards by those who are less regular. He worries if these people are not firmly corrected, and he seeks to have them corrected. He worries if the work is not precisely regulated so that at every moment everyone knows exactly what is right and wrong, etc., etc.

His solution is to enter into a system where doubt is impossible. This looks like "faith," but is it?

Someone will say: Why be so subtle about it? Why split psychological hairs? Even supposing they are artificial and immature interiorly, these monks are objectively fulfilling their obligations, and it would be hard to tell the difference between them and the really mature monks whose seriousness and regularity are based on fully responsible identities before God and man. These others are at least able to act like good religious, and since they also desire to be good monks, who is to say that they are not so? These people have good will, good intentions, and they are "obedient." They do not rock the boat. They help keep order. They are "edifying." Why complain? Let us be grateful that we have so many such monks. They may not be ideal, they may be a little stiff and unnatural, but who knows if they are not saints, after all?

It is quite true that no one can say what God thinks of these men and of their good will. It is not for us to question the fact that he will reward their efforts to love him according to their own ability. But the fact remains that we are talking about the human and personal development which is in the line of man's natural maturing and which is therefore willed by God for all. If these people, without any moral fault, are to some extent deficient in maturity, the absence of fault does not make their deficiency a good in itself, something that others can accept knowingly as good. If this passive and evasive response to the identity problem is a false solution, then its falsity must be noted for what it is. They may think they want to give God everything, but by their (inculpable) failure to really mature and attain to full personal stature, they are keeping themselves in a state where they really cannot give him the fullness of service and love to which he is entitled. This is proved by the fact that these people often crack up and become psychotic, which happens when it is no longer possible for them to maintain the artificial and rigid black-and-white, right-and-wrong view of the monastic life on purely external motives. Because they lack inner identity and inner truth, they cannot face the real problems of life if these bear down on them too hard. But the monastery may, it is true, provide them with a permanent refuge in which they can always more or less successfully avoid facing reality in themselves and in others.

It is often evident that such lives are really to a great extent humanly sterile, no matter how much we may rationalize them as "holy," edifying, meritorious.

For example, unlike those who are mature and solid monks and live their vocation with deep personal motives and faith, these people are often eccentric in their conduct and bizarre in their theology. Their devotions are often marginal and queer. They generally lack sound judgment and even common sense. They are often quite incapable of normal human relationships, and their contacts with others are stilted and artificial—or else perhaps they go to the other extreme and become clinging and sentimental. They are always raising strange and useless questions or making naive propositions. They are usually harmless and well-intentioned, but sometimes they become critical and go about ferreting out the "faults" of others and denouncing them. In one word, these people are in many ways deficient and impoverished, and their external regularity is just about all they have. Instead of developing their true identity they have acquired a pseudo-identity. They are not persons but only "characters."

What is much more important: the apparent uselessness and sterility of the lives of the externally compliant religious who are approved, who do not rock the boat, who do not raise doubts and questions, who conform, who are passive, is a constant source of doubt to others in whom the identity problem is more acute.

In other words: those who experience doubt, who question their vocation, who have to face the fact that they might be wrong, or even that they might have made profession without sufficient motives, are brought into a state of crisis by observing those who have adopted the false "compliant" solution. They cannot perhaps formulate their serious misgivings, but they know and experience the fact that there is "something wrong with this edifying behavior." (It is important to note that this is for them a genuine and personal experience. It is therefore something real. It is something to work with. It is also important for the monastery and for the community. It is important for us. It may be telling us something we badly need to know.) They may have a valid and disquieting intuition of the real lack of identity and lack of authenticity in these others. They are really aware, however dimly, that the "false solution" of those who have evaded the issue and simply complied, is indeed false. But because they themselves have no deep convictions of their own, because they do not experience their own values as personal and authentic, because they do not fully dare to commit themselves to some other solution which is more genuine, they remain in a state of doubt, frustration, resentment.

It is at this point, we must face it squarely, that the behavior of the externally "good religious" who, in good faith, unconsciously, certainly without guilt, has in fact compromised with one of the most basic demands of his humanity (the demand for authenticity and personal integrity) is a scandal to those who are still deeply aware of their need to attain to a fully human and personal identity, to become authentic human persons in order to give themselves to God as monks.

What follows is of course that the religious truth of monastic profession is brought into question. From failure on the natural level comes a questioning of the supernatural.

Time after time, young monks, novices, postulants, try to express their anxiety and their distress over the fact that, though they cannot formulate it, they feel that the life of some of the older monks as it is concretely lived and "approved," as it is manifested in the monks who have "made it" and are apparently the ones who are most adapted to the monastic life, is inauthentic, an evasion. They feel it is unreal because it is less than human. They feel instinctively that there is something wrong with a sweeping claim that all this rigidity and formality, this artificiality in otherwise good and normal human beings, is really "supernatural." This claim is something that they find deeply disturbing, and gradually they have to admit that they have genuine motives for being disturbed by it. Are they right?

(Here of course an important qualification is necessary: First of all, this intuition of inauthenticity can be greatly exaggerated, and those who have gradually decided that they can't face the monastic life any more do tend to build up too strong a case against the poor monks they see in the community. Even the more artificial ones are not as bad as all that: with their limitations they always retain a certain simplicity, genuineness and goodness which it is unjust and uncharitable to overlook. And then there are in every community a few excellent priests and brothers who, while not being in every respect ideal, are really authentic and genuine Christian persons, mature, simple, direct, honest, and totally human. These are always recognized and respected for what they are, though their presence may be conveniently overlooked by the monk who is intent on arguing his way out the front door.)

Yet these "critics" still love the monastic life. They still see something very real, very desirable, very healthy, in fact something irreplaceable in the spirit of the Rule of St. Benedict (in its honesty and simplicity) and in authentic monastic tradition, insofar as it all reflects the sanity and wisdom of the Gospels. They still want to "truly seek God." But they feel they can no longer reconcile the "search for God" and for truth with an external and routine existence in which they cannot experience in themselves any opening up of their own inner truth. It seems to them that the mere carrying out of actions which they personally find meaningless, in the trust that this will somehow prove meritorious and will be rewarded in heaven, reflects upon God himself. Can God really ask man to sacrifice the most basic realities of identity and meaning in order to live a life that seems absurd? Does this not call into question the very idea of God? We may try to assuage this doubt by mystical concepts—the "dark night" and so on—but mystical formulations are not called for here. These people are not in the mystical night of the superhuman illuminations; they are in the subhuman and psychological night of depersonalization, of facelessness, lack of identity. God is not asking them to be subhuman and to remain without identity. He wants them to become persons so that they can love him and give themselves totally to his truth.

In any event, to resume what has been said so far: it quite often happens that, in practice, a young American who enters the monastery and there comes face to face with his identity crisis tends to solve it "honestly" by coming to recognize that he does not have sufficient motives for staying or that, even if he has vows, there is such good reason for his leaving that it now seems to be a greater good for him to leave.

If this is in fact true, it is quite an indictment of our system. And perhaps the realization of this is what makes us unwilling to really go too deeply into the question. The question remains: can we adjust our life and our view of our life in such a way that it will be capable of being lived in a more authentic and honest way by modern youth, that is to say, can we offer them a life in which they will really be able to find themselves, realize their identity, authentically grow and develop spiritually as well as mentally and emotionally?

Are we capable of offering modern youth a life in which, if they are generous and honest (which they usually are), they can become completely mature Christians and monks?

One might at this point discuss something that always arises in connection with this problem of "authenticity": the question of our "antiquated observances." To what extent can they retain a deep meaning for modern Americans? This is certainly something that people question quite often. The fact that as novices they may at first be willing to accept certain rudimentary spiritual explanations of our monastic behavior does not necessarily mean that they accept the observances in their hearts. They are probably just shelving the question—until it comes up later in connection with a postprofession vocation crisis.

But the question of observances and of their meaning is too complex to go into here. And once again, the usages and the way they are observed are symptoms rather than roots of the trouble.

One thing must be said: mere modernization of usages, of liturgical practice, of rules, of behavior, will not solve the basic problem, which lies much deeper. The agitation and very active concern with which so many are plunging into the work of changing our customs, our liturgy, etc., certainly have a good aspect. It certainly is related to a general renewal of monastic life which is manifesting itself everywhere. But at the same time, insofar as this need for change is flavored with a kind of desperation, it may be seen as proceeding from people who are still struggling with this deep identity problem and who hope against hope that changes of rule and ritual will solve it for them.

It must be stated categorically that the problem cannot be solved from the outside. No amount of "modernization" will make an alienated personality experience himself as fully real, though it may help him to confront his problem more squarely.

Nor can the problem be solved by legislation.

Very often in the efforts made to devise new solutions and get them legislated, we see immature people acting out their problem in relation to authority, in relation to control, and it may still be the adolescent problem of identity, which they are trying to handle in this way.

They are perhaps trying to persuade themselves that they are "real," that is to say, that their ideas and opinions, their tastes and needs have an authentic value.

But if I am the kind of person who cannot believe that my ideas and convictions have authentic value unless they are the object of a whole gamut of legislative acts on the part of the order and the Church, then I prove by that fact that I do not believe in myself, that I cannot take my convictions seriously, that I do not experience my own inner motives as real until they are certified as real by external and official approval.

This does not mean that a mature person never consults anyone else and never seeks advice. He certainly asks advice and accepts it when it is needed and useful. He can also adjust himself to the will and need of another and renounce his own way in order to do what another wants of him. But in all this he knows when he himself is convinced, because he experiences his own convictions as inner realities, not just as "feelings" or "impressions" or dubious manifestations of something or other needing confirmation by someone else before he can admit that he has them.

It is sometimes assumed as axiomatic that every action of the monk must be subject to external control, even, in some cases, that every thought of the monk must be subject to external control. To renounce one's autonomy to the point of abandoning all spontaneous and independent reflection, intellection, volition, even feeling, is sometimes presented as an ascetic ideal. But this is an impossibility, and even the idea that such a thing is desirable can do irreparable harm. The attempt to live in this manner and to make others do so is gravely damaging to souls and is a flagrant violation of Christian truth and of the integrity of the human person made in God's image. Our monastic life can at times suffer seriously from this overcontrol.

To be more exact, it used to suffer seriously from it. In practice there is much more spontaneity and variety allowed today. Complete submission to absolute external control is rarely demanded any more in practice, but it is still accepted in theory as right and good, as the "supernatural" and "monastic" way for a monk to live. This creates problems both for those who are seriously attempting to submit in all things and abandon all responsibility for themselves into the hands of others and for those who are in doubt about the validity of their motives and the honesty of remaining indefinitely "minors" in the religious life.

Overcontrol thus tends to do just the opposite from what it is theoretically expected to do.

In theory it is supposed to be a manifestation of faith and supernatural spirit. It is supposed to strengthen faith and the supernatural spirit. In actual fact it breeds doubt, and it eventually undermines both faith and vocation.

Overcontrol of an immature religious does not make him mature, does not strengthen him. It merely suppresses for the time being the questions he ought to be raising and the initiatives he ought to be taking. And its chief effect is to keep him in a state of doubt. It makes him inert, hesitant, confused, helpless and frustrated.

Actually, there is great harm not only to the religious but also to the community in maintaining him in a state of doubt, ignorance and insecurity.

Here are some of the effects of overcontrol on immature monks:

a. By deliberately withholding information from them, and thus keeping them insecure, superiors unwittingly create in their subjects an altogether inordinate need and desire for information. For instance, the immature monk in his identity crisis now becomes convinced that knowledge is altogether essential for his maturity. Hence the veritable panic with which so many young religious now are hunting for knowledge, for education, for information, for information which they feel they have lacked and which they are trying to catch up with. This is one of the more usual and more urgent symptoms of our present crisis.

b. By keeping the subject in constant doubt about himself, by making him repeatedly experience himself as a being of dubious worth, a questionable object, besides preventing him from having inner peace which is necessary to a solid interior life and for growth, one makes him all the more likely either to doubt everything and everyone, or else encourages a blind dependency which in the end cannot help becoming pathological if the person is seriously vulnerable.

c. By fomenting this constant doubt in the heart of the individual monk, one actually creates in him a very ambivalent attitude toward authority. The young monk may experience himself acutely as not worthy of trust, not worthy of being informed, not "able" to know and understand, etc. This may precipitate all kinds of desperate maneuvers to allay doubt, to change the attitude of authority. It ends by causing a great deal more trouble for the superior.

In résumé: It is likely that in the case of modern American youth the phenomenon of overcontrol in our monasteries will result only in confirmed self-doubt on their part, coupled with a deep and eventually hostile suspicion of authority. In a word, overcontrol is dangerous and self-defeating. It is a source of many serious problems and it really solves nothing.

Let us not make the mistake of thinking that overcontrol is really a religious value in disguise, that it really has to do with religious obedience and with surrender to God. Let us not imagine that overcontrol answers a real need on the part of the postulant who comes from an anarchic and libertine society in which there is nothing but license and self-will rampant on all sides.

We must be quite clear about one thing above all: overcontrol is one of the salient features of the secular world today. It is particularly related to godlessness and materialism.

Indeed one might argue that it is the largely unsuccessful but nevertheless thorough systematization of control in secular life that is to a great extent responsible for the apparent lawlessness of certain reactions (delinquency etc.). These rebellions are in their turn frantic and desperate attempts to meet overcontrol with genuine independence and authentic identity. Because overcontrol is precisely so powerful, the attempts usually fail.

The world is dominated by the questionable, but inevitable, power of mass society.

We will not here go into all the manifestations of overcontrol, which is just as evident in our affluent consumer society as it is in the rigid totalitarian societies beyond the iron curtain. The manifestations are different, that's all. With us the control is largely anonymous and decentralized but nonetheless effective for being anonymous. It would be easy to cite hundreds of ways in which, by advertising etc., the consumer is treated consistently as a minor and is maintained in a state of psychological passivity and dependence, so that he is "unable to resist." (It is important to keep the consumer from having too much of a mind of his own, yet at the same time, to create the illusion that he is in the know by feeding him all kinds of bogus information about the product, plus elaborate and "efficient" instructions about how to open the package and make use of the product.)

To sum it all up in one word, our postulants come to us from a society in which man is alienated, in which he is systematically deprived of a serious identity, in which he cannot believe in his dignity, in which he has good reason to be profoundly skeptical of everything and everyone, and in which he tends to renounce all hope of experiencing himself as real and genuinely worthwhile. It is a society in which he has not much left but to resign himself, with a sigh, to passivity with a can of beer in front of the TV.

The term alienation is used of a human being who is systematically kept, or who allows himself to be kept, in a social situation in which *he exists purely and simply for somebody else.*

His reason for existing and for acting is not in himself, but in someone else's profit. That is to say that what he does is vastly more profitable and pleasant for someone else, and he gets little or nothing out of it himself. His life lacks meaning. As far as he personally is concerned, there is no reason for him to exist at all. Life is not worth living. (Of course he can manage, if he is strong, to salvage a little meaning and satisfaction. This was possible, as Viktor Frankl has shown, even in the ultimate meaninglessness and alienation of the concentration camp. The prisoner in the concentration camp is the type of the completely alienated man, who is totally under the control of the power of mass society. Is this the monastic ideal?)

(Let us not imagine that this "existing for another" is compatible with perfect love. The alienated man cannot love. He has nothing to give. Nothing is his. The lover is able to give himself completely to another precisely because he is his own to give. He is not alienated. He has an identity. He knows what is his to surrender. The alienated man has no chance to surrender. He has simply been "taken over" by total control.)

How will an "alienated" person act and experience the realities of life in a monastery?

In his spiritual life he will tend not to experience realities directly, but secondhand. In the liturgy, for example, instead of deeply feeling and understanding the meaning of the chants, texts, rites, and sacred action directly and personally as relevant to his own response to Christ the Savior and his relationship of brotherhood with the other monks as fellow disciples of Christ, he will experience the fact that in doing these things he is doing what is right: he is doing what is approved by the Church; he is doing what the superiors and professors of liturgy have described as the highest form of worship.

In his reading, he will not so much read books that deeply interest him and arouse a profound intellectual, affective and spiritual response which is personal to him and which he experiences as light to follow God's paths. He will rather experience the fact that what he is reading is entirely familiar and safe, that there is nothing about it that is disturbing. It echoes the ideas and experience that have been publicly praised and approved by others, especially by Reverend Father, Father Master, etc.

In the question of monastic renewal, the "alienated" person may doubtless take a fairly active part in new movements, yet without abandoning his alienation. Let us suppose that he admits to consciousness just enough realization of his condition to suggest that a change is needed. He will then "experience" in himself not the real, profound and personal need for a radical change that goes with genuine renewal and implies a certain anguish, insecurity, and risk. He will rather experience the fact that a certain line of change is now approved by forward-looking theologians and publicists. Hence he will accept these ideas not with any intention of involving himself in the anguish and uncertainty of a real renewal, but simply in order to experience himself as "with" the approved ones. His very desire for change is a desire not for the anguish of renewal and self-commitment, but for the safety of having made the right change, the right adjustment, without too much difficulty. "Everything will have changed and it will be all right." Everything will have changed except his alienation.

After having at considerable length studied aspects of the identity problems (without by any means exhausting them, or indeed even scratching the surface), let us briefly conclude with some of the implications for the monastic life and for renewal.

Monastic renewal must now more than ever aim at authenticity.

But we must take care to note a very special aspect of authenticity which has become crucially important now. It will no longer be enough to guarantee a kind of "juridical authenticity," that is to say, a monastic practice which is faithful to the documents of the past. More than ever a merely literal authenticity (fidelity to the letter) will be not only unsatisfactory but disastrous.

The authenticity which the modern monk sincerely and rightly desires, whether or not he may be fully conscious of it, is first of all a fidelity to his own truth and his own inner being as a person. The very first thing of all (something that was much less precarious in the past) is the authentic affirmation of his own identity. Without this starting point, everything else will be lost.

But a monastic life that tends systematically to deny and frustrate the monk in this quest of his own inner authenticity first of all will necessarily threaten the authenticity of his vocation. It will leave him confronted with the choice: either to submit, sacrifice his integrity and his fidelity to this first demand of conscience and live like a zombie—or else to leave the monastery. For many it will reduce itself to this hard choice. Only the mature will be able to adjust to the monastery in spite of everything and live as true monks even though the spirit of the community may be to some extent inauthentic.

We cannot even begin to understand the task of monastic renewal and of a really meaningful aggiornamento, unless we take account of this danger.

Being aware of the need of the postulant for inner and personal authenticity first of all, and taking account of the fact that we cannot afford to admit people who are not capable of seriously confronting the problem themselves, we will conclude that we must in no circumstances tolerate the survival of a spirituality which seems, either explicitly or implicitly, to require the sacrifice of personal authenticity and integrity. That would be the sacrifice of truth. It would be a living lie.

We must be very careful indeed not to tolerate any ambiguity on this score, for example by approving concepts of humility and obedience which seem to say that the complete abdication of one's personal autonomy and dignity is a basic value in monastic asceticism. We must not preach an obedience that is mere passive compliance, a humility that is the glad acceptance of depersonalized abjection, a spirituality that glorifies, as "abnegation," the total abdication of all human worth and all identity. This must be seen for what it is: a debasing of man which gives no glory to God, but is bad theology and false supernaturalism, and which seriously endangers the faith of those who allow themselves to be caught in it for a while, only to leave later disgusted and disillusioned.

This has very important theological implications because a spirituality which despises nature and contemns the human person is basically divisive and Manichaean. It implies a strongly dualistic concept of God and his creation in which creation seems to be opposed to the goodness of God and completely *alien* to God; indeed creation seems in this light to be cursed by God rather than blessed and redeemed. Thus instead of using the goods of nature which God has given us, we tend to fear and despise them. We reject them and trample on them with contempt. But when it comes to our own freedom, our integrity, our dignity as persons, we cannot afford to do this! To contemn the human person and his identity is to contemn the image of God reflected in man, his creature and his Son.

We must on the contrary recognize that nature is not irreconcilable with grace, and by the Incarnation and Redemption, nature has become penetrated and hallowed by grace. Nature has become the rich field in which grace brings forth its harvest. To sterilize the fruitful capacities of nature is then to sterilize grace itself by depriving it of the ground in which its seed will grow and fructify.

In the contemplative life above all, lack of identity is a disaster.

The monastic life demands first of all a profound understanding and acceptance of solitude. The spirit of the monastic life, even of the cenobitic form of the monastic life, is the spirit of solitude and of the desert, the spirit of the life lived like that of St. John the Baptist, Elijah, and St. Anthony, alone in the presence of God ("By the Living God in whose presence I stand," said Elijah, in I Kings 17:1).

But this capacity for solitude is nothing else than the full affirmation of one's identity, that is to say, the complete acceptance of oneself as willed by God and of one's lot as given by God. It is also the complete and loving acceptance of the ability to choose and to love, the capacity and the necessity for choice which one must make in the presence of God, under the eye of God, in the light of his truth and of his redemptive love.

This affirmation of identity is not proud; it is not by any means a *non serviam*, for the fullest identity is found only in the readiness to serve. It is the *Ecce ancilla Domini* of the Mother of God. (*Non serviam* means in effect the refusal to accept oneself and one's identity, one's place and one's mission, as gifts of God. It means the affirmation of a false identity, and therefore of nothingness, set up over against being, and requiring to be defended by prevarication.)

It should therefore be quite clear that the failure to accept and understand the basically solitary character of the monastic life means to some extent a failure of the monk to fully achieve his identity and authenticity in that life.

Those monks today who are conscious of the problem of authenticity, and who feel that the only solution for the need of individual monks for identity must be resolved in active apostolic work and dealing with other people, are quite probably thinking realistically in terms of the modern thinkers, from Marx down to Teilhard de Chardin, Emmanuel Mounier, etc., whose thought is essentially oriented to activity and even to some extent suspicious of contemplation. This is perhaps due to the deformations and evasions that have been tolerated and preached in the name of "the contemplative life." It is true that our life can be made to seem nothing more than canonized inertia. But this is a total falsification of the meaning of monasticism.

It is for us not to surrender our monastic life and its tradition but to get down to its real meaning and to revive its genuine values.

The choir, we must admit it, is at least for choir religious and novices quite often the scene of the most serious difficulties with personal integrity and authenticity of prayer.

It is in choir that the monk often feels himself most completely depersonalized, most totally subject to overcontrol, most thoroughly alienated.

This of course may be due to the accumulated failures of many monks over many years creating an atmosphere of frustration, negativism, and thinly veiled despair in many choirs. There is no question that the choir is and can be very trying. But is this not due in large part to ignorance and even to a kind of refusal to consider the real nature of choral prayer?

Is this not in turn due to a deeper ignorance not only of Christian asceticism but of the basic truths of theology?

The purely individualistic concept of asceticism and of prayer is, paradoxically, very harmful to the development of true personal identity. The identity of the person is fully realized only in a conscious and mature collaboration with others. The "atomized" concept of the choir as a group of individuals, each enclosed in his private solitude and recollection, results in depersonalization, stupor and indifference. The phenomenon of sleep in choir and in meditation is simply an evasion from identity and presence.

It is true that American vocations are ill-prepared for genuine collective prayer, praying with others in any real communal sense.

Is this not due in great part precisely to the problem we have been discussing? It is the person who has fully realized his identity and accepted it that is able not only to face God in solitude but also to meet his brother in love and collaboration. He is the one best fitted to "pray with" others in unity.

The person who has an identity crisis will have it in choir more than anywhere else, because there it is most difficult to evade.

In choir he is apparently reduced to nonentity (in terms of the individualism with which he is familiar). The prayers are "not his" and yet they are so "universal" that they tend to escape him and he cannot even get the secondhand experience of satisfaction with them because they are "official." He may feel totally disoriented and lost.

For this reason, of course, there is a tremendous push for the vernacular in the monastic liturgy, a push so anguished and so concerted that it surely represents a real need. Those of us who are satisfied with the Latin liturgy, and who have been able in the past to taste its deep and genuine realities, will probably have to content ourselves with an English office that will be in itself much less excellent, but which will better serve the needs of a new generation no longer capable of tolerating a Latin office that is not understood. We must frankly admit that we owe them this and that it is only right to let them have it. It is to be hoped that the Latin office will not altogether disappear: there may still be room for one community or other here and there where it could be kept up, precisely because it has such great intrinsic worth (as artists and musicians in the wicked world frequently remind us).

In the most characteristic practices of the contemplative life of the monastery, silence, enclosure, *lectio* and *oratio,* and even *contemplatio,* the identity crisis poses very serious problems.

First of all, the identity crisis makes monastic silence almost intolerable for someone who is anxiously seeking to experience his own reality by seeing himself understood and accepted by others. This is a very normal adolescent trait, and it accounts for the fact that young novices and professed are often so wildly communicative. If they have to remain silent and alone, they become overwhelmed with doubt of their own reality (not in a metaphysical sense, but in our life they cannot experience themselves as "being there" with any certitude because they just have no way of really telling where they stand and what they want and what they really mean).

The immature person, when forced to be silent, tends to experience his inauthenticity and has no escape from it. Communication with others, even about nothing, at least offers some diversion. No need to insist on this common and rather well understood fact of our life. It simply indicates that those who are not mature enough to accept the discipline of silence cannot be admitted. To admit them and then provide recreation for them will not solve the problem; it will simply diminish the seriousness of the monastic life for the more mature ones, without helping the immature to become serious monks.

In the matter of prayer, contemplation and "mystical theology" one extremely important point must be mentioned.

The "alienated" and somewhat immature person, the one who may still be trying to negotiate his identity crisis, may and often does, in the beginning, seem to have some evidence of contemplative prayer. And if this is not the case, their "dryness" and "darkness" may very easily be taken for the kind of thing mystical writers have characterized as the Night of the Senses. (An incautious director might even take the extreme distress of a depersonalized monk as "Night of the Spirit.")

Of course there is absolutely no point in trying to determine whether these people, usually good and sincere, are receiving real graces of prayer. Whether they are or not, the pattern is usually this: they come to the monastery, they find themselves sheltered, their lives are completely regulated, the burden of responsibility is lifted from their shoulders, they are surrounded by benign authority figures who give evidence of liking them and even of taking them seriously. In this situation, these novices and young monks may experience a new feeling of relief, of self-acceptance, and they assume that their troubles are over. Strongly supported, they relax, they remain passive in an experience of contentment and love (which is rooted in the fact that they feel "safe" and "accepted" for the first time, perhaps, in their lives). This contentment is of course most evident in moments of prayer, and their prayer is easily prolonged. This happiness has a place in their lives no doubt, but it may turn out to be completely meaningless insofar as it represents nothing but the momentary renunciation of self-concern and anxiety that comes from totally leaning on another—not God in this case but the superior, the rule, the ambient of safety provided by the community.

One might say that this respite might quite possibly be used, and a good spiritual father can perhaps take advantage of it to help in solving the identity crisis by bringing the young monk to face himself.

It would however be a very great mistake to take the dryness and trials of an anguished, depersonalized young monk for a "mystical purification." It is not so at all. The alienated man can certainly feel in himself an awful sense of meaninglessness, of dryness, helplessness, void. But this is because he is not fully a person and because he lacks some of the normal natural resources of a mature person. He is a diminished and spiritually handicapped man. He can certainly be helped, but it will not help him at all to encourage him by the false assurance (often given in perfectly good faith) that his emptiness marks him as a higher kind of being, a "contemplative" and a "mystic."

Nothing is more disillusioning than persons of limited and mediocre humanity, less than mature, incapable of genuine love for others, narrow, impoverished, lacking in imagination and even in common sense, who have been taught that they are somehow quite extraordinary beings and that their very limitations are signs that they are in the "mystical way." Established firmly in complacency and illusion by this error, they remain as a scandal and a portent to those whom God has perhaps brought to the monastery with real potentialities for the life of prayer.

One final word about work.

It is in our work above all that the most obvious and most tangible opportunities for personal development exist. This does not mean that we should therefore get more and more involved in work and even go out into the parishes. But it does mean that we must take frank and honest advantage of the real value of monastic work.

First of all, let us recognize the profound human importance of hard manual labor in a natural setting! Factory work and office work are not the same thing and will not fill the bill. They may be to some extent unavoidable, but we should take care not to reduce our work merely to "making money" and therefore doing what is most profitable.

At least in a monastery, the spiritual, psychological and biological value of physical work ought to be recognized. Work is for the spiritual good of the monk first of all, and therefore it follows that even though the profit of the monastic business may be somewhat reduced, there should always be a good proportion of field work and work in the woods, even though these operations may not pay. It would be totally shortsighted, unmonastic and un-Benedictine to "take more care for temporal things" and deprive the monks of outdoor work in the midst of nature on purely materialistic grounds. On the contrary, the greater profit of the monastery, in all respects, will certainly be safeguarded in the long run. The monks will be healthier, they will be more at peace, they will pray better, they will work better in every job.

Also it must be admitted that it is at manual work that the monk can best deal with the identity problem. It is at work that he can begin to experience genuine responsibility (assuming he is allowed to do so). It is at work that he can begin most simply and spontaneously to experience himself as a real person, by seeing before him the results of his efforts, in a concrete contribution to the life of his brothers. This is certainly most important. It accounts for the fact that at least here in this community quite a few novices ask to pass from the choir to the brothers and assert that they feel that the "brothers life is much more real." This is precisely because of the work and because of the relatively less control to which the brothers are subjected.

Finally it is in manual labor that the young monk can come to appreciate his identity by respecting the identity of others in collaboration with them on useful tasks. It is here too that a certain amount of leeway in talking can be a great help (instead of the nonsensical ideal of an artificial and depersonalized "recreation" which would only make the problem of authenticity more acute). If a young monk or novice is placed as apprentice under an older monk who really knows his job and from whom he himself can learn to become a good workman, it will do more than anything else to help him mature and grow in his vocation.

In conclusion, let us recognize that if in the monastery the work, the liturgy, the study and so on are all overorganized and made artificial, if they are more and more removed from the sphere of *nature* and brought indoors to the office or assembly line, if the monastery comes to resemble a big business and a plant surrounded by noise and clatter, the monks will certainly lose very much. They will tend to be more and more alienated, taking refuge from routines in which they cannot take a serious human interest because they are the same impersonal and organized routines they left in the world.

If this happens to a monastery, then there is no hope of renewal no matter how much you tinker with the liturgy, no matter how much you psychoanalyze the monks, no matter what trivial rewards you grant them in the form of amusements and diversions or trips and vacations.

The monastic life today stands over against the world with a mission to affirm not only the message of salvation but also those most basic human values which the world most desperately needs to regain: personal integrity, inner peace, authenticity, identity, inner depth, spiritual joy, the capacity to love, the capacity to enjoy God's creation and give thanks. If the world fails to find these things in the monastery, then there is little value in following the latest in liturgy, having the most efficient machines and operating a profitable business.

Our first task is to be fully human and to enable the youth of our time to find themselves and develop as men and as sons of God. There is no need for a community of religious robots without minds, without hearts, without ideas and without faces. It is this mindless alienation that characterizes "the world" and life in the world. Monastic spirituality today must be a personalistic and Christian humanism that seeks and saves man's intimate truth, his personal identity, in order to consecrate it entirely to God.

IV

Dialogue and Renewal

The task of renewal in the monastic and cloistered orders is just as urgent and just as challenging as it is everywhere else in the Church, though the problems and risks involved may in fact appear to be less dramatic. In order to understand this task of renewal we have to remember that the Vatican Council did not simply command religious to reform from the top down. The renewal of religious life, including the cloisters and monasteries of contemplatives, is a work in which the religious themselves must actively share. Indeed, it would seem that the share of the "ordinary religious" may prove in some sense decisive. In other words, there is a big difference between a "renewal" which requires active participation at every level and a reform which starts at the top with the action of superiors and reaches the subject passively through new laws and new decrees to be accepted and obeyed. Ultimately, of course, there must be new legislation. But it is understood that the legislation should be much more flexible and that it should leave room for a larger measure of self-determination in communities where the subjects themselves will (we hope) play a more active role in guiding their own communal destinies.

Not only are subjects participating in the work of giving their lives a new shape and a new scope, they are also to some extent going to the root of their contemplative vocation trying to rediscover its true meaning. This means a reexamination of the very essence of their life and vocation. Not that the essence of the life will be necessarily changed: but a new understanding of that essence has to be arrived at. In other words, it is no longer sufficient to take for granted the accepted and conventional ideas of what the contemplative life is all about. The contemplative ideal must be rediscovered in new terms. There is a difference between what stems from living tradition (from tradition as fully alive now) and what is accepted passively and without question from a dead past. What is valid is Spirit and Life. It is from God. What is invalid is dead—it is mere human custom.

It is no longer possible merely to impose sixteenth-century ideas on the postulant who enters the cloister from "the world" of the twentieth century and expect him to accept everything without question. The modern world, speaking through the modern postulant, will make itself heard in the cloistered dialogue—perhaps with devastating effect. But the cloistered orders, like all others, must take this voice into account if dialogue and renewal are to be effective. On the other hand, this voice is not the only one that deserves to be heard, nor is it automatically and in every case entitled to say the last word on the grave problems of contemplatives.

There are two ways in which the monastic community can look at the postulant whom it expects to recruit from "the world"—ways which may reflect differences, and perhaps rather profound differences, in one's concept of the Church, the monastic life and the "world." The first way considers the monastic order (the Church too, by implication) as the embodiment as well as the guardian of a fixed traditional ideal which can never be questioned. It also considers that this ideal can be easily discovered—by asking those who know: the superiors.

Without examining too closely what the authentic monastic tradition really is, this outlook simply assumes that what "is there," what is "given," what is more or less "established," is also in fact perfectly traditional. Thus we find that an "accepted spirituality" is considered without investigation or question to embody a living tradition and to say the last word on what is and is not "contemplative" or "monastic." Though not really official, this "spirituality" has common currency in the order, is taken for granted by superiors and is received by subjects without question and even without serious interest, as if it could not really be questioned. As a result, the real monastic tradition becomes drained of life and sap and becomes more or less inert. By virtue of a passively accepted, vague, indefinite "spirituality," tradition tends to be transformed into routine. Yet this accepted attitude toward monastic observance, embodied in formal regularity and in a somewhat schematic teaching, stands radically opposed to all other ideologies, especially to that of "the world."

Hence the postulant is regarded as one who comes to the order with the intention of being stripped of an old ideology and clothed with a new one—the "accepted spirituality." And of course more than ideas are at stake: a whole new way of life will reflect the new ideas or indeed the new ideas will perhaps come as a result of the new behavior. If the novice learns to walk humbly, sit humbly, cough humbly, etc., he will also think humble thoughts. At least we hope so. But in any case, he now has wrong ideas and he will soon be given right ideas.

There is of course a genuine charitable concern for the spiritual needs of the postulant, but it is taken for granted, first, that the community perfectly well understands his needs and his possible problems (they are all characteristic problems of "the world" and can all be schematically reduced to a few simple headings: pride, self-satisfaction, self-seeking, self-will), second, that the solution to his problems and the fulfillment of his needs is ultimately a simple matter. It is in fact assumed that the postulant, by the mere fact of desiring to enter the monastic order, thereby signifies his recognition that he is "wrong," that he wishes to escape from the errors and the ambiguities of his worldly state, that he is resolved to have done with these errors in their totality and, indeed, recognizes that all that is of the world is simply error and sin. Thus there is no necessity to examine his needs with subtle and discreet analysis. He has one need: the need for the doctrine and discipline he is to receive in the monastery. And in order to do this he needs to escape from the world. Having once escaped it, there remains one need above all: the need to be kept from returning to it, at any cost.

Therefore the novice has only to embrace the rule and the observances, to renounce and forswear his own ideas and opinions and accept with perfect docility any teaching, however superficial, that is given him. Whatever he is taught is "right." This teaching need not be especially stimulating or "intellectual." Indeed the value of intellectuality is questioned, though learning is respectable, provided that it means the learning of acceptable and well-understood time-tried attitudes: the "accepted spirituality." (Note that the teaching given tends to be not so much the personal doctrine of a "spiritual father" based on his experience but, rather, what is taken for granted by a whole generation. Not that this "spirituality" has a definite authoritative status, a precise teaching: it may be comfortingly vague. Its chief advantage is that it is not likely to get anyone excited. It is safe. And you can live by it without having to think!)

Why is this doctrine rather than another to be taught? First, because it is already accepted. In actual fact, this accepted spirituality recommends itself because it is the most complete justification of the community in its actual condition. If it permits changes, they will all be very slight because in fact only the slightest changes are felt to be needed. Anything else would strike at the "essence of the monastic life." It is true that "times have changed," but are they not rather the "times" of the "world"? The truth is one and eternal. It does not change. Of course there must be accidental changes. But they are worthwhile precisely insofar as they can be made with the minimum of disturbance. In fact their chief recommendation is perhaps that they are more apparent than real. They can be made without anything really happening.

A "good monk" is then one who has thoroughly learned this accepted spirituality and put it into practice, thus becoming at once an exemplar of the current teaching and its confirmation. The presence of the "good monk" is a kind of concrete guarantee that the teaching itself is practical and that it can and does succeed (if it can succeed in some cases therefore it must be capable of succeeding in all cases). The successful carrying out of this program is rewarded by a life of happiness and peace, since the monk feels that he is approved, accepted, and that his efforts are rightly directed, in fact blessed by God. The orientation of faith, in this situation, is toward what has always been there. It is consequently accepted and unquestioned.

This being the case, the average postulant can be judged by his willingness to understand, accept and follow the accepted spirituality and the ordinary rules. The ability to do this is a sign that he is capable of being formed "according to the spirit of the order."

To put it quite simply, such a one shows unmistakable signs of having a divine vocation. He agrees with us from the very start and we have reason to be assured that he will cause us no trouble, nor will he raise any doubts in our own minds as to the absolute rightness of what we have always accepted ourselves.

There is no question that this approach is in many ways quite simple and practical. It may, in its application, be somewhat oversimplified, even to the point where it becomes slightly inhuman in its apparent indifference to the peculiar and personal needs of some modern vocations. But it assumes that these special needs can legitimately be sacrificed to the common good, which is reduced to the peaceful efficient application of the accepted norms to all without exception or difference. And, in times of general stability, it may happen that in fact exceptional vocations consent to this without too much anguish, though of course not without effort and self-immolation. They can accept the sacrifice demanded of them without too much questioning and are able to adjust their motives. And because this happens in some cases, or many cases, it is taken to be reasonable evidence that it ought to happen in *all* cases. It is even elevated to the rank of a universally valid principle, for all situations and at all times.

But when for various reasons the Church herself, in a time of crisis and of reform, calls into question certain human customs and practical principles that have been accepted for a long time, and when some of these are seen to have possessed a validity that was temporary rather than permanent and universal, then immediately the force of an "accepted spirituality" tends to be questioned, all the more so because in becoming quasi-official it may in fact have lost some of the necessary elements of suppleness, of life and of *charis* (in the sense of spiritual beauty, attractiveness, appeal) which inspire genuine love of the monastic vocation. Then at the same time it may become apparent to younger religious that those who have devoted themselves with all sincerity and trust to carrying out the teachings of the accepted spirituality have suffered certain human impoverishments and limitations in consequence; though they have perhaps developed and have attained to an admirable poise and even wisdom, supported by the observances which they faithfully practice, this wisdom suddenly seems to have no reference to the realities of life, whether in the monastery or anywhere else. Thus the relevance of the monastic ideal itself comes to be questioned, and young religious begin to wonder whether the most basic doctrines of the spiritual life, as taught and practiced in the monastery, have any real significance. When this questioning begins, as we have seen, the whole structure of faith suddenly seems to be threatened, insofar as the mere questioning of the validity of an accepted spirituality seems to involve a doubt of the principle of authority, doubt of the Church, doubt of God revealing himself in and through the Church, and ultimately doubt of God himself. Thus the monk who is convinced that he must identify everything that is "accepted" as traditional, and therefore as the teaching and the will of God himself, suddenly finds that in doubting the meaningfulness of this or that monastic observance he appears to be doubting God. But this lamentable misapprehension can hardly be articulated. Nor is any encouragement offered for it to be so. It sometimes remains unspoken and often unconscious. Perhaps more often the monastic conscience is formed to such a way that the mere "temptation" to question the absolute and eternal validity of this or that practice may cause terror in the heart of the monk who sees himself as it were putting his foot on the slippery path to total apostasy. In any case, conscious or unconscious, where this misapprehension exists, it becomes the cause of grave difficulties. These can seldom be resolved once they have deeply taken hold on a young monk, and as a result the monastery becomes, for him, the only solution.

Unfortunately, he has learned to accept as axiomatic the idea that he belongs in the monastery, that his needs can be satisfied only in and by the monastery, and that any needs he may have which cannot be fulfilled in the monastery are highly questionable, indeed "natural" and therefore suspect of degeneracy or at least of uselessness.

When it becomes necessary for such a monk to leave the monastery, in which he is no longer able to extricate himself from intellectual confusion and spiritual anguish, he returns to the world without really getting rid of his doubts and his hesitancies. He goes back to secular life with a heart full of ambiguity, self-questioning, perhaps self-hatred, and in any case profound distress.

The consequence of this first way of looking at the postulant and at the order's obligation to him is that at the present time there will be very few postulants who will be able to assimilate this rigid and absolute idea of monasticism and resign themselves to live by it. One can simply tighten up the requirements, writing off the new generation as more or less monastically hopeless, and then at the same time attempt to quietly and unobtrusively adapt the accepted spirituality, relaxing its rigidities and making room for a more tolerant consideration of the needs of the modern postulant, while assuming it to be obvious that this is what we meant to do all along.

The principle, however, remains this: that the postulant comes to the order with "wrong ideas," and consequently even his expression of what he feels to be urgent personal and spiritual needs will usually be wrongheaded and inspired by unregenerate self-love (or perhaps by a neurosis), which cannot be reconciled with the monastic life. The right idea of the monastic life is the idea which is commonly held by and taught in the order, and the first requirement of faith and humility in a prospective monk is to accept this in all docility as an unquestionable premise.

There is, however, another concept of the monastic life, which implies a somewhat different view of the Church, and which is perhaps more complex and less absolute. It is doubtless more difficult to understand in theory and certainly more difficult to put into practice. It involves definite risks of misinterpretation and of misapplication, and from the institutional point of view it may seem, and indeed may actually be, less practicable and more hazardous than the other.

Basing itself on more general principles from the Bible and from the Rule of St. Benedict and primitive monastic documents (rather than on detailed and more recent legislation, observance and spiritual doctrine), this view understands the monastic community as an assembly of Christians called together by the grace of God in order that they may live the life of discipleship together under a Rule and an abbot, helping one another to attain to eternal life by means which will (in their minor details) depend largely on the situation in which they are actually living.

According to this view, the monastic community is in possession not so much of a body of detailed and more or less infallible and rigid principles, governing all the minutiae of one's daily life and worship and systematizing all one's communal relationships, but rather the Holy Spirit, working through the humility and charity of the brethren in their loving acceptance of their Rule and their spiritual father, enables them all to keep the commandments and counsels of Christ within a framework of rather flexible observances and practices which are not regarded as so perfect that they cannot be changed without extraordinary legislation.

Depending less on the support of legislation in black and white, the community puts its trust in the love and grace of Christ. Believing that the Holy Spirit has been granted to the community to be a source of light and life, and acting in a spirit of openness and sincerity, the brothers under their spiritual father seek to work out together actual solutions to their own problems. They may certainly come up with answers that are far from ideal in theory, but it may happen by God's grace that these are the particular answers which bring to all of them a possibility of authentic peace, fruitfulness and growth in Christ. Naturally these solutions will not lack the support of whatever official approval may be necessary.

Into this conception of the monastic life enters a correlative conception of the world. There is no question, of course, that the monk lives as one who is basically alien to the ways of the world (*a saeculi actibus se facere alienum*). So says St. Benedict. But nevertheless the peculiar difficulties and vicissitudes of life in the world are relevant to the monastic life which is considered precisely as a remedy and as a fulfillment: a remedy for the ills contracted in the world and a fulfillment of legitimate needs which the world of this particular time arouses without being able to satisfy.

The first concept of the monastic life also promises a fulfillment which the world cannot give, a fulfillment which is attained by
the simple and uncompromising way of renunciation (of the world)
and obedience (to the accepted observances and practices of the
monastery, as applied in detail by the superior). But in this first case
there is no concern for needs, legitimate or otherwise, that may have
been brought to consciousness by the mentality of "the world."
Whatever came to mind in the world remains more or less irrelevant
to the monastic calling, which is so far "out of this world" that it has
nothing more to do with it. So the "needs of modern man" precisely
as modern and contemporary are regarded as irrelevant.

Contemporary man is regarded, by the first view, as "contemporary" precisely in his worldliness. In having a "need" to renounce
his worldliness, he has *ipso facto* a need to renounce his contempo-
raneousness. He ceases to be contemporary with his fellow man in
entering the monastery, just because in that same act he ceases to be
worldly, and becomes an unworldly being, concerned only with the
needs of his soul and with eternity. Of course, it can be argued that
eternity is contemporaneous with all time and in this sense the monk
becomes contemporary, in an abstract and universal way, with absolutely all ages and all times. A malicious intelligence might also
conclude that in so doing the monk becomes contemporary with no
one and, in fact, altogether abandons the realm of the human.

The second view, on the contrary, recognizes, not without a certain anguish, that there is no other time than the present and that
to be contemporary is the price of existence itself. Man has a responsibility to his own time, not as if he could seem to stand outside it
and donate various spiritual and material benefits to it from a position of compassionate distance, but man has a responsibility to find
himself where he is, namely in his own proper time and in his place,
in the history to which he belongs and to which he must inevitably
contribute either his responses or his evasions, either truth and act
or slogan and gesture. Even his gestures of evasion and withdrawal
may unfortunately be decisive contributions to a void in which history can take on a demonic orientation. And so the second form of
monasticism exists in confrontation with a world and with a time to

which it feels it must respond. Not that it must become implicated by a loss of its own special perspective. For the first thing that the monk can contribute to the world of his time is precisely a perspective that is not of the world. The monk owes the world of his time an unworldliness proper to this time, and the contemporary monk is real insofar as he manages, by the grace of God and the charism of his vocation, to achieve a contemporaneous unworldliness. He is in the world and not of it. He is both in his time and of it.

Hence we see the error of imagining that being out of the world also involves being out of one's own time—i.e., in the past, since the past is imagined as having acquired an eternal validity by the fact that it is past.

It would perhaps be more truly monastic to say that the monk who is effectively liberated from the servitudes and confusions of "the world" in its negative and sterile sense ought to be enabled by that very fact to be more truly present to his world and to his time by love, by compassion, by understanding, by tolerance, by a deep and Christlike hope.

The second view of monasticism can therefore be called in a certain sense "worldly," not that it concerns itself with the ends and means of secular life as such, but it takes into account with sympathy and understanding the legitimate aims which "the contemporary world" feels itself called to obtain for man, such as peace, personal fulfillment, communion with other men in a warm and creative social environment, etc. It regards these aspirations as real and relevant to everyone and therefore to monks, and it sees with compassion that man today is frustrated in his most sincere efforts to attain these things. It does not despise or condemn him because his efforts are undertaken seemingly "without God" or in an "irreligious" spirit since it sees that he is basically sincere and in good faith and that these aspirations, good in themselves, doubtless come from God. The monk should be in the world of his time as a sign of hope for the most authentic values to which his time aspires.

Thus the monastic community will take seriously the earnest and valid effort of secular thought to reach out toward these values but will understand that thought in the light of the Bible and of the

Fathers, finding there a very propitious climate for ideas which seem to a great extent doomed to sterility in the aridity and violence of modern urban and technological life.

This is not the place to develop this idea in all its implication. One consequence of this attitude concerns us here: in looking at the postulant, the monastic community will no longer assume that he comes to the monastery with ideas and aspirations that are all wrong, but that some of the deepest needs of his heart, even though they may not be explicitly religious needs, are genuinely human and specifically contemporary needs which the monastic life is also called upon to fulfill. And so to ignore these human needs, to reject them as irrelevant, and to turn the whole attention of the postulant to other seemingly more lofty, more eternal, more unworldly, more spiritual and more religious aims, may in fact turn out to be arbitrary, unjust, and even unrealistic. For that reason, this procedure will ultimately tend to vitiate the postulant's vocation precisely in its religious and spiritual authenticity. For one cannot establish the religious authenticity of a vocation by trying to distill away all the human and contemporary components that may be there in it. On the contrary, the truth of a vocation, its religious truth, depends on the fundamental respect for the human components which have been placed there by heredity, by the postulant's history, by his own freedom acting in union with grace, and therefore by God himself.

There is no question that in implementing the postconciliar legislation on the religious life, the monastic order will naturally adopt the second of the two attitudes we have outlined above.

The Council decree *Perfectae Caritatis* on the renewal of the religious life praises the contemplative orders and urges them to maintain "at their holiest" their "withdrawal from the world and the practices of their contemplative life." But it also states that the language of praise and approval for the contemplative orders as "the glory of the Church and an overflowing fountain of heavenly graces" does not exempt them from the obligation of complete renewal. The decree says significantly: "*Nevertheless* their manner of living should be revised according to the aforementioned principles and standards of appropriate renewal" (n. 7).

Among the principles referred to are the following:

"Communities should promote among their members a suitable awareness of contemporary human conditions and of the needs of the Church" so as to enable the members to make "wise judgments in the light of faith concerning the circumstances of the modern world [and] come to the aid of men more effectively" (2 d).

"The manner of living, praying and working should be suitably adapted to the physical and psychological conditions of today's religious. . . . The way in which communities are governed should be reexamined in the light of these same standards. . . . Constitutions, directories, custom books . . . are to be suitably revised. . . . This task will require the suppression of outmoded regulations" (3).

But also: "The fact must be honestly faced that even the most desirable changes made on behalf of contemporary needs will fail of their purpose unless a renewal of spirit gives life to them. Indeed such an interior renewal must always be accorded the leading role even in the promotion of exterior works" (2 e).

In the section that deals specifically with monks, the decree says:

"While safeguarding the proper identity of each institution, let monasteries be renewed in their ancient and beneficial traditions and so adapt them to the modern needs of souls that monasteries will be seedbeds of growth *(seminaria aedificatiois)* for the Christian people" (n. 9). (The injunction to "safeguard the proper identity" of each "institution" refers to the previous sentence in which the decree says some monks serve God "by devoting themselves entirely to divine worship in a life that is hidden" and others "by lawfully taking up some apostolate or works of Christian charity.")

Note that in speaking of papal cloister for nuns the decree says that while the cloister is to be maintained, "outdated customs are to be done away with" and "in such matters consideration should be given to the wishes of the monasteries themselves" (n. 16).

Without doubt a notable change of attitude has already taken place. Communities certainly show an increased willingness to consider realistically the needs of the new generation, and one no longer categorically assumes that the new wave is made up entirely of morons, rebels, neurotics and dope fiends. It is almost conceded that in their quixotic way the young manifest a certain amount of good sense. Unfortunately there is still very much of a spirit of patronage in this benign endeavor to recognize the engaging and positive qualities of youth. Do we really believe that monasticism can actually survive in an actual *dialogue* with the modern postulant? Or with the novice? Or with the young monk?

Here we must admit there are problems, some of them rather complex. It would be a little silly to take for granted that one who has no experience whatever of the monastic life is, upon entering, in a secure position to reform everything in the first week. When all monastic tradition unanimously assumes that the worthy postulant manifests a sincere desire to listen and to learn rather than immediately to teach, this is surely not to be taken as an eccentric and antique formula fit for the museum. It is after all not unfamiliar to modern man, for example, in the world of athletics. Coaches are not normally patient with temperamental freshmen who know more about football than anybody else.

On the other hand, let us admit we can no longer safely insist that the postulant passively accept our cursory diagnosis of his ills just because we have a familiar remedy at hand to fit that particular diagnosis. ("You are proud, therefore you need to submit to humiliation, and to begin with you must accept the fact that I know you better than you know yourself, and if you don't agree on that point, it shows from the very start how proud you really are!" A most convenient vicious circle which dispenses with all effort to understand the subject's real needs!)

The postulant who has come to the monastery looking for something may not necessarily be looking for what we think. Yes, of course, *si revera Deum quaerit.* "Does he truly seek God?" But what entitles me, as novice master, to imagine that *my* particular way of seeking God is the only way possible and that *my* spirituality, *my* prayer, *my* idiosyncrasies, *my* monastic likes and dislikes, *my* interpretations, are normative for all monks of all time? Such an assumption teaches, louder than any words, that I have no humility myself and am therefore disqualified from trying to teach it to another. I do not have the elementary humility to respect his own personal integrity, his uniqueness, his differences, his own singular and personal need.

All this is quite simply to say that the Holy Spirit speaks in very many ways, and one of the ways in which he speaks is precisely through the need, the poverty, the limitation of our fellow man.

A merely external practice of silence and enclosure will never do anything by itself to guarantee the inner transformation of consciousness which the contemplative life requires. We have to reexamine all our practices with a serious willingness to admit that our present conceptions may simply be inadequate. They need to be made much deeper and much more alive—and perhaps given an entirely new perspective. In this way we will show ourselves truly alert to the new needs of a new generation, aware that in this alertness we are being open to grace, obedient to the love of the Holy Spirit, and in the end more authentically monks than if we simply insisted on making two fatal assumptions: (1) that the idea of monasticism which we happen to hold, and which happens at the moment to have a quasi-official look, is the only right view and is therefore of the essence of the monastic life and therefore unchangeable; (2) because we are right in this respect, we are right in every other respect too: we can safely assume that the man who comes in from the world is infected with every error and that if he does not manage to assimilate our own favorite view of monasticism this is merely a proof that he is bad material, dead wood, a fruitless tree, fit only to be rooted up and cast into the fire. Attachment to these two rather arrogant assumptions will guarantee the early end of the monastic life in any community that clings to them with perseverance.

V
Renewal
and Discipline*

The monastic life can be seen as a dialectic of freedom and discipline if we remember that it implies, by its very nature, some kind of distance and transcendence with regard to ordinary social and cultural life. The monk is "out of this world" insofar as he is liberated from the routine demands of "worldly" life. His liberation enables him, however, to give to the world something it needs: a capacity for creative and spontaneous celebration, a deeper understanding, a freer response to the basic existential challenge that summons us to make sense out of our life—to make our own sense out of life. Not just to accept someone else's answers, but to discover by personal experience and to verify existentially the inner meaning and value of human life on earth. Note that I am speaking of the monastic ideal, not of the actuality, which can easily turn out to be the exact opposite.

The element of "distance" from the ordinary unthinking way of life—the element of solitude, withdrawal "into the desert," of silence, of ascesis, of poverty, humility, obedience—all this is necessary for the monk. But why? Simply because "monastic tradition says so"? or simply to give the monk "something to do"? or to "make him more virtuous"? The traditional ideas of worldliness and asceticism, of dis-

---

*The author noted that the following pages' informal, offhand observations intended in part to answer some question raised by the lively exchange on the "decline" of the Trappists in the *National Catholic Reporter,* January 11, 1968. "In a letter of mine, published in that issue, I stressed the element of freedom essential to the monastic life but also remarked on the importance of discipline."—Ed.

cipline, renunciation, self-denial, prayer, have come under criticism because of the way they have been presented: now in terms of arbitrary and compulsive perfectionism, now in terms of formalist institutionalism. Obviously there is no point in the vicious-circle argument which postulates an austere Trappist image and then practices austerity in order to keep the image authentic. It is not a matter of image. It is not a matter of putting up a front or even of making a contract (to live austerely) and then living up to it. The reasons for discipline lie deeper.

St. Paul long ago remarked on the obvious analogy between the training of athletes and the discipline of Christian self-denial. Over the course of long ages of routine understanding, Paul's analogy was somewhat materialized and his self-denial came to be regarded, by those who thought only superficially, as a matter of "payment" for an ultimate commodity: beatitude. This materialistic view of sacrifices as *quid pro quo,* for which one would "collect" in the afterlife, influenced the nineteenth-century view of Christian asceticism in monasteries. But really, there is more to it. If one "trains" and disciplines his faculties and his whole being, it is in order to deepen and expand his capacity for experience, for awareness, for understanding, for a higher kind of life, a deeper and more authentic life "in Christ" and "in the Spirit." The purpose of discipline is not only moral perfection (development of virtue for its own sake) but self-transcendence, transformation in Christ "from glory to glory, as by the Spirit of the Lord." The death and crucifixion of the old self, the routine man of self-seeking and conventionally social life, leads to the resurrection in Christ of a totally "new man" who is "one Spirit" with Christ. This new man is not just the old man in possession of a legal certificate entitling him to a reward. He is no longer the same, and his reward is precisely this transformation that makes him no longer the isolated subject of a limited reward but "one with Christ" and, in Christ, with all men. The purpose of discipline is then not only to help us "turn on" and understand the inner dimensions of existence, but to transform us in Christ in such a way that we completely transcend our routine existence. (Yet in transcending it, we rediscover its existential value and solidity. Transformation is not a repudiation of ordinary life but its definitive recovery in Christ.)

Monastic discipline and freedom are correlatives. In traditional ascetic terms, our passions, appetites, needs, emotions, create certain limitations which hamper and frustrate a certain kind of development if we allow ourselves to remain too dependent on them. They blind us, weaken us, unnerve us, make us cowards, conformists, hypocrites. They are roots of bad faith. The craving for a certain kind of comfort, reassurance and diversion can be satisfied only if one is willing to accept certain social conditions: to fulfill a prescribed role, to occupy a definite place in society, to live according to acceptable social norms. If we fulfill the role imposed on us by others, we will be rewarded by approval. These roles impose definite limitations, but in return for accepting the limitations, we enjoy the consolation of companionship, of understanding, support and so on. We are made to feel that we "belong" and are therefore "all right." The monastic idea, originally, was to explore the possibilities that were opened up once these limitations were removed, that is to say, once one "left the world." The comforts and joys of ordinary social life, married love, friendly converse and recreation among other people, business, a place in the city and the nation, were to some extent renounced. Sometimes the renunciation was made in crude terms, as if ordinary social life were "evil." This must not mislead us. It was simply a question of obscurely realizing that, in some way, the limitations imposed by social life stood in the way of something else, and the monk was one who wanted to look into this "something else."

The monastic life has always had something of this element of "exploration" about it (at least in periods when it has been *alive*). The monk is a man who, in one way or other, pushes to the very frontiers of human experience and strives to go beyond, to find out what transcends the ordinary level of existence. Aware that man is somehow sustained by a deep mystery of silence, of incomprehensibility—of God's will and God's love—the monk feels that he is personally called to live in more intimate communication with that mystery. And he also feels that if he does not respond to this summons, he cannot be happy because he cannot be fully honest with himself. To evade this would be to reject a certain kind of truth, a certain inner reality, and ultimately to forfeit his self-respect as a human being.

I am simply trying to translate into more modern terms the familiar idea that has hitherto been expressed in the words "a monastic vocation" or "a contemplative vocation." The idea of this vocation is not necessarily confined to one special kind of discipline. There may be various different ways. Different aspects of training may be emphasized: now community life, now solitude; now ascesis, now work; now *lectio,* now silent prayer; now liturgy, now meditation; now a thoroughly sacramental piety, and now a life of spiritual risk outside the cadres of ritual and institution. But all these, some more and some less, are oriented to a kind of exploration "beyond frontiers." The claim of a cenobitic and liturgical monasticism is that it is safer and more universal because it does not push the frontiers too far and maintains a more normal human (social) measure. Yet the cenobium itself is a little Church, a sacred community, in which the Lord is present to his own in the breaking of the bread. The frontiers are dissolved, not from our side but from his. And of course this is a universal truth underlying all the paradoxes about "monastic exploration." In the end, there really are no frontiers. We would not seek God unless he were not already "in us," and to go "beyond ourselves" is just to find the inner ground of our being where he is present to us as our creative source, as the fount of redemptive light and grace. Whether as hermit or as cenobite, as pilgrim or as laborer, as hesychast or liturgist, the monk seeks in some way to respond to the summons: "Behold the Bridegroom comes: go out to meet him!" The need for discipline is the same need for watchfulness, for readiness, as in the parable. The ones who wait for the Lord must have oil in their lamps and the lamps must be trimmed. That is what monastic discipline is all about. It implies the cultivation of certain inner conditions of awareness, of openness, of readiness for the new and the unexpected. Specifically, it implies an openness to, a readiness for, what is not normally to be found in an existence where our attention is dissipated and exhausted in other things. True, one important new insight in the current monastic renewal is an awareness that "the world" cannot be summarily dismissed as irrelevant to the Christian life. But this is above all a salutary reaction against a kind of sclerotic, artificial, automatic routine of pious thinking: the mechanical assumption that to put on a religious habit, retire to a cloister and embrace a complex set of observances somehow guarantees a deepening of life and gives our existence its true meaning. As if one automatically became enlightened and liberated merely by the rote learning of a cloistered ideology.

Here we might pause a moment to consider something that, to my knowledge, has never been studied: the influence of science and scientific method on the monastic mentality and on the monastic concept of discipline. Anyone who is acquainted with early monastic and patristic literature is aware that, for the Fathers, discipline and ascesis were not simply surefire methods which paid off in results, provided you followed all the instructions and carried out all the proper steps in the right order. This concept of discipline in the life of prayer did however arise in the fifteenth and sixteenth centuries, about the same time as the concept of scientific method developed (Bacon, Descartes). It quite evidently influenced the Jesuits—perhaps not so much Ignatius himself who was more subtle and more experienced—but doubtless the Ignatian school. The idea was that if you set up the right conditions, a kind of laboratory for prayer, and if you carried out the experiment according to instructions, you would get the desired result. You could work things out efficiently so that you obtained the precise kind of grace you were looking for. This concept has by now evolved into the simple pharmacology of contemplation: you take the right pill and you turn on. Hence the idea of discipline was corrupted into a kind of methodology and, as in the case of social sciences for instance (where the same kind of transposition took place), instead of really praying and meditating, people became obsessed with their "method" and observed themselves at prayer, checking on the method and wondering why they were not getting the desired results. Without going further into this important question, it has to be said here and now that this transformation of a discipline in a broad, human measure and of a theological climate of love and grace into a methodology of will and concentration has been fatal to Catholic contemplation. Fortunately, a few rare people like Caussade persistently and quietly counteracted this error, led by a kind of sanity and tact which emphasized openness to grace, passivity, and a deeper, less rationalistic kind of attention. For the discipline of prayer (especially in the old monastic tradition) is not a matter of forcing the issue and getting what you want, but of learning the ways of the spirit and of grace, and of being ready and open to respond to the unpredictable working of a God whose ways are "not our ways."

It can be seen that the long centuries in which the monastic order was deeply embedded in the structure of Christian civilization, while very fruitful and rich both for monasticism and for European culture, did in the end produce a kind of routinism which can only be overcome by a thorough return to sources. The whole issue of monastic discipline has been confused, especially for Americans, by the fact that it has in practice been reduced to blind submission to a set of nineteenth-century customs. Fidelity to the monastic vocation has been too often confused with the ability to swallow, without criticism or question, a bittersweet and rather unpalatable mixture of quasi-Jansenist rigorism, pietistic formalism, a literal-minded, myopic theology and anthropology, plus a certain self-complacency about admitting that one was indeed the salt of the earth and that one's prayers were really keeping the cosmos from falling apart. At the price of a dogged insistence on devout observance and a head hard enough to resist severe nervous breakdown from one year to the next, one could thus rationalize his existence as thoroughly monastic, pleasing to God, and even in some sense "contemplative." After all, one never went anywhere or knew anything. One had all but forgotten the wicked world. Presented in this light, monastic discipline was self-discrediting. Those who have broken away from the ordinary monastic patterns and have tried to open up new perspectives have naturally discarded this idea of discipline before everything else. Rightly so.

At this point we must face one of the main dilemmas of the "monastic order" or of monasticism as institution. The monastic vocation is a summons to *metanoia, conversatio morum,* a whole new life.

If this new life is nothing more than a change on the cultural and religious levels it will fail to satisfy the deepest and most authentic demands of the monastic vocation. In other words, the postulant who feels himself called to become a new man, a more authentic person, more profoundly true to his Christian calling and to the gospel, feels an obscure dissatisfaction with his former life "in the world" and entrusts himself to the monastic community believing that it will show him the way to deepen and expand his awareness as a Christian by developing his whole being "in Christ." What happens is that he is instructed in the observances and ideology of a very specialized, cloistered style of life. He receives a special formation which adapts him to life according to a particular cultural and religious pattern. This monastic and religious culture, handed down from the deeply Christian Middle Ages, has certainly a real validity of its own. Nor is it totally irrelevant to *all* modern men. Many, especially in Europe, have been able to take full advantage of these cultural and religious means and have profited by them in the same way that the monastic fathers did in the past. They have found that Gregorian chant, the reading of the Fathers, monastic ascesis as understood in terms of early Benedictinism and twelfth-century Citeaux, and the Bible have helped them find the way to a real self-transcendence, an interior transformation, which has met the requirements of their interior call from God. Within the structure of monastic life, but not enslaved by externals, they have developed interiorly and acquired a kind of wholeness, certitude and peace. They are fully mature Christians and monks because they have made use of these cultural means and at the same time gone beyond them in their own personal way. But many of the younger generation, while embracing the monastic observance and "culture" with complete generosity, have not managed to find the same kind of meaning in them. In the past, the tendency was to blame the young for this. Now we are more ready to understand that it is nobody's "fault." These young monks have felt, perhaps more rightly than we realize, that entering a monastery has meant little more than leaving one kind of culture and society in order to learn the complex rubrics and roles of another. They have felt that this amounts to little more than an external change and that religious rationalizing and purification of intention really do nothing to make it interior and profound. They learn a whole new role, a whole new system of attitudes and ideas, but interiorly they remain dissatisfied, disoriented, empty, and in the end they feel not only that they have somehow been cheated, but that if they continue to play the same external roles, they themselves are cheating. For one reason or other, the external role does not betoken—still less bring about— any interior renewal of a very deep kind. Merely to lead sheltered and more or less sinless lives—this is not what they can accept as a valid transformation in Christ. (Perhaps in this respect the older generation was more patient and less demanding. The young are less easily satisfied.)

In any case, what happens is that the learning and practice of monastic observances, rituals, do not constitute a real discipline though they may indeed provide an appropriate setting for the learning and practice of such a discipline. True discipline is interior and personal. It is something more than just learning a certain kind of conduct and possessing coherent religious justifications for that conduct. It is one thing to say that when I make a profound bow I intend to express love and adoration for God, but another to really grow and develop in that love and adoration. For some people, the bow and its explanation may tend to become more of a hindrance than a help. In other words, there may come a time when the young monk realizes that in order to meet the real, deep demand of the call that once brought him to the cloister, he has to leave the cloister. The machinery of cloistered life is now imposing limits that prevent his authentic development. The tragedy may be that when he leaves he gets into a still less profitable situation and loses even the little that he had in the monastery.

Monasticism after Vatican II* will obviously pass through a transition in which there will be a great deal more permissiveness since, in fact, people will be trying out all kinds of new formulas. This permissiveness will (and in fact does) vary from community to community. On one hand, there will be communities which, for one

---

*The author was writing in February, 1968.

reason or other, will effectively try to work out the problems of renewal within the familiar institutional framework of the large monastery with its multiple projects, big plant, varied commitments and
its fidelity to established cultural patterns. In Europe this will mean
a certain evident continuity with a millennial past. In America it
will mean more or less continuity with the nineteenth century of
which we are, nevertheless, somewhat dubious and ashamed. It is
after all a notable monument of religious camp. And it is at the same
time all we have as "tradition." The tendency will be to modernize
in the sense of to "Americanize" and to tend more and more to
"protestantize" our life, to liberalize it with borrowings from sociology, psychotherapy, etc.: in a word, to suburbanize the monastic
life. This will be the case because people, after all, need to have some
bearings to identify themselves by, and having renounced the crude
otherworldliness of the nineteenth-century immigrant and ethnic
Catholicism, American monks are situating themselves, naturally
enough, where they are: twentieth century in America. But if a Trappist monastery becomes after all indistinguishable from any other
marginal, seminary-type outfit in the Great Society, it will have lost
its reason for existing. Thus, while we will certainly be flexible, permissive, tolerant, open-minded, and will explore in the sense of experiment with new patterns, we must nevertheless remember our
identity as monks. That identity cannot be preserved without a discipline oriented to real inner transformation, to the development of
the "new man."

In this connection, I think we ought to be more conscious of and
attentive to the kind of paramonasticism which is very alive in this
country. I mean, frankly, movements like the hippies, like the beats
before them, like all those who are interested in Yoga and Zen, like
(in other respects) the peace movement, the civil rights movement.
All these movements have elements that can be called monastic
in the sense that they imply a very radical and critical break with ordinary social patterns. They have their asceticism, their "discipline,"
in the various kinds of sacrifices they make in order to "break" with
their own past, with their normal milieu, with the society of their
parents, or with a social order with which they violently disagree. It is

common knowledge that while monks have largely given up fasting, kids in the peace movement are liable to fast several days (with *no* food) on a peace vigil which may also be a prayer vigil. Whether or not one may agree with those who burn their draft cards, they are certainly making a more radical "break with the world" in this particular area than the postulant who walks into the monastery, is automatically exempt from all further concern about the draft and is fully approved by society. I do not mean to say that all these things are necessarily "right" and that monks are "wrong." I am just saying that the monks cannot afford to ignore these poor relations. They represent an attitude toward the world which is analogous to that of the monk. They also, in many cases, seek to explore the frontiers of experience and perception in ways at once more serious and more dangerous than monks do. Whatever one may think of psychedelic drugs, as a sociological fact they clearly indicate that the desire for inner experience is not something buried in the medieval past. The fact that the Beatles took LSD and then went to an Indian monk and guru for guidance, then dropped LSD when he told them to, and practiced meditation under his instruction, is certainly salutary for so-called contemplative monks. And it is a simple illustration of what I mean in talking of discipline. This edifying scenario has a special interest because it reminds us of something too often ignored in practice. Monastic ascesis has tended to be in general what one might call an ascesis of virginity, presupposing that there is a special excellence in a life in which passion has never reached full expression and satisfaction but has been sublimated from the beginning in divine love. Such excellence is certainly real, but it is a special charism. It is not the only formula for monastic ascesis and perfection. We remember that in the religious tradition of Hinduism, for example, it is considered normal for a man (or woman) to undertake the solitary and ascetic life of prayer after having been married and having brought up children. The charismatic life of virginity retains its own value, but we must also emphasize that for modern people a monastic life that is embraced when there has been no fully normal and mature sexual development may remain ambiguous and problematic. Paradoxically, we often find that young men come to

the monastery in order to discover finally, with more reliable certitude, that their vocation is marriage. There are many married people
who, after ten or fifteen years of married life (or longer if they are to
bring up their children) would definitely like to separate and take on
a different kind of life, more solitary and disciplined and perhaps in
some sense monastic. Our customs and even the laws of the Church
provide them with little or no encouragement. They would probably
make very good "monks"—perhaps much better ones than their
children.

The idea of discipline implies a clear recognition of an elementary
human fact: permissiveness is all right if you are content to drift
along with a stream that carries you more or less safely by itself. We
can to a great extent trust our nature and culture to guide us once
we have learned the relatively easy and habitual norms they impose.
But this easy permissive, drifting existence is bought at a price: it excludes certain other dimensions of life which cannot be found unless
to some extent we work hard to discover them. Of course one must
always admit of exceptions. There may be people who drift along
permissively and who attain an unusual degree of wisdom. But usually you will find that even their apparent permissiveness is the result
of a break, a sacrifice of certain easy adjustments and of a conventional role. The man who wants to deepen his existential awareness
has to make a break with ordinary existence, and this break is costly.
It cannot be made without anguish and suffering. It implies loneliness and the disorientation of one who has to recognize that the old
signposts don't show him his way and that, in fact, he has to find the
way by himself without a map. True, the monastic life provides other
signposts and other maps: but the trouble is that too often the signposts point merely to a dead end, and the maps are like those curious
productions of fourteenth-century cartographers which inform us
that "here are many dragons." The real function of discipline is not
to provide us with maps but to sharpen our own sense of direction
so that when we really get going we can travel without maps.

Monastic discipline is therefore by no means a matter of training
in pious deportment and moderation, a system of modesty, prudence and self-control, which guarantees a certain capacity for recol-

lection and pays off in inner peace. Such discipline is nothing more than conformity to rule in a specified style of life. It is simply a matter of learning to play one's part, to fulfill one's monastic role, and, I suppose, to "edify." True monastic discipline does not begin until this leaves off: and presumably one can begin without passing through any formal schooling in "monastic etiquette." Such schooling may or may not be useful, but clearly it is not what I am talking about, and I cannot believe it is essential to any serious monastic renewal. It may help, for those who are interested. On the other hand, there does seem to be a definite danger that those who have lost patience with discipline as etiquette and recollection may, in discarding it, get rid of all discipline whatever. The result will then be an entirely casual monasticism without any structure, any forms and recognizable shape and perhaps even without any serious motivation or real purpose. Even this may have its advantages temporarily, but it will have to be only temporary, a breathing spell in which the experiment discovers its own motives and its own identity. During such a lull, one may hope that a permissive and entirely unstructured situation may be helpful, provided there is real stuff in the men who live in it. On the other hand, if a group of "reformers" are banded together in a nebulous idea with no cohesion except that provided by half-conscious aspirations, fears and resentments held more or less in common, mere permissiveness and casualness will never serve. The danger of acting out neurotic drives will be too great. The result will then be regression and disintegration, both for the group and for the individuals in it.

The question of discipline naturally raises another, and even more critical, question of authority. Indeed, the discrediting of discipline, the suspicions attached to it, are largely the result of crude authoritarianism. Those who are distrustful of authority are distrustful of discipline, and vice versa. Usually there are at least a few plausible reasons for their distrust. But in the end, we must admit that monastic training demands some kind of authority as it demands some kind of discipline. Obviously, the concept of the Lord Abbot vested in pontificalia and graciously offering his ring to be kissed for a thirty days' indulgence—or perhaps forbidding his subjects "by virtue of the vow" to read *The New Yorker*—has had its day. But such authority never had any real inner strength. It was bolstered up externally by legal sanctions. What is needed in monasteries is a recognition of authority that is strong with the strength of love and of gospel truth. This authority may be seen perhaps in the rare charismatic teacher, but we will be more practical if we look for it in the believing community, united in Christ, in the humility of Christian love and of the spirit, seeing one another in the obedience of faith and gathered around one they have chosen to make the final practical decisions in running their community. Discipline in such a setting is less a matter of personal austerity and will ("character training") than of openness to the demands of the Spirit of Love to the needs of one's brothers and of the community.

Nevertheless we cannot neglect the importance of personal ascetic training, as also of spiritual fatherhood (where this can be found). The life of inner contemplative prayer is something that has to be learned by trial and error, under some sort of experienced guidance. One of the great problems of "the contemplative life" is that such guidance has usually been too rudimentary, too superficial, too improvised, too slack—or else too arbitrary, too compulsive, too legalistic and too insensitive to the real needs of the individual vocation. Hence monks never really learn to pray, to meditate, to "discern the spirits" and to find their way in the uncharted territory they have come particularly to explore. The spatial metaphor must not mislead us. Obviously, there is no "territory" at all "within us" and we do not "travel." Nevertheless the idea of development is something we naturally tend to visualize in spatial terms (for instance in a graph). The purpose of discipline is, however, to make us critically aware of the limitations of the very language of the spiritual life and of ideas about that life. If on an elementary level discipline makes us critical of sham values in social life (for example, it makes us realize experientially that happiness is not to be found in the usual rituals of consumption in an affluent society), on a higher level it reveals to us the limitations of formalistic and crude spiritual ideas. Discipline develops our critical insight and shows us the inadequacy of what we had previously accepted as valid in our religious and spiritual lives. It enables us to abandon and to discard as irrelevant certain kinds of experience which, in the past, meant a great deal to us. It makes us see that what previously served as a real "inspiration" has now become a worn-out routine and that we must go on to something else. It gives us the courage to face the risk and anguish of the break with our previous level of experience. It enables us, in the language of St. John of the Cross, to face the Dark Night in full awareness of our need to be stripped of what formerly gratified and helped us. To adjust to a new level of experience is at first painful and even frightening, and we must face the fact that the crisis of real growth in the contemplative life can bring one perilously close to mental breakdown. That is why it is so helpful to have the support of someone who knows what it is all about.

Growth in experience implies a serious self-doubt and self-questioning in which values previously held seem to be completely exploded and no other tangible values come to take their place. This may even take the form of a crisis of religious faith in which our whole conception of God and of our relationship to him may be turned upside down. There may seem to be "no God" at all, or else our relationship to him may seem so desperate that we feel as though we are damned, in our moments of darkness. This, as St. John of the Cross shows, marks the beginning of a whole new experience of faith on a completely different level. The passage from a stage in which one loves and worships God as a beautiful object of desire to a stage in which God ceases to be object and loses all definite limitations in our mind is something which cannot easily be described: but it is a perilous, though necessary, experience. Discipline prepares us for this. But the passage itself is not a matter of discipline. It is brought about "mystically" by the secret action of God in a way of which we cannot be fully conscious. Obviously, serious problems will be raised by any kind of "discipline" which simply seeks to maintain one at a single satisfactory level of experience (that of a fervent novice) and represents any "going beyond" as illusion or infidelity. A discipline that in fact *blocks and prohibits* development can produce nothing but tragic inertia. In such a case, crisis and upheaval are desirable reactions! They keep us in touch with reality. If in fact many monks have (in quiet despair) sought psychiatric help rather than spiritual direction, this is not to be wondered at. Psychiatry has advanced more valid claims to seriousness than most contemporary "spiritual direction." The two are entirely distinct. We need only remark on the obvious fact that some psychiatric help may be an absolutely necessary preliminary to a serious spiritual life, and psychiatry may (with important qualifications however) usefully intervene in the grave crises of mature contemplative development. (Obviously the psychiatrist must be one who knows what the monastic life is all about!) But spiritual discipline is something else again. And we must not lightly set aside the possibility of mystical prayer and charismatic developments in the course of a monastic life. The purpose of discipline is to favor such developments. One of the faults of the old narrow and rigid nineteenth-century spirituality was that it excluded all this a priori (while venerating the most naive accounts of it in the lives of the saints). The modern activistic approach also takes up a categorically antimystical position—and does so, if possible, even more savagely than did our fathers. Contemplative nuns are repeatedly assured that if they like to spend a long time in silent, thoughtless prayer, they are just neurotic, and no distinction is made between narcissistic absorption and genuine, intuitive, simple prayer.

The overemphasis on rationalizing and logic to the exclusion of everything intuitive and the repudiation of the aesthetic from the contemplative life have perverted the idea of monastic discipline with a kind of arid rationalism. Descartes has laid a curse on the Catholic life of prayer. What has to be rediscovered is the inner discipline of "the heart," that is to say, of the "whole man"—a discipline that reaches down into his inmost ground and opens out to the invisible, intangible, but nevertheless mysteriously sensible reality of God's presence, of his love, and of his activity in our hearts. The old familiar literature in this field (the debates of people like Saudreau, Poulain, and Garrigou-Lagrange) may have lost all sense and savor for us, and there is not much new literature of any real value about the mystical life. Nevertheless the classics of monasticism and contemplation are there to be reinterpreted for modern readers, and above all the Greek and Russian (hesychast) tradition can infuse a new life into our rationalist Western minds. Oriental ways of contemplation (Zen, Yoga, Taoism) can no longer be completely neglected by us. Sufism and Hassidism have a great deal to say to monks because of their explicit or implicit biblical content and because they are so closely related to a monastic type of spirituality. (Hassidic and Sufi communities are not strictly monastic in our sense but, very interestingly, provide a monasticism for people "in the world but not of it.") Modern psychoanalysis, social anthropology, comparative religion, some schools of philosophy, also have much to contribute to a rethinking of monastic discipline. Contact and communication of monastic communities among themselves, dialogue with one another and with other groups, scholars, psychoanalysts, Zen People, hippies, etc., can be of great importance for monks today. A concept of monastic discipline that merely excludes and rejects all that does not take place within the walls of the monastery is definitely not for our age (except in individual cases when a mature—or maybe just an old—religious may have found his or her "way" in this kind of isolation).

Much more could be said about all these points. My purpose is simply to reaffirm that without discipline the monastic quest, which seeks typically to explore regions of faith, of love, of experience and of existence beyond the limits of ordinary Catholic routine, can never lead to anything serious. Let us be quite clear that although there may be a real need for new attitudes and new approaches, and though the whole question of the *how* of monastic discipline needs to be rethought, there is no change in the need for discipline itself. This means first of all a need for control and liberation on the level of appetite and physical need. One cannot seriously pretend to "explore" unusual realms of experience if one is enslaved by a need for kicks on the sensual level. There is also no change in the need for those values which have traditionally been described in terms of humility, obedience, detachment, poverty, etc. It is quite true that the whole idea of humility needs to be rethought in terms that will make it real to modern people. It is true that obedience must be rediscovered, not as submission to legalistic authority but as openness to the hidden will of God. But basically, the discipline involved here is that of a crucifixion which eliminates a superficial and selfish kind of experience and opens to us the freedom of a life that is not dominated by egoism, vanity, willfulness, passion, aggressiveness, jealousy, greed. Finally, discipline means solitude of some sort, not in the sense of selfish withdrawal but in the sense of an emptiness that no longer cherishes the comfort of various social "idols" and is not slavishly dependent on the approval of others. In such solitude one learns not to seek love but to *give* it. One's great need is now no longer to *be* loved, understood, accepted, pardoned, but to understand, to love, to pardon and to accept others just as they are, in order to help them transcend themselves in love. Anyone who undertakes to be a monk knows, by the very fact of his vocation, that he is summoned by God to a difficult, lifelong work in which there will always be anguish and great risk. If he evades this work under any pretext whatever (even under the pretext of conforming to an exterior ritual or ascetic observance which does not really suit his inner needs), he must know that he cannot have any peace with himself or with God because he is trying to silence the deepest imperative of his own heart.

We must not (in thinking romantically and emotionally) make discipline an absolute good in itself. Discipline has its uses. What we want is to rediscover the right use of discipline, and this implies a recognition that it may in fact be used wrongly. For instance: suppose that one has certain objectives in the life of prayer and is set on obtaining these. He tries first one kind of discipline, then another. The discipline that appears to him to be "good" is the one which seems to bring him closest to his objective. But one may in this way use discipline to one's own (and the community's) great disadvantage if it turns out in fact that the objectives sought are irrational, or unreal, or self-contradictory, or unproductive, or simply not viable at all. This would be the case with disciplines whose effect would simply be to create, rapidly and convincingly, an illusion of holiness, of prayer, of union with God—in other words, of disciplines whose chief effect would be to enable one to "turn on" with a minimum of delay and inconvenience. This is the problem of psychedelics, and it is also a problem of ascetic methods. I would therefore, without going into details, suggest that we need to apply the cutting edge of discipline a little closer to the root and make use of it first of all to question our objectives themselves. Monastic discipline today will have to concern itself not with obtaining unquestioned contemplative "goals" that are accepted as valid merely because they are thought to be ideally "monastic." Rather, discipline must question these goals themselves and find out, not whether they are "monastic," but first of all whether they have, or can have, any reality whatever. In this sense it is to our advantage to accept, at least provisionally, the rather severe critique which is directed against the contemplative life. Instead of simply trying to repel all hostile arguments by forcing the issue and tightening up discipline to prove that we mean business and that therefore our goals must be sound (this is no logic at all—nor can it be justified as a mystique), we might profitably admit that much that passes for "contemplation" is mere narcissism and self-love, placed at a convenient remove of subjectivity and mystery where it cannot be reached by criticism. ("Oh, you just don't understand. One has to experience these things to understand them.") Discipline and experience must, on the contrary, reach into this area and criticize what goes on there. The problem is then not to barricade oneself in cloistered subjectivity and in a silence from which the critic is excluded: one must learn to make "silence," "solitude," the "desert," and so on, areas of more relentless criticism. Effective discipline will then not confirm us in error (which would be the case if we merely used it to "get what we want") but will enable us to unmask and correct our errors. This may sound very obvious, but as a matter of fact it is not obvious at all in practice. Discipline can so easily be used in the service of bad faith and religious hocus-pocus, with the emotional assumption that the intensity of one's conviction is a proof of its rightness (and discipline is used merely to intensify one's conviction). Thus, for example, the ascetic who punishes himself and then gets a nice warm feeling in the solar plexus as a reward becomes mechanically self-justifying—and confirms himself in illusion. Our discipline needs first of all to question and, if necessary, to discredit some of these "good" self-justifying feelings and convictions of ours. Our discipline should lead us to discover not how right we are but how wrong we are. If in the course of this discovery we give up our monastic enterprise altogether, well, perhaps it was never real in the first place. If, on the other hand, we radically revise our whole idea of what we came here for and continue to seek what we came to seek, but in a different way and with an entirely different (and more humble) understanding, our discipline will be serving a useful purpose.

VI

The Place
of Obedience

The draft schema on Religious presented in the third session of the Second Vatican Council was severely criticized because it did nothing to meet a desperately felt need for a renewed theology of the religious life. Such a theology is obviously demanded if the religious life is going to be brought up to date in accordance with the *Constitution on the Church*.

The remarkable thing about this *Constitution* is the shift of emphasis which, instead of considering the Church primarily and principally as a hierarchical society and a strictly organized institution, affirms that the Church is the community of the faithful, the Mystical Body of Christ, the people of God. It thus affirms the primacy of spiritual life and its fruitfulness over organizational rigidity, juridical exactitude, and temporal power. Certainly the Church is a society with laws, an organized institution; but the laws and organization are for the sake of love, of life. They exist to safeguard the freedom of the Spirit within the framework of earthly society. Thus the institution, its power and its influence do not become ends which every Christian must serve, even at the cost of his own inner spiritual fruitfulness and growth. The end is the transformation and consecration of all life to God by the leaven of holiness and, hence, by the spiritual vitality and fruitfulness of the members of Christ. Thus a static concept of the Church as organization is replaced by a dynamic concept of the Church as a living body moved by the invisible and divine Spirit of truth and love imparted to her by the Risen Christ.

This is why we do not speak today of the *reform* of religious life but rather of its *renewal*. Renewal is something deeper, more living and more total than reform. Reform was proper to the needs of the Church at the time of the Council of Trent when the whole structure of religious life had collapsed, even though there was still a great deal of vitality among religious. Today the structure and the organization are firm and intact: what is lacking is a deep and fruitful understanding of the real meaning of religious life. Simply to imitate the Tridentine reform and legislate a tightening of discipline within the now familiar framework would ignore the very real problem of religious, and not least the problem of obedience and authority in the modern context.

The obedience which is vowed by a religious is not the obedience of a child to a parent, nor the obedience of a citizen to civil authority, nor is it properly understood merely as the obedience of a subject to juridically constituted authority, even though this may be within a religious framework. Hence the renewal of religious obedience will not be accomplished simply by an increase of promptitude and exactness, though these are certainly not to be overlooked. The religious, and particularly the monk, desires the *bonum obedientiae* (one might almost translate St. Benedict's phrase as the "benefit of obedience") because it is a means to closer union with God. It is, in fact, the chief way by which the monk returns to God, as St. Benedict says in the opening sentences of his Prologue. Now a merely external and juridical obedience, no matter how exact, is hardly to be prized as an especially efficacious way to union with God. The obedience of the monk must therefore be the obedience of faith, deeply rooted in his belief in Christ as his Lord and Savior, in his earnest desire to live as a perfect disciple of Christ, in his love for Christ who for our sakes became "obedient unto death" (Phil. 2:8).

Monastic obedience is seen by the monk as a way to imitate the obedience and love of Christ his Master. Since Jesus "emptied himself taking the form of a servant" (Phil. 2:7), the monk will seek also to empty himself of his own will and to become a servant, above all because this is Christ's "new commandment." "The Son of Man came, not to be ministered unto, but to minister" (Matt. 20:28). At the Last Supper, Jesus plainly demonstrated his meaning to his disciples when he washed their feet and told them: "If I, being your Lord and Master, have washed your feet, so you should also wash one another's feet: for I have given you an example, and as I have done, so must you do also" (John 14:14–15). The monk who desires to live as a true disciple of Christ will therefore seek to humble himself before all his brothers and to serve all his brothers, and not only his superiors, because if he does not do this he is "putting himself above the Master" (John 14:16–17).

Religious obedience must be seen first of all in this context of love and discipleship. Only then do its formal and juridical aspects fall into the right perspective. The monk must obey, not because he has become the subject of the Abbot who has all the authority of a Roman paterfamilias, but because he is a disciple of Christ and because, in faith and humility, he wishes to see his own function as a service to be exercised in all humility and love. The Abbot desires not only to get his own will carried out, or to see that the Rule is strictly enforced, or to guarantee that the community is well-disciplined and prosperous, but to help his monks to seek and find God more truly, more sincerely, more intelligently, and more efficaciously.

It is to be expected that this crisis of obedience will loom very large in the views of superiors. But this very fact may tend to perpetuate certain unfortunate confusions if superiors continue to regard obedience, consciously or unconsciously, as ordered primarily to the good order and efficient functioning of the religious institute. Any "renewal" of obedience that begins from such a viewpoint will hardly be more than a consolidation of what amounts in fact to a spiritual disorder. This disorder consists in considering that the monk exists for the sake of his institution and in order to keep it going, and that his good and his sanctification are to be found above all in the obedience which places him totally at the service of his superiors in working for the interests—and, we may add, the prosperity and prestige—of the community. While this concept of obedience may perhaps be more justified in modern active congregations (though even there it would lead easily to abuse), *it has no justification whatever in the monastic context.*

The whole purpose of monastic obedience, the *disciplina* of the regular life, the docile acceptance and following of spiritual and traditional norms, is the sanctification of the monk and in fact his liberation from temporal agitations and concerns in order that he may learn to listen to God in his heart and to obey God.

The unfortunate tendency to regard the problem of obedience and authority as primarily one of *order* obscures much deeper theological implications. Religious, especially in America, tend to seek immediate practical solutions and adjustments that will make their life run more smoothly and effectively here and now. Hence there is considerable interest in psychology and psychiatry, and great trust is placed in techniques that have been used in social sciences. It is certainly good to know what may be the less obvious motivations and forces at work to generate our common problems. But basically the problem of obedience is inseparable from the theology of the religious life, and solutions on the level of psychology, sociology or even canon law and disciplinary reform will all be useless without new theological perspectives. However, let us consider first of all the concrete and psychological dimensions of the case.

It is quite possible that the whole Church is now facing a crisis of authority—a crisis of order. If so, the crisis will doubtless be especially acute among clerics and religious. But it will probably be a crisis of *understanding* even more than one of *will*. The hesitations, doubts, and outspoken questions of so many religious (in this matter of authority and obedience) arise not from a simple refusal to comply or from a rebellious assertion of self-will—though they are often seen in this light only. They more often arise from a fundamental lack of understanding and agreement concerning the real meaning of the religious vocation.

Let us not forget that modern man, or modern woman, at least in the "advanced countries," is desperately concerned with the problem of giving meaning to a life that is so easily reduced to mere empty routine by the alienating pressures of commercial and technological organization. We are often very keenly aware of the danger of becoming mere "mass men," frustrated, unidentified cogs in a huge impersonal machine.

Hence the religious often develops the same unformulated objections and resentments that characterize the "mass man." He finds himself deeply involved in the very futility and alienation he came to the monastery to escape. (In this case the desire to "escape" a meaningless existence is surely legitimate.) His feeling that his vow of obedience means more than a commitment to work for the organization and the prestige of the order is basically sound—but he does not know how to formulate it. And in fact he confronts a theology that has developed as an unconscious justification for the state of affairs in which he finds himself.

The summons to offer himself as a victim of holocaust on the altar of religious perfection, without even a reasonable hope that the sacrifice will make sense or be of real use to human persons, but only to the impersonal "Institute," leaves him in a state of serious doubt about the worth of the religious life itself. To diagnose this as cowardice or lack of generosity is more often than not equivocation. These same religious, in a situation that they are better able to comprehend, can give themselves most generously. Clichés about "blind obedience" make the modern religious feel, and not without reason, that his objections are simply being waved aside without even being considered.

Theology has, up until recently, viewed the religious life almost exclusively in terms of sacrifice and immolation (an outlook that corresponded to the medieval liturgical forms in which the Host was primarily a Victim immolated in the distant and invisible sanctuary, in the midst of mysterious words and rites which the faithful observed in devout, uninitiated silence). Certainly the religious life is a sacrifice, and so is the Mass. But just as theology now stresses the Eucharist as a sign of fraternal unity and demands active and intelligent participation in a common act of worship, so the old theology of the religious life needs to be completed and filled out with a new perspective in which the obedience of love rooted in faith becomes at once a sign and a principle of living unity in Christ, and a way of "returning to the Father" in and with the loving obedience of Christ. This "Eucharistic" concept of obedience is aimed not at an abstract, impersonal "common good" but at a concrete, personal, indeed mystical unity of love in Christ. Instead of a "common good" that remains external to the religious and affects his life only superficially, the fruit of obedience is the living and life-giving Spirit who is at once God's gift to each and the unifying bond of all.

Here, instead of the religious being forced back into the isolation of his individual will, which he exerts in order to obtain for himself an abstract and juridical reward, he is drawn into the living dynamism of fervor and love which gives meaning to his own life by enabling him to contribute personally to the meaningful life of his brothers in Christ.

Obedience then becomes an expression of the new life and the new creation which restores the simplicity and peace of paradise (*paradisus claustralis*) to a communal life in which each is the servant of all, and each finds fulfillment in a meaningful service of love that is inspired and vivified by the presence of Christ in his Spirit.

The end of Christian obedience is then not merely order and organization, not the abstract common good, but God himself, the epiphany of God in his Church and in the microcosm of the new creation which is the monastic community.

Once this is understood, the totality of the demand of obedience becomes obvious by itself. Evidently the individual must renounce his own will in everything and obey God in everything. His obedience to *God* is without limit because it is simply a fulfillment of his basic orientation to God by baptism, made more specific and concrete by his religious vow.

This *in no sense* means all abdication of his basic human rights and dignity in order to become an inert and uncomprehending utensil in the hands of a religious superior. It means a dedication and consecration of liberty in which the superior first of all must see that he is obliged to serve and preserve the spiritual liberty and dignity of his subjects. The superior cannot demand blind and total subjection to his own authority in order that he may make an arbitrary use of his subjects for his own ends or for those of the organization considered as such (for example, in order to make more money). He has to enlist the freedom of his subjects for the service of God and of love. He must realize that all other ends are subordinated to the spiritual good of the subjects as persons and as a community, and to the good of the souls they serve.

This does not by any means eliminate either the element of sacrifice, of heroically difficult obedience, or of complete immolation, but it presents them in a totally different light. The religious spends himself and devotes himself to the work of God in Christ with all the more good will and energy since he is able to see how he is in fact fulfilling his vocation and responding to its deepest exigencies of love and surrender to the truth of Christ. His work is not a blind, uncomprehending act of submission to the mandates of an inscrutable authority—mandates in which he has fundamentally no interest whatever because they really have no vital relation to his own vocation or to the true good of souls.

The work of obedience implies a loyal collaboration between superior and subject in which *both* strive, each according to his function, to understand and carry out the will of God. It is not that the superior arbitrarily makes his own will the will of God by issuing a command but that he objectively and in the fear of God seeks the divine will and, in doing so, does not neglect to consider first of all the spiritual good of his subjects. The subject, on the other hand, must remember that he is not on a plane of democratic equality with his superior and that collaboration with his superior must mean more than an informal dialogue in which the subject may decide, if he likes, that he is not bound to do the will of the superior even when the command is objectively legitimate.

However, obedience is in truth a dialogue between two responsibilities—that of the subject and that of the superior—and in carrying out his superior's command the subject cannot allow himself to abdicate moral responsibility and act as a mere utensil. It is also a dialogue between two forms of *service*. Superiorship is a service, just as much as the obedience of the subject. The superior serves God and his subjects by assuming the responsibility of decision and command. The subject serves God within the framework of law and command, but not without making mature decisions of his own. His decision to obey is not an abdication of freedom but a mature use of freedom. The superior owes his subject the information and confidence which will make mature obedience possible, and the subject owes his superior intelligent and loyal cooperation.

If this is true in ordinary everyday religious life it is also true in the special work of aggiornamento and religious renewal which has been undertaken by the Church today. While the major superiors and the competent councils and chapters must of course finally decide what adaptations are to be put into effect, in accordance with the Rule and Constitutions, it is nevertheless essential that all the members should actively participate in the renewal of religious life by assessment of the meaning and value of their vocation, clarifying the relevance of their particular religious ideal for themselves and for their time, evaluating the contribution they might make to the understanding and aid of the contemporary world, defining the relevance in a present-day context of certain observances belonging to the past, and bringing to the attention of superiors the real everyday needs and problems of subjects.

The true monk is one who, fully aware of his own limitations, has surrendered to the love of Christ in order to praise the mercy of God and serve him joyously in common with others who have made the same surrender. This is simply a special modality of the ordinary Christian life in which the vows are to be seen not just as peculiar and difficult obligations, but as means to guarantee the authentic purity of the gospel life in religious communities. It is here above all that renewal is demanded because in point of fact, as theologians observe with increasing frequency, the vows have often come to be used as evasions and pretenses—for example, where poverty becomes a purely abstract formality, by virtue of which the religious enjoys all the comforts of life "with permission" and without the exercise of juridical proprietorship—or the burden of responsibility.

The authenticity of the religious commitment is what makes all religious life (even that which is contemplative and cloistered) apostolic. So, the measure of apostolicity in religious communities is not to be sought purely and simply in the amount of active work they accomplish but in the purity of their faith as expressed in the genuine simplicity of a truly humble and open Christian life.

Hence it would be an illusion for the monastic orders to increase their commitment to active life at the expense of their essential monastic *conversatio*. This is not addressed to those monastic congregations which have schools and parishes. Their problems are of a different and special order, since they do in fact commit themselves to provide an active and apostolic service, whereas the contemplative monasteries have quite another function—that of preserving the purity of the monastic and contemplative tradition in a world in which that tradition is increasingly misunderstood and menaced, not only by people outside the monastery, but even by the monks themselves.

A spirit of *openness* is most important in any renewal of monastic life. Observances which are "closed" and incomprehensible even to the religious themselves will almost inevitably generate a spirit of pretentiousness and artificiality which is incompatible with true gospel and monastic simplicity. Such observances must either be rethought so that they recover a living meaning or they must be discarded and, if necessary, replaced by others that fulfill the function which they have ceased to fulfill.

In any case it is clear that one of the central concerns of the Church in the monastic life, as in the liturgy and everywhere else, is to ensure that renewal is more than tightening up the exactitude of rubrical or juridical observance. In monastic life as in liturgy, renewal means a restoration of authentic meaning to forms and acts that must recover their full value as sacred signs. And these signs, whether in religious observance, monastic witness, contemplative solitude or liturgical worship, should always be clear and evident not only to those who give them form and shape by their living practice, but to all who may happen to see them. The renewal of the monastic life must be first of all a renewal of authentic meaning and of understanding, and only after that a renewal of zeal in carrying out what is understood.

In considering this renewal of the "significance of signs" in the monastic life we must remember that the sign and the thing signified are always inseparable. No matter how much we may attempt to renew the meaning of the sign, the meaning will not change in any real way if the thing signified does not change. Thus if the actions and ceremonies of monastic liturgy are informed by a spirit of institutional ambition, if they spring from organizational arrogance and self-complacency rather than from charity and from an earnest desire to obey the gospel of Christ, then no matter how one may alter the "sign," it will still proclaim the thing that is really signified. Hence one cannot renew the religious life in depth merely by superficially altering some of the ceremonies and rites which are meant to bear witness to the inner spirit. However, once the change of the inner spirit has seriously begun, a renewal in the clarity and significance of the sacred signs will be of great help in bringing all to a clearer understanding and deeper appreciation of the work of renewal.

The meaning of communal life, of the vows, of monastic work, of worship, meditation and prayer can therefore not be permitted to remain arbitrary or abstract. Everything must converge on the central living mystery of unity in Christ and illuminate it—or rather spread the illumination which it receives from it. The function of the monastic community is to manifest this mystery, and the "spirit" of each order is in fact simply the way in which the order interprets its vocation to understand and to live some particular aspect of the mystery of Christ. Usually this "spirit" was manifested to the founder and made itself fairly clear in the first generations of the order's history. And so, for example, the sons of St. Benedict pray in the liturgy of his feast "that the Lord may renew in his Church the Spirit that St. Benedict served, so that we, being filled with the same Spirit, may strive to love what he loved and to carry out in our works the things that he accomplished." So in the monastic life, renewal consists in rediscovering the meaning and spirit of monasticism as it was understood and lived by the early monks. Obviously the "return to sources" has been an important element in the monastic movement of the past hundred years.

The Church in recent years has insisted upon two essential aspects of the contemplative life: first that it must be and must remain what it has always traditionally been: a life oriented directly to God alone (si *revera Deum quaerit!*) in physical separation from the world, i.e., in solitude. But at the same time the Church insists that the contemplative life is and must be fully and completely apostolic. My purpose is not to define the "apostolate of contemplatives" or to introduce nuances into the rather crude idea of the monastery as a "dynamo of prayer" in which the monks are generating spiritual power for the workers in the active ministry. If the active apostolate does not proceed from the apostle's own union with God, the lack cannot be supplied by somebody else's holiness. The monk's prayer of petition and his inner consecration doubtless bring down grace upon the world. But the ancient monastic idea of the *vita apostolica*—source of the traditional understanding of our "apostolic vocation"—is centered in the witness of complete renunciation in obedience to the gospel, what the early Cistercians called the *formula perfectae paenitentiae*, the life of obedience to the gospel in humility, poverty and love.

It is by this spirit of apostolic renunciation that the monk, in spite of his essential solitude, can be open to the needs and to the anguish of the world and hence exercise his apostolate which is above all the apostolate of understanding and of compassion.

Here again, what is demanded of the monk is not the cold and perhaps stupefied "unworldliness" which may at bottom be no better than egoism, but a Christ-like selflessness and purity of heart which can take upon itself the sins and conflicts of the world and "baptize" them with the tears of repentance.

VII

Openness and Cloister

The work of religious renewal is naturally geared for the tempo of the majority who are in the active, apostolic life. The terms in which programs of renewal are articulated will therefore be dynamic, outgoing, aggressive, even in a certain sense "worldly." Since the contemplative orders (especially communities of cloistered women) have unfortunately come to depend on others to formulate and also to solve their problems for them, this may put them in a rather awkward position.

Speaking as a member of a contemplative order, I think this can teach us something. It is high time we contemplatives (and I include the nuns) learned to stand on our own feet and solve our own problems in our own terms. We have to think for ourselves and help one another. We would be very mistaken if we tried to apply the norms and solutions of active religious to the very different problems of the contemplative life.

Many cloistered communities have been seized with panic and confusion when confronted with the demands of renewal, simply because these demands have been formulated in terms that do not really apply to contemplatives. Instead of studying these demands in the light of our own special vocation, and learning to translate them into terms viable for the renewal we ourselves need as badly as anyone else, some of us have tended to reject them en bloc and to hold on desperately to the only solutions whose validity we can vouch for by experience. In many cases this means simply clinging to the past. But our younger religious have very grave problems with the legacy of the past, however valid it may once have been. Experience has shown us that if we simply *refuse* the challenge of renewal, and do no more than maintain archaic values, the cloistered life has no future. The day of grilles, double locks, conversations through veils and curtains, mysterious whisperings through the turn, even more mysterious Masses celebrated out of sight behind a wall—this day is done.

What does aggiornamento mean for contemplatives? Naturally, this is a very big question, and it is one which radically divides whole communities—usually along the lines of seniority. The young are a little more inclined to impatience and desperation. They may desire change at any cost, and demand the introduction of new ideas that work in the active life, on the assumption that these must be valid for everybody. The old, on the other hand, have an existential appreciation of certain values that are fully known only to those who have lived under conditions of discipline and sacrifice which no longer prevail. The more intelligent of these older religious are aware that these values can perhaps be preserved in a completely new form, but others identify the values with the framework of rule and discipline of the "old days." They cling to externals of observance that the new generation cannot understand and cannot accept. This is particularly true in the matter of "openness" and "dialogue."

Should contemplatives be "open to the world"? This is a question that has plunged some communities into what amounts to an identity crisis because it has been formulated in the wrong terms. It is interpreted to mean: Should Carmelites leave the cloister and teach school? Should Trappists run parishes? In other words, are cloistered religious now going to be drafted for service in routine organized work for which they do not feel themselves qualified and for which, in fact, they have no vocation? Stated in such terms, the question is merely silly. The Church has no intention of abolishing the contemplative orders, and she hopes that they will have the good sense not to abolish themselves. What the Church wants is not the destruction of the contemplative life, but its renewal. Now, the renewal of the contemplative orders does fit into the overall program of renewal in the entire Church. One important element in the program, as formulated by Vatican II, is "openness to the world." Contemplatives are not exempt from this, but they have to understand it in their own terms. In other words, they must consider how, and to what extent, they can be "open to the world" without losing their identity as contemplatives.

To some contemplatives, the idea of "openness to the world" is incomprehensible. It contradicts what they believe is fundamental to their vocation. The essence of the cloistered life consists in their being "enclosed." They argue that the cloistered life cannot be open in any real sense without ceasing to be cloistered. This seems to them a matter of simple logic. When you embrace the contemplative, cloistered life, you turn your back on the world, you renounce the world, you forget the problems and concerns, you pray for it without needing to know what you are praying for.

You turn away from the world to God because the world is opposed to God. The cloistered ideal then becomes an ideal of "pure contemplation" in which everything is organized in view of a state of perfect recollection: everything is arranged so that one will be entirely purified not only of attachment to the world but even of all interest in it, all concern for it, all memory of it.

But "openness" to the world means involvement in the affairs of people outside the cloister, identification with them in their desires, problems, struggles, dangers; it means vital concern about a world of total war, genocide, race riots, social injustice, misery, poverty, violence, lust, every kind of disorder. All this is wicked and ungodly. Far from divine, it is diabolical. How can one think of such things and maintain the inner peace, the purity of recollection, the serenity of spirit in which one will hear the sweet ineffable call to divine union?

Rejection of the world, "contempt for the world," then results in a crudely automatic polarization: everything that happens outside the cloister is considered hateful, ridiculous, erroneous, ungodly, or at least trifling. Everything that happens in the cloister and according to the sacrosanct rules of the cloistered life is wise, pleasing to God, full of redemptive power, and supremely significant. The God who is nauseated by the actions of worldlings outside the cloister is consoled and delighted by the actions of observant religious within the cloister. This distorted interpretation of the gospel texts about re-

nouncing the world in our own hearts becomes an excuse for phari-
saical complacency. Contemplatives despise the world because they
imagine themselves to be superior to it in every way. The cloister is
the guarantee of that superiority. If they resume contact with the
world, they lose their superiority and become like everybody else.
The beautiful image is tarnished. They no longer feel secure in the
thought that God loves them better than anybody else.

Obviously, this is caricature. But this distortion has been made
positive by a valid traditional concept of the contemplative life—one
which has been taken for granted for sixteen hundred years! Yet
there are many things which have been taken for granted longer than
that which the Church is now questioning.

Is the contemplative life to be considered a state of interior recollection and an affective absorption in God considered as Infinite
Love, or is it a response to the concrete *Word of God* manifesting to
us his will and his love not only for ourselves as individuals but for
the whole family of man redeemed by the Cross of Christ? Is our
love of God to take the form of blissful repose in consolation and
inner peace or is it a total response which draws us out of ourselves
beyond all concern over how we happen to *feel*? Is the cloistered life
a mere cult of ordered serenity or is it complete self-forgetfulness in
obedience to God? Is the cloistered life merely to escape from the
troubles and conflicts of the world to a condition of security and
peace in which we "rest" and "taste" the consolations of intimacy
with God? Or does it mean sharing the anguish and hope of a world
in crisis in which millions struggle for the barest essentials of human
existence?

Should not the contemplative life be seen in terms of *event* and *encounter* rather than simply as a "viewing" and "tasting" of essential
love? Is love an *object* or is it a *happening*? Is God present to us in
idea or in *act*? Is the contemplative life built on a dynamic of word
and obedience, call and response, or is it a static project in which
minds and hearts seek to become impregnated with a spiritual essence of love? If contemplative love is something which one acquires
or receives in secret and jealously preserves from contamination,
then one can build walls around it for safekeeping. But if contempla-

tive love is a response to someone who is supremely free and whose "thoughts are not our thoughts, whose ways are not our ways," then we cannot really pin him down to purely predictable relationships. We have to be "open" in the sense that we are ready and available in all possible situations, including those of human encounter and exchange. Christian love, including contemplative love, starts from the basic realization that those who are unable to relate to others in a valid human encounter are also handicapped in their relations to the encounter with God.

The current problems of the contemplative life stem in large measure from the way these questions have been answered in the past. Everything now depends on our capacity to reconsider them in the light of the gospel and of contemporary human problems.

Most of the statements proposed about the contemplative life as a life of withdrawal, of "perfect recollection," with stress on negation, with being "undistracted" and so on, tend to have a Platonic rather than a Christian emphasis. These conceptions were valid as long as they fitted into the framework of a consciously religious civilization.

The whole worldview of medieval civilization was structured on the ideas of eternity and divine transcendence. Secular life itself was understood in this framework of unworldliness. At the same time we have forgotten how completely the monks of the Middle Ages were integrated into the secular life of their time. The Cistercians of northern England in the twelfth century played somewhat the same role in their society as General Motors plays in American society today. The wool from the Cistercian granges was one of the most important factors in the economy of medieval England. The renunciation of the world practiced by the Cistercians of the Middle Ages paradoxically gave them a key place in the world of their time, and their asceticism, their mystical life, were understood to be an essential contribution to a religious culture in which everyone participated. The same is true in a different way of the Carmelite reform in sixteenth-century Spain. But today the symbolic dramatization of the contemplative witness, appropriate to a different kind of culture, has acquired a different meaning in a specifically irreligious culture.

We must now learn to distinguish between "religiosity" and "discipleship of Christ." "Religion" was an essential part of medieval culture. "Irreligion" is an essential part of modern culture. What is of importance today is not to get modern man to accept *religion* as a human or cultural value (he may do so or he may not) but to let him see that we are witnesses of Christ, of the new creation, of the Resurrection, of the Living God: and that is something that goes far beyond the cultural phenomenon of religion. The contemplative life will therefore need to be understood, not in terms of religious observances which dramatize the more devout attitudes of a bygone society, but in terms of living experience and witness, that is to say, in terms of complete Christian authenticity. What is important now is not so much to preserve order and regularity in observance but to produce *real contemplatives,* disciples who have found and have known him whom the Father has sent into the world and who are able to bear witness to his reality by their characters, by their lives and by the transformation of their consciousness.

Today a new and more biblical understanding of the contemplative life is called for: we must see it as a response to the dynamic Word of God in history; we must see it in the light of biblical eschatology. The contemplative finds God not in the embrace of "pure love" alone but in the prophetic ardor of response to the "Word of the Lord": not in love considered as essential good but in love that breaks through into the world of sinful men in the fire of judgment and of mercy. The contemplative must see love not only as the highest and purest experience of the human heart transformed by grace, but as God's unfailing fidelity to unfaithful man. The contemplative life is not only Eros (the yearning of the human heart for the vision of beauty), but also Agape (surrender to the inexplicable mercy which comes to us from God entirely on his own terms, in the context of our personal and social history). Once this has been said, Eros cannot be excluded. However, it remains always secondary.

God speaks to us not only in the Bible, not only in the secret inspirations of our hearts, but also through the public and manifest events of our own time and, above all, through the Church. The radical change in the Church's attitude toward the modern world was one of the significant events that marked Vatican II. In the light of the Council it is no longer possible to take a completely negative view of the modern world. It is no longer possible, even for contemplatives, to simply shut out the world, to ignore it, to forget it, in order to relish the private joys of contemplative Eros. To insist on the cultivation of total recollection for the sake of this Eros and its consolations would be pure and simple selfishness. It would also mean a failure to really deepen the true Christian dimensions of Agape, which are the real dimensions of the contemplative life. This is where so much confusion arises.

Lack of theological knowledge, ignorance of the true riches of Christian tradition and of the Church's wisdom, have made contemplatives take a short view of their vocation, one that is almost "materialistic" (emphasis on walls, grilles, veils, withdrawal, mutism). But the same ignorance may well carry them to the opposite extreme. Some apparently imagine that by throwing off the veil, running around talking to everyone, and getting themselves involved in every kind of official active task, they can justify their existence in the eyes of the world. To please "the world" they repudiate their call to contemplation. We have to be careful not to discredit a false idea of contemplation in such a way that we discredit true contemplative life and get rid of the cloister so that everyone can plunge into action, but to renew the true contemplative life as an authentic, rare but vitally necessary charism in the Church. Now, the call of the Church to "openness" is essential to renewal itself, even for contemplatives. Hence "openness" is *necessary* for contemplatives. It is by no means a mere concession, something permitted to modern people who would otherwise become tense through too much concentration and withdrawal. In one word: openness is now seen to be not only not opposed to cloistered contemplation but even as necessary for its deepening and its renewal.

But why is this the case? Once again, the only way to validate such a claim is by appealing, not to psychology, not to the pragmatic necessities of the moment, but to theology itself. Openness to the world is demanded by the realization that the world of today, in which man's whole future for good or for evil now rests in his own hands, is for all men the place of God's epiphany as Judge and as Savior, as the Lord of history. On the other hand, as we all know too well, those who are completely immersed in the world with its violence and confusion may certainly have a very real experience of its problem, but they may also see these problems so close at hand that they lose their perspective. Their view of things needs to be completed by the perspective of those who see life from another angle. In order to see the world from this "other angle" there must necessarily be places where people live, under special conditions, devoting themselves to meditation, study, prayer and worship, not for themselves but as a service to the entire Church. This service is what now needs to be properly understood and defined. Here is where "openness" is important. If the contemplative is totally out of touch with the realities and crises of his time, he loses all claim to that special fullness and maturity of wisdom which should be his. The Church has always expected that her contemplatives should be men and women who have attained a greater depth of prophetic wisdom, a more profound understanding of the Word and love of God, so that they may be more perfect witnesses of the Kingdom and of the new creation. That is why John the Baptist—"the voice of one crying in the wilderness"—has traditionally been the model of monks: not just because he fasted and lived in the desert, but because it was he who was first able to recognize the Messiah. Needless to say, our contemplatives are not always distinguished by this superior wisdom at all, and the charism of prophetic wisdom has unfortunately too often become distorted by eccentricity and illuminism. (No need to retail here the taste for bizarre devotions, for curious inner feelings, for apocalyptic surmises, or for preternatural happenings which have flourished in the cloister due to excessive rigidity and too much enclosure.)

There is therefore a twofold need for "openness" in contemplative communities. Contemplatives need to be more "open" for their own good and for the renewal of their contemplative life by a saner contact with contemporary reality. But also, assuming that the contemplative life itself is authentic, others need to share in its advantages. Openness works two ways. On both sides there is giving and receiving. The result is, or should be, a real increase of charity, a greater love of the contemplative for the world created and redeemed by God, a greater love of the noncloistered person for God, found and experienced more deeply in temporary contact with the cloister. Needless to say, those who have been deputed by the Church not only to pray for the world but also to attain a deeper level of experience and understanding should also, at least in some cases, be able to teach the ways of prayer to others living outside the cloister, besides providing them with a place of quiet and rest and interior renewal.

There can be no question whatever of the Church asking contemplatives to engage in work for which they are not qualified, work which others can do far better than they. There is no need for contemplative Carmelites to teach third-grade arithmetic. There is no need either for Cistercians to get out into the parishes and preach. What the Church needs is for contemplatives to share with others their privilege of silence, worship and meditation, their ability to listen more deeply and more penetratingly to the Word of God, their understanding of sacrifice, their inner vision.

Anyone who has been called to share with others the fruits of contemplation knows well enough that this sharing is not a distraction and not a threat to the contemplative life. On the contrary, much discipline and humility are necessary for one who tries in all honesty to share with others an undistorted view of the truth. The task of conveying to others clearly and sincerely what one knows of the problems of the Christian life, without saying more than one knows and without resorting merely to catch phrases borrowed from books, is a great help for one's own life in Christ. Of course, not all are called to do this kind of thing habitually, and many members of contemplative communities will have no reason to worry about it.

Now an important question: What is meant by "openness"? As a matter of fact, it is not quite certain just what openness is going to mean in practice for contemplatives: that is something we have to discover by experiment. I would suggest the following as a useful description of what openness might imply for cloistered orders. Here I am not making nice distinctions for men and women, but just taking the contemplative life in general.

a. First of all, being "open to the world" means being aware of and responsive to the real situation of people in the world, the critical problems of the world. These problems are basically spiritual problems. The world is in a state of spiritual crisis. In fact we are now in one of the most crucial periods of development in the whole evolution of man. We are literally at the crossroads of our destiny. Most people either ignore the spiritual dimensions of the crisis or else they are incapable of apprehending the real issues in any way whatever. The contemplative, by *selective* information and *well-chosen* exposure to sound commentary, should be able to identify intelligently and compassionately with modern man in crisis. Simple aloofness, withdrawal, and refusal of concern would make the contemplative a scandal to his brother in the world.

Parenthetically: this is another case where the lack of originality and initiative are grave handicaps in the contemplative life. There is obvious risk in an uncritical use of modern media: we have to face the fact that what passes for news is often merely the retailing of pseudoevents. What passes for entertainment is the subject of articulate and constant protest on the part of intelligent people. It would be absurd for naive contemplatives to be agog over material which those outside the cloister regard as cultural garbage, and there is very real danger of their doing so, since they lack the critical sense to discern what is valuable and what is not. There is need for qualified persons to select and distribute information that would be really pertinent in the contemplative life and to provide a minimum of intelligent comment showing its relevance to our life in Christ. Someone ought to undertake a weekly mimeographed newsletter for contemplatives: this would be a real service. It would save religious the tedium of plowing through the newspapers and magazines to find something useful amid the bewilderment of pseudoevents and religious fads. This mimeographed service could also include a list of references to articles in useful sources like *Herder Correspondence, Informations Catholiques Internationales,* etc.

b. Being "open to the world" means being more accessible to people of flesh and blood who are brought by God, in one way or other, to our doorstep. The poor, materially and spiritually. Our relatives and friends. Men and women who are looking for something they need, without being able to identify it precisely, and who come to the cloister for rest, reflection and retreat. Here, too, there have to be certain limits, and contacts with the outside must be *selective*. There is no point in simply turning the monastery into a busy retreat house. In any case, it would seem that "retreat movements" and "closed retreats" are losing their significance. What people seek today is not so much the organized, predigested routine of conferences and exercises, but an opportunity to be quiet, to reflect, and to discuss in informal, spontaneous and friendly encounters the things they have on their minds. At this point we might add that there is today a far greater interest in contemplation among non-Christians and even nonbelievers than there is among the ordinary run of Christians. Contemplative communities may find that they have a great deal to say to these people who seek spiritual insight but who, generally speaking, are bored to death with preachers and utterly deaf to Christian apologetics. The only Christian communities that still retain some meaning for these people are contemplative communities.

c. Does openness to the world imply going out of the cloister more freely? The contemplative life would lose its meaning if it did not preserve a certain amount of solitude and silence. But we must admit that merely keeping everyone locked up is no guarantee of an authentic contemplative life. There are times when a contemplative needs to leave the cloister. Obviously there is no point in a contemplative merely going out "socially" and spending time in idle conversation or "having fun." But there may be reasons why a contemplative should leave his cloister in order to obtain information or experience that would be valuable for him and for his community. Obviously this too will be a highly selective matter. But it should be quite normal to go to other monasteries in order to take courses in theology, Scripture, liturgy and so on. This should be possible for nuns also. Cloistered nuns can and should be open to the extent of attending certain important meetings and conferences (for superiors, novice mistresses, etc.). Monks might in exceptional cases travel to engage in ecumenical dialogue or discussions where their presence would be really useful. Contemplatives have a special slant on the theological and spiritual problems of the Church and of the world. They should be able to make their own contribution to discussions of these problems and should be allowed, with other qualified experts, to participate in affecting the good of the whole Church. Above all, they should take a most active part in solving the problems of contemplative communities themselves and should be able to give help where it is really needed. On the other hand, if a contemplative religious becomes so caught up in these activities that he is no longer able to live a contemplative life, then the reason for his "services" no longer exists. He is qualified to help others insofar as he is what he is supposed to be: a contemplative. No matter what may be the need for action and service on the part of the contemplative, that need must yield to the minimal demands of the contemplative life itself. In the contemplative life, action exists for the sake of contemplation and vice versa. The openness of the contemplative is justified insofar as it enables him to be a better contemplative and to share with others the fruit of his contemplation.

Finally, one very important point. In the past, the structures of the contemplative life have acquired too much rigidity and uniformity. Emphasis on exterior regularity and on uniform observance tended to stifle personal development and took little or no account of special needs or personal vocations, for instance to greater solitude. Contemplative "openness" must develop not only in relation to the outside world but also, and above all, within the community itself. Free and spontaneous contacts between the religious themselves are absolutely necessary. Religious must communicate frankly and sincerely in a personal way and not only in the set of formalized relationships which have been favored in the past. The structure of community relations in the contemplative life has been too inflexible, too impersonal, and in many cases artificial to the point of stultification.

Relationships must once more become "natural" and human in the best sense of those words. This means inevitably a greater freedom and tolerance in the matter of communication. In other words, it means materially less silence. On the other hand, to balance this freedom of communication, the legitimate needs of individual religious for greater solitude and silence must also be respected. The community that grows in charity and self-understanding will also spontaneously recognize these special needs—and favor them in a spirit of real love, knowing that they imply no derogation of the common life. The mature contemplative (who may not always be necessarily a very brilliant or gifted person) can contribute a great deal to the common life by his or her silent and solitary prayer. Even those who are not yet fully formed need the experience of periods of solitude and silence in order to grow in the life of prayer. Contemplative communities should recognize the value of encouraging these personal aspirations.

The "openness" that is asked of contemplatives by the Church is then not a mere matter of relaxation, not an expedient for making life more livable. The real purpose of openness is to renew life in the Spirit, life in love. A greater love and understanding of people is no obstacle to a true growth in contemplation, for contemplation is rooted and grounded in charity. A more generous sharing of the values of the contemplative life will increase our love instead of diminishing it. It will also increase our understanding of and appreciation for our own vocation. Obviously, a great deal of prudence will be required, but we should not be so afraid of mistakes that we fail to make necessary changes. If we face change in a courageous spirit of faith, the Holy Spirit will take care of the rest.

VIII

Is the World a Problem?*

Is the world a problem? I type the question. I am tempted to type it over again, with asterisks between the letters, the way H*y*m*a*n K*a*p*l*a*n used to type his name in *The New Yorker* thirty years ago. And as far as I am concerned that would dispose of the question. But the issue is doubtless too serious for a blank page with "Is the world a problem" running down the middle, full of asterisks. So I have to be serious too and develop it.

Maybe I can spell this question out politely, admitting that there are still cogent reasons why it should be asked and answered. Perhaps, too, I am personally involved in the absurdity of the question; due to a book I wrote thirty years ago, I have myself become a sort of stereotype of the world-denying contemplative—the man who spurned New York, spat on Chicago, and tromped on Louisville, heading for the woods with Thoreau in one pocket, John of the Cross in another, and holding the Bible open at the Apocalypse. This personal stereotype is probably my own fault, and it is something I have to try to demolish on occasion. This is one of the occasions.

Now that we are all concerned about the Church and the World, the Secular City, and the values of secular society, it was to be expected that someone would turn quizzically to me and ask: "What

---

* On the original title page the author had written:
> *Et quand donc suis-je plus vrai*
> *que lorsque je suis le monde?*
> —Camus

about you, Father Merton? What do you think?"—and then duck as if I were St. Jerome with a rock in my fist.

First of all, the whole question of the world, the secular world, has become extremely ambiguous. It becomes even more ambiguous when it is set up over against another entity, the world of the sacred. The old duality of time-eternity, matter-spirit, natural-supernatural and so on (which makes sense in a very limited and definite context) is suddenly transposed into a totally different context in which it creates nothing but confusion. This confusion is certainly a problem. Whether or not "the world" is a problem, a confused idea of what the world might possibly be is quite definitely a problem, and it is that confusion I want to talk about. I want to make clear that I speak not as the author of *The Seven Storey Mountain,* which seemingly a lot of people have read, but as the author of more recent essays and poems which apparently very few people have read. This is not the official voice of Trappist silence, the monk with his hood up and his back to the camera, brooding over the waters of an artificial lake. This is not the petulant and uncanonizable modern Jerome who never got over the fact that he could give up beer. (I drink beer whenever I can lay my hands on any. I love beer and, by that very fact, the world.) This is simply the voice of a self-questioning human person who, like all his brothers, struggles to cope with turbulent, mysterious, demanding, exciting, frustrating, confused existence in which almost nothing is really predictable, in which most definitions, explanations and justifications become incredible even before they are uttered, in which people suffer together and are sometimes utterly beautiful, at other times impossibly pathetic. In which there is much that is frightening, in which almost everything public is patently phony, and in which there is at the same time an immense ground of personal authenticity that is right there and so obvious that no one can talk about it and most cannot even believe that it is there.

I am, in other words, a man in the modern world. In fact, I am the world just as you are! Where am I going to look for the world first of all if not in myself?

As long as I assume that the world is something I discover by turning on the radio or looking out the window I am deceived from the start. As long as I imagine that the world is something to be "escaped" in a monastery—that wearing a special costume and following a quaint observance takes me "out of this world," I am dedicating my life to an illusion. Of course, I hasten to qualify this. I said a moment ago that in a certain historic context of thought and of life this kind of thought and action once made perfect sense. But the moment you change the context, then the whole thing has to be completely transposed. Otherwise you are left like the orchestra in the Marx brothers' *Night at the Opera* where Harpo had inserted "Take Me Out to the Ball Game" in the middle of the operatic score.

The confusion lies in this: on one hand there is a primitive Christian conception of the world as an object of choice. On the other there is the obvious fact that the world is also something about which there is and can be no choice. And, historically, these notions have sometimes got mixed up, so that what is simply "given" appears to have been chosen and what is there to be chosen, decided for or against, is simply evaded as if no decision were licit or even possible.

That I should have been born in 1915, that I should be the contemporary of Auschwitz, Hiroshima, Viet Nam and the Watts riots are things about which I was not first consulted. Yet they are also events in which, whether I like it or not, I am deeply and personally involved. The "world" is not just a physical space traversed by jet planes and full of people running in all directions. It is a complex of responsibilities and options made out of the loves, the hates, the fears, the joys, the hopes, the greed, the cruelty, the kindness, the faith, the trust, the suspicion of all. In the last analysis, if there is war because nobody trusts anybody, this is in part because I myself am defensive, suspicious, untrusting, and intent on making other people conform themselves to my particular brand of death wish.

Put in these terms, the world both is and is not a problem. The world is a "problem" insofar as everybody in it is a problem to himself. The world is a problem insofar as we all add up to a big collective question. Starting then from this concept of a world which is essentially problematic because it is full of problematic and self-doubting freedoms, there have been various suggestions made as to what to do about it.

At present the Church is outgrowing what one might call the Carolingian suggestion. This is a worldview which was rooted in the official acceptance of the Church into the world of imperial Rome, the world of Constantine and of Augustine, of Charlemagne in the West and of Byzantium in the East. In crude, simple strokes, this worldview can be sketched as follows: We are living in the last age of salvation history. A world radically evil and doomed to hell has been ransomed from the devil by the Cross of Christ and is now simply marking time until the message of salvation can be preached to everyone. Then will come the judgment. Meanwhile, men, being evil and prone to sin at every moment, must be prevented by authority from following their base instincts and getting lost.

They cannot be left to their own freedom or even to God's loving grace. They have to have their freedom taken away from them because it is their greatest peril. They have to be told at every step what to do, and it is better if what they are told to do is displeasing to their corrupt natures, for this will keep them out of further subtle forms of mischief. Meanwhile the Empire has become, provisionally at least, holy. As figure of the eschatological kingdom, worldly power consecrated to Christ becomes Christ's reign on earth. In spite of its human limitations the authority of the Christian prince is a guarantee against complete chaos and disorder and must be submitted to—to resist established authority is equivalent to resisting Christ. Thus we have a rigid and stable order in which all values are fixed and have to be preserved, protected, defended against dark forces of impulse and violent passion. War on behalf of the Christian prince and his power becomes a holy war for Christ against the devil. War too becomes a sacred duty.

The dark strokes in the picture have their historical explanation in the crisis of the barbarian invasions. But there are also brighter strokes, and we find in the thought of Aquinas, Scotus, Bonaventure, Dante, a basically world-affirming and optimistic view of man, of his world and his work, in the perspective of the Christian redemption.

Here in the more peaceful and flourishing years of the twelfth and thirteenth centuries we see a harmonious synthesis of nature and grace in which the created world itself is an epiphany of divine wisdom and love and, redeemed in and by Christ, will return to God with all its beauty restored by the transforming power of grace, which reaches down to material creation through man and his work. Already in St. Thomas we find the groundwork for an optimistic Christian affirmation of natural and worldly values in the perspective of an eschatological love. However, this view too is static rather than dynamic, hierarchic, layer upon layer, rather than ongoing and self-creating, the fulfillment of a predetermined intellectual plan rather than the creative project of a free and self-building love.

In the Carolingian worldview it somehow happened that the idea of the world as an object of choice tended to be frozen. The "world" was identified simply with the sinful, the perilous, the unpredictable (therefore in many cases the new and, even worse, the free), and this was what one automatically rejected. Or, if one had the misfortune to choose it, one went at once to confession. The world was therefore what one did not choose. Since society itself was constructed on this concept of the world, Christian society ("Christendom") conceived itself as a world-denying society in the midst of the world, a pilgrim society on the way to another world. It was fitting that there should be in the midst of that society, and in a place of special prominence and choice, certain people who were professional world-deniers, whose very existence was a sign of *contemptus mundi* and of otherworldly aspirations. Thus from a certain point of view this renunciation and unworldliness of monks became a justification of worldly power and of the established social and economic structures. The society that, by its respect for consecrated unworldliness, confessed its own heavenly aspirations was certainly the realm of Christ on earth; its kings and its mighty were all alike pilgrims with the poor and humble. If all kept their proper place in the procession the pilgrimage would continue to go well. This is all obvious to everyone who has ever read a line about the Middle Ages, and its obviousness is presently being run into the ground by critics of monasticism. What these critics overlook is that though the theory was austere and negative, in practice the "sacred" and basically "clerical" and "monastic" Christendom produced a world-affirming, nature-respecting, life-loving, love-oriented, fruitful and rich culture. It had its limitations and its grave flaws. But the monastic and contemplative ideal of the Middle Ages, based on an ideological rejection of the world, actually recovered and rediscovered the values of the world on a deeper and more imperishable level, not merely somewhere aloft in a card file of Platonic ideas but in the world itself: its life, its work, its people, its strivings, its hopes and its existential day-to-day reality. The world-denying monastic ethos found itself willy-nilly incorporated in a life-affirming and humanistic climate. No one who has really read Anselm, Thomas, John of Salisbury, Scotus, Bonaventure, Eckhart, and the rest can seriously doubt this.

Nevertheless, this stereotyped hierarchic idea of the world's structure eventually ceased to be really fruitful and productive. It was already sterile and unreal as early as the fifteenth century. And the fact that the Church of the Second Vatican Council has finally admitted that the old immobilism will no longer serve is a bit too overdue to be regarded as a monumental triumph. The *Constitution on the Church in the Modern World* is salted with phrases which suggest that the fathers were, at least some of them, fully aware of this.

In any case, one of the essential tasks of aggiornamento is that of renewing the whole perspective of theology in such a way that our ideas of God, man and the world are no longer dominated by the Carolingian-medieval imagery of the sacred and hierarchical cosmos in which everything is decided beforehand and in which the only choice is to accept gladly what is imposed as part of an immobile and established social structure.

In "turning to the world" the contemporary Church is first of all admitting that the world can once again become an object of choice. Not only can it be chosen, but in fact it must be chosen. How? If I had no choice about the age in which I was to live, I nevertheless have a choice about the attitude I take and about the way and the extent of my participation in its living ongoing events. To choose the world is not then merely a pious admission that the world is acceptable because it comes from the hand of God. It is first of all an acceptance of a task and a vocation in the world, in history and in time: in my time, which is the present. To choose the world is to choose to do the work I am capable of doing, in collaboration with my brother, to make the world better, more free, more just, more livable, more human. And it has now become transparently obvious that mere automatic "rejection of the world" and "contempt for the world" is in fact not a choice but the evasion of choice. The man who pretends that he can turn his back on Auschwitz or Viet Nam and act as if they were not there is simply bluffing. I think this is getting to be generally admitted, even by monks.

On the other hand the stereotype of world rejection is now being firmly replaced by a collection of equally empty stereotypes of world affirmation in which I, for one, have very little confidence. They often seem to be gestures, charades, mummery designed to make the ones participating in them feel secure, to make them feel precisely that they "like participating" and are really doing something. So precisely at the moment when it becomes vitally important for the destiny of man that man should learn to choose for himself a peaceful, equitable, sane and humane world, the whole question of choice itself becomes a stark and dreadful one. We talk about choosing, yet everything seems more grimly determined than ever before. We are caught in an enormous web of consequences, a net of erroneous and even pathological effects of other men's decisions. After Hitler, how can Germany be anything but a danger to world peace? To choose the world therefore is to choose the anguish of being hampered and frustrated in a situation fraught with frightful difficulties. We can affirm the world and its values all we like, but the complexity of events responds too often with a cold negation of our hopes.

In the old days when everyone compulsively rejected the world it was really not hard at all to secretly make quite a few healthy and positive affirmations of a worldly existence in the best sense of the word, in praise of God and for the good of all. Nowadays when we talk so much of freedom, commitment, "engagement," and so on, it becomes imperative to ask whether the choices we are making have any meaning whatever. Do they change anything? Do they get us anywhere? Do we really choose to alter the direction of our lives or do we simply comfort ourselves with the choice of making another choice? Can we really decide effectively for a better world?

The "suggestion" that has now most obviously replaced that of the Carolingians is that of Karl Marx. In this view, history is not finished, it has just reached the point where it may, if we are smart, begin. There is no predetermined divine plan (although frankly the messianism in Marx is basically biblical and eschatological). After a long precarious evolution, matter has reached the point, in man, where it can become fully aware of itself, take itself in hand, control its own destiny. And now at last that great seething mass of material forces, the world, will enter upon its true destiny by being raised to a human level. The instruments by which this can be accomplished— technology, cybernetics—are now in our power. But are we in our own power? No, we are still determined by the illusions of thought patterns, superstructures, devised to justify antiquated and destructive economic patterns. Hence if man is to choose to make himself, if he is to become free at last, his duty can be narrowed down to one simple option, one basic commitment: the struggle against the (imperialist) world.

With a shock we find ourselves in a familiar pattern: a predetermined struggle against evil in which personal freedom is viewed with intolerance and suspicion. The world must be changed because it is unacceptable as it is. But the change must be guided by authority and political power. The forces of good are all incarnate in this authority. The forces of evil on the contrary are incarnate in the power of the enemy system. Man cannot be left to himself. He must submit entirely to the control of the collectivity for which he exists. "Man" is not the person but the collective animal. Though he may eventually become free, now is not the time of freedom but of obedience, authority, power, control. Man does not choose to make himself except in the sense that he submits to a choice dictated by the authority of science and the messianic collective—the party which represents the chosen eschatological class. Hence though in theory there are all kinds of possible choices, in reality the only basic choice is that of rejecting and destroying the evil "world"—namely capitalist imperialism and, in the present juncture, the United States.

Hence the ambiguities of Communist dogma at the moment: the choice of peace is of course nothing else than the choice of war against the United States. In other words, we have turned the page of *Aïda* and we are now playing "Take Me Out to the Ball Game," but it is the same crazy Marx brothers' opera. Freedom, humanism, peace, plenty and joy are all enthusiastically invoked but prove on closer examination to be their opposites. There is only one choice, to submit to the decision handed down from on high by an authoritarian power which defines good and evil in political terms.

This, as I see it, is the present state of the question. The Church has finally realized officially that the classic worldview, which began to develop serious flaws five hundred years ago, is no longer viable at all. There is something of a stampede for security in a new worldview.

In this endeavor the dialogue with Marxism is going to be of crucial importance not only for Christians but for Marxists. For if it is a true dialogue it will possibly involve some softening and adjustment of doctrinaire positions and an opening to new perspectives and possibilities of collaboration. Obviously, however, the dialogue with official and established Marxism—the Soviets or Red China—is not to be considered yet as a meaningful possibility. But the conversations that have begun with the type of revisionist Marxism represented by the French thinker Roger Garaudy may certainly have some effects. But what effects? Good or bad? It is all too easy for enthusiastic Catholics, having tasted a little of the new wine, to convince themselves that "turning to the world" and "choosing the world" mean simply turning to Marx and choosing some variation—Maoist, Soviet, Castroist—of the Communist political line. There is no question that since the Council a few Catholic thinkers and publicists in Europe and South America are tending in this direction. Their tendency is understandable, but I do not find it altogether hopeful.

The majority of Catholic thinkers today are, however, working in the direction of a modern worldview in which the demands of the new humanism of Marx, Freud, Teilhard, Bonhoeffer and others are fully respected and often heartily endorsed. For them, the tendency is no longer to regard God as enthroned "out there" at the summit of the cosmos, but as the "absolute future" who will manifest himself in and through man, by the transformation of man and the world by science oriented to Christ. Though this certainly is not a view which conservative theologians find comforting, it represents a serious attempt to reexpress Christian truths in terms more familiar to modern man. It demands that we take a more dynamic view of man and of society. It requires openness, freedom, the willingness to face risks. It also postulates respect for the human person in the human community. But at the same time it seems to me that it may have serious deficiencies insofar as it may ignore the really deep problems of collective technological and cybernetic society. To assume, for instance, that just because scientific and technological humanism can theoretically be seen as "perfectly biblical" ("nothing is more biblical than technology," says Père Daniélou) does not alter the profound dehumanization that can in fact take place in technological society (as Daniélou also clearly sees). The fact that man can now theoretically control and direct his own destiny does nothing to mitigate the awful determinism which in practice makes a mockery of the most realistic plans and turns all men's projects diametrically against their professed humanistic aims. The demonic gap between expressed aims and concrete achievements in the conduct of the Viet Nam war, for instance, should be an object lesson in the impotence of technology to come to grips with the human needs and realities of our time.

I have a profound mistrust of all obligatory answers. The great problem of our time is not to formulate clear answers to neat theoretical questions but to tackle the self-destructive alienation of man in a society dedicated in theory to human values and in practice to the pursuit of power for its own sake. All the new and fresh answers in the world, all the bright official confidence in the collectivity of the secular city, will do nothing to change the reality of this alienation. The Marxist worldview is the one really coherent and systematic one that has so far come forward to replace the old medieval Christian and classic synthesis. It has in fact got itself accepted, for better or for worse, by more than half the human race. And yet, while claiming to offer man hope of deliverance from alienation, it has demanded a more unquestioning, a more irrational and a more submissive obedience than ever to its obligatory answers, even when these are manifestly self-contradictory and destructive of the very values they claim to defend.

The dialogue with Marxism is an obvious necessity. But if in the course of it we simply create a vapid brew of neomodernist and pseudoscientific optimism I do not see what has been gained, especially if it leaves people passive and helpless in the presence of dehumanizing forces that no one seems quite able to identify exactly and cope with effectively. In this sense, the world is certainly a problem. Its idea of itself is extremely ambiguous. Its claims to pinpoint and to solve its own greatest problems are, in my opinion, not very convincing. Its obligatory answers are hardly acceptable. I am not in love with them!

When "the world" is hypostatized (and it inevitably is) it becomes another of those dangerous and destructive fictions with which we are trying vainly to grapple. And for anyone who has seriously entered into the medieval Christian, or the Hindu, or the Buddhist conceptions of *contemptus mundi, Mara* and the *"emptiness of the world,"* it will be evident that this means not the rejection of a reality, but the unmasking of an illusion. The world as pure object is something that is not there. It is not a reality outside us for which we exist. It is not a firm and absolute objective structure which has to be accepted on its own inexorable terms. The world has in fact no terms of its own. It dictates no terms to man. We and our world interpenetrate. If anything, the world exists for us, and we exist for ourselves. It is only in assuming full responsibility for our world, for our lives and for ourselves that we can be said to live really for God. The whole human reality, which of course transcends us as individuals and as a collectivity, nevertheless interpenetrates the world of nature (which is obviously "real") and the world of history (also "real" insofar as it is made up of the total effect of all our decisions and actions). But this reality, though "external" and "objective," is not something entirely independent of us that dominates us inexorably from without through the medium of certain fixed laws which science alone can discover and use. It is an extension and a projection of ourselves and of our lives, and if we attend to it respectfully, while attending also to our own freedom and our own integrity, we can learn to obey its ways and coordinate our lives with its mysterious movements. The way to find the real "world" is not merely to measure and observe what is outside us but to discover our own inner ground. For that is where the world is, first of all: in my deepest self. But there I find the world to be quite different from the "obligatory answers." This "ground," this "world" where I am mysteriously present at once to my own self and to the freedoms of all other men, is not a visible objective and determined structure with fixed laws and demands. It is a living and self-creating mystery of which I am myself a part, to which I am myself my own unique door. When I find the world in my own ground, it is impossible for me to be alienated by it. It is precisely the obligatory answers which insist on showing me the world as totally other than myself and my brother that alienate me from myself and from my brother. Hence I see no reason for our compulsion to manufacture ever newer and more shiny sets of obligatory answers.

The questions and the answers surely have their purpose. We are rational and dialectical beings. But even the best answers are themselves not final. They point to something further which cannot be embodied in a verbal ground. They point to life itself in its inalienable and personal ground. They point to that realm of values which, in the eyes of scientific and positivistic thought, has no meaning. But how can we come to grips with the world except insofar as it is a value, that is to say, insofar as it exists for us?

There remains a profound wisdom in the traditional Christian approach to the world as to an object of choice. But we have to admit that the habitual and mechanical compulsions of a certain limited type of Christian thought have falsified the true value-perspective in which the world can be discovered and chosen as it is. To treat the world merely as an agglomeration of material goods and objects outside ourselves, and to reject these goods and objects in order to seek others which are "interior" and "spiritual," is in fact to miss the whole point of the challenging confrontation of the world and

Christ. Do we really choose between the world and Christ as between two conflicting realities absolutely opposed? Or do we choose
Christ by choosing the world as it really is in him, that is to say, created and redeemed by him, and encountered in the ground of our
own personal freedom and of our love? Do we really renounce ourselves and the world in order to find Christ, or do we renounce our
alienated and false selves in order to choose our own deepest truth in
choosing both the world and Christ at the same time? If the deepest
ground of my being is love, then in that very love itself and nowhere
else will I find myself, and the world, and my brother and Christ. It is
not a question of either-or but of all-in-one. It is not a matter of ex-
clusivism and "purity" but of wholeness, wholeheartedness, unity
and Meister Eckhart's *Gleichheit* (equality) which finds the same
ground of love in everything.

The world cannot be a problem to anyone who sees that ultimately Christ, the world, his brother and his own inmost ground are
made one and the same in grace and redemptive love. If all the current talk about the world helps people to discover this, then it is fine.
But if it produces nothing but a whole new divisive gamut of obligatory positions and "contemporary answers" we might as well forget
it. The world itself is no problem, but we are a problem to ourselves
because we are alienated from ourselves, and this alienation is due
precisely to an inveterate habit of division by which we break reality
into pieces and then wonder why, after we have manipulated the
pieces until they fall apart, we find ourselves out of touch with life,
with reality, with the world and most of all with ourselves.

IX

Contemplation in a World of Action

This is not intended merely as another apologia for an official, institutional life of prayer. Nor is it supposed to score points in an outdated polemic. My purpose is rather to examine some basic questions of *meaning*. What does the contemplative life or the life of prayer, solitude, silence, meditation, mean in the atomic age? What can it mean? Has it lost all meaning whatever?

When I speak of the contemplative life I do not mean the institutional cloistered life, the organized life of prayer. This has special problems of its own. Many Catholics are now saying openly that the cloistered contemplative *institution* is indefensible, that it is an anachronism that has no point in the modern world. I am not arguing about this—I only remark in passing that I do not agree. Prescinding from any idea of an institution or even of a religious organization, I am talking about a special dimension of inner discipline and experience, a certain integrity and fullness of personal development which are not compatible with a purely external, alienated, busy-busy existence. This does not mean that they are incompatible with action, with creative work, with dedicated love. On the contrary, these all go together. A certain depth of disciplined experience is a necessary ground for fruitful action. Without a more profound human understanding derived from exploration of the inner ground of human existence, love will tend to be superficial and deceptive. Traditionally, the ideas of prayer, meditation and contemplation have been associated with this deepening of one's personal life and this expansion of the capacity to understand and serve others.

Let us start from one admitted fact: if prayer, meditation and contemplation were once taken for granted as central realities in human life everywhere, they are so no longer. They are regarded, even by believers, as somehow marginal and secondary: what counts is getting things done. Prayer seems to be nothing but "saying words," and meditation is a mysterious process which is not understood: if it has some usefulness, that usefulness is felt to be completely remote from the life of ordinary people. As for contemplation: even in the so-called "contemplative life" it is viewed with suspicion! If "contemplatives" themselves are afraid of it, what will the ordinary layperson think? And, as a matter of fact, the word "contemplation" has unfortunate resonances—the philosophic elitism of Plato and Plotinus.

It is a curious fact that in the traditional polemic between action and contemplation, modern apologists for the "contemplative" life have tended to defend it on pragmatic grounds—in terms of action and efficacy. In other words, monks and nuns in cloisters are not "useless," because they are engaged in a very efficacious kind of spiritual activity. They are not idle, lazy, evasive: they are "getting things done," but in a mysterious and esoteric sort of way, an invisible, spiritual way, by means of their prayers. Instead of acting upon things and persons in the world, they act directly upon God by prayer. This is in fact a "superior kind of activity," a "supreme efficacy," but people do not see it. It has to be believed.

I am not interested, for the moment, in trying to prove anything by this argument. I am concerned only with its meaning to modern people. Obviously there are many who *believe* this in the sense that they accept it "on faith" without quite seeing how it is possible. They accept it on authority without understanding it themselves and without trying to understand it. The argument is not one which appeals to them. It arouses a curious malaise, but they do not know what to do about it. They put it away on a mental shelf with other things they have no time to examine.

This view of the contemplative life, which is quite legitimate as far as it goes, places a great deal of stress on the prayer of petition, on intercession, on vicarious sacrifice and suffering as work, as action, as "something accomplished" in cloisters. And stress is laid on the idea that the prayers and sacrifices of contemplatives produce certain definite effects, albeit in a hidden manner. They "produce grace" and they also in some way "cause" divine interventions. Thus it happens that a considerable volume of letters arrives in the monastery or convent mailbag requesting prayers on the eve of a serious operation, on the occasion of a lawsuit, in personal and family problems, in sickness, in all kinds of trouble. Certainly, Catholics believe that God hears and answers prayers of petition. But it is a distortion of the contemplative life to treat it as if the contemplative concentrated all his efforts on getting graces and favors from God for others and for himself.

This conception of God and of prayer is one which fits quite naturally into a particular image of the universe, a cause-and-effect mechanism with a transcendent God "outside" and "above" it, acting upon it as Absolute First Cause, Supreme Prime Mover. He is the Uncaused Cause, guiding, planning, willing every effect down to the tiniest detail. He is regarded as a Supreme Engineer. But men can enter into communication with him, share in his plans, participate in his causation by faith and prayer. He delegates to men a secret and limited share in his activity insofar as they are united with him.

I am not saying that there is anything "wrong" with this. I have expressed it crudely, but it is perfectly logical and fits in naturally with certain premises. However, the trouble is that it supposes an image of the universe which does not correspond with that of post-Newtonian physics. Now, in the nineteenth century and in the modernist crisis of the early twentieth century there was one response to that: "If our view of the universe does not correspond with that of modern science, then to hell with science. We are right and that's that." But since that time it has been realized that while God is transcendent he is also immanent and that faith does not require a special ability to imagine God "out there" or to picture him spatially removed from his creation as a machine which he directs by remote control. This spatial imagery has been recognized as confusing and irrelevant to people with a radically different notion of the space-time continuum. Teilhard de Chardin is one witness among many—doubtless the best known—to a whole new conception, a dynamic, immanentist conception of God and the world. God is at work in and through man, perfecting an ongoing Creation. This too is to some extent a matter of creating an acceptable image, a picture which we can grasp, which is not totally alien to our present understanding, and it will doubtless be replaced by other images in later ages. The underlying truth is not altered by the fact that it is expressed in different ways, from different viewpoints, as long as these viewpoints do not distort and falsify it.

Now it happens that the immanentist approach, which sees God as directly and intimately present in the very ground of our being (while being at the same time infinitely transcendent), is actually much closer to the contemplative tradition. The real point of the contemplative life has always been a deepening of faith and of the personal dimensions of liberty and apprehension to the point where our direct union with God is realized and "experienced." We awaken not only to a realization of the immensity and majesty of God "out there" as King and Ruler of the universe (which he is) but also to a more intimate and more wonderful perception of him as directly and personally present in our own being. Yet this is not a pantheistic merger or confusion of our being with his. On the contrary, there is a distinct conflict in the realization that though in some sense he is more truly ourselves than we are, yet we are not identical with him, and though he loves us better than we can love ourselves we are opposed to him, and in opposing him we oppose our own deepest selves. If we are involved only in our surface existence, in externals, and in the trivial concerns of our ego, we are untrue to him and to ourselves. To reach a true awareness of him as well as ourselves, we have to renounce our selfish and limited self and enter into a whole new kind of existence, discovering an inner center of motivation and love which makes us see ourselves and everything else in an entirely new light. Call it faith, call it (at a more advanced stage) contemplative illumination, call it the sense of God or even mystical union: all these are different aspects and levels of the same kind of realization: the awakening to a new awareness of ourselves in Christ, created in him, redeemed by him, to be transformed and glorified in and with him. In Blake's words, the "doors of perception" are opened and all life takes on a completely new meaning: the real sense of our own existence, which is normally veiled and distorted by the routine distractions of an alienated life, is now revealed in a central intuition. What was lost and dispersed in the relative meaninglessness and triviality of purposeless behavior (living like a machine, pushed around by impulsions and suggestions from others) is brought together in fully integrated conscious significance. This peculiar, brilliant focus is, according to Christian tradition, the work of Love and of the Holy Spirit. This "loving knowledge" which sees everything transfigured "in God," coming from God and working for God's creative and redemptive love and tending to fulfillment in the glory of God, is a contemplative knowledge, a fruit of living and realizing faith, a gift of the Spirit.

The popularity of psychedelic drugs today certainly shows, if nothing else, that there is an appetite for this kind of knowledge and inner integration. The only trouble with drugs is that they superficially and transiently mimic the integration of love without producing it. (I will not discuss here the question whether they may accidentally help such integration, because I am not competent to do so.)

Though this inner "vision" is a gift and is not directly produced by technique, still a certain discipline is necessary to prepare us for it. Meditation is one of the more important characteristic forms of this discipline. Prayer is another. Prayer in the context of this inner awareness of God's direct presence becomes not so much a matter of cause and effect as a celebration of love. In the light of this celebration, what matters most is love itself, thankfulness, assent to the unbounded and overflowing goodness of love which comes from God and reveals him in his world.

This inner awareness, this experience of love as an immediate and dynamic presence, tends to alter our perspective. We see the prayer of petition a little differently. Celebration and praise, loving attention to the presence of God, become more important than "asking for" things and "getting" things. This is because we realize that in him and with him all good is present to us and to mankind: if we seek first the Kingdom of Heaven, all the rest comes along with it. Hence we worry a great deal less about the details of our daily needs, and we trust God to take care of our problems even if we do not ask him insistently at every minute to do so. The same applies to the problems of the world. But on the other hand, this inner awareness and openness makes us especially sensitive to urgent needs of the time, and grace can sometimes move us to pray for certain special needs. The contemplative life does not ignore the prayer of petition, but does not overemphasize it either. The contemplative prays for particular intentions when he is strongly and spontaneously inspired to do so but does not make it his formal purpose to keep asking for this and that all day long.

Now, prayer also has to be seen in the light of another fundamental experience, that of God's "absence." For if God is immanently present he is also transcendent, which means that he is completely beyond the grasp of our understanding. The two ("absence" and "presence") merge in the loving knowledge that "knows by unknowing" (a traditional term of mysticism). It is more and more usual for modern people to be afflicted with a sense of absence, desolation, and incapacity to even "want" to pray or to think of God. To dismiss this superficially as an experience of "the death of God"—as if henceforth God were completely irrelevant—is to overlook one significant fact: that this sense of absence is not a one-sided thing; it is dialectical, and it includes its opposite, namely presence. And while it may be afflicted with doubt, it contains a deep need to believe.

The point I want to make is this: experience of the contemplative life in the modern world shows that the most crucial focus for contemplative and meditative discipline, and for the life of prayer for many modern men, is precisely this so-called sense of absence, desolation, and even apparent "inability to believe." I stress the word "apparent" because, though this experience may be to some extremely painful and confusing and raise all kinds of crucial "religious problems," it can very well be a sign of authentic Christian growth and a point of decisive development in faith, if they are able to cope with it. The way to cope with it is not to regress to an earlier and less mature stage of belief, to stubbornly reaffirm and to "enforce" feelings, aspirations and images that were appropriate to one's childhood and first communion. One must, on a new level of meditation and prayer, live through this crisis of belief and grow to a more complete personal and Christian integration by experience.

This experience of struggle, of self-emptying, "self-naughting," of letting go and of subsequent recovery in peace and grace on a new level is one of the ways in which the *Pascha Christi* (the death and resurrection of Christ) takes hold on our lives and transforms them. This is the psychological aspect of the work of grace which also takes place beyond experience and beyond psychology in the work of the sacraments and in our objective sharing of the Church's life.

I am of course not talking about "mystical experience," or anything new and strange, but simply the fullness of personal awareness that comes with a total self-renunciation, followed by self-commitment on the highest level, beyond mere intellectual assent and external obedience.

Real Christian living is stunted and frustrated if it remains content with the bare externals of worship, with "saying prayers" and "going to church," with fulfilling one's external duties and merely being respectable. The real purpose of prayer (in the fully personal sense as well as in the Christian assembly) is the deepening of personal realization in love, the awareness of God (even if sometimes this awareness may amount to a negative factor, a seeming "absence"). The real purpose of meditation—or at least that which recommends itself as most relevant for modern man—is the exploration and discovery of new dimensions in freedom, illumination and love, in deepening our awareness of our life in Christ.

What is the relation of this to action? Simply this. He who attempts to act and do things for others or for the world without deepening his own self-understanding, freedom, integrity and capacity to love will not have anything to give others. He will communicate to them nothing but the contagion of his own obsessions, his aggressiveness, his ego-centered ambitions, his delusions about ends and means, his doctrinaire prejudices and ideas. There is nothing more tragic in the modern world than the misuse of power and action to which men are driven by their own Faustian misunderstandings and misapprehensions. We have more power at our disposal today than we have ever had, and yet we are more alienated and estranged from the inner ground of meaning and of love than we have ever been. The result of this is evident. We are living through the greatest crisis in the history of man; and this crisis is centered precisely in the country that has made a fetish out of action and has lost (or perhaps never had) the sense of contemplation. Far from being irrelevant, prayer, meditation and contemplation are of the utmost importance in America today. Unfortunately, it must be admitted that the official contemplative life as it is lived in our monasteries needs a great deal of rethinking because it is still too closely identified with patterns of thought that were accepted five hundred years ago but which are completely strange to modern man.

But prayer and meditation have an important part to play in opening up new ways and new horizons. If our prayer is the expression of a deep and grace-inspired desire for newness of life—and not the mere blind attachment to what has always been familiar and "safe"— God will act in us and through us to renew the Church by preparing, in prayer, what we cannot yet imagine or understand. In this way our prayer and faith today will be oriented toward the future which we ourselves may never see fully realized on earth.

X
The Contemplative and the Atheist

In all the great religious traditions men and women have dedicated themselves to contemplative lives in which, under special conditions of silence, austerity, solitude, meditation and worship, it has been possible for them to deepen and broaden their spiritual consciousness. In so doing, they have become able to explore realms of experience which, though unusual, have profound implications for the ordinary lives of their fellow men. Whether from the point of view of psychology, ethics, art, religion, or simply in the development of man's deepest capacities, the contemplative experience is in touch with what is most basic in human existence.

In religious cultures these contemplatives have tended to form recognized elites in special monastic institutions. But it is not necessary that this drive for spiritual discovery be socially organized: it can spring into existence spontaneously outside the cloister or hermitage, even under the most unfavorable conditions. For the contemplative life is not merely a matter of escaping the world, singing psalms, or mastering traditional techniques of meditation: it is also and above all a personal charism.

Thus there are contemplatives not only in monasteries but also in the midst of secular life. But in all contemplative traditions, it has been found necessary that those who have attained to some depth of religious insight should to some extent guide others who seek to attain the same experience of truth in their own lives. Thus, though the contemplative lives in silence and seeks to maintain a certain freedom from involvement in feverish and pointless activity, he does not simply turn his back on the world of other men. Like them he remains rooted in this world. He remains open to the world and is ready, when necessary, to share with others something of his own experience, to the extent that this may be desirable or possible. He also realizes his need to listen to other men and learn from them. But above all he seeks to go deeper into that divine source from which all life springs and to understand the destinies of man in the light of God.

At a time when the Catholic Church herself has entered into a spontaneous and living dialogue with modern man on all levels of his existence, should Catholic contemplatives also speak to modern man and listen to him, question him and be questioned by him?

The "Message of Contemplatives" presented to the Synod of Bishops in 1967 reflected a deep concern on the part of men who, though dedicated to lives of silence and solitude, felt they also had a duty to share the fruit of their experience with their fellow men struggling in the modern "crisis of faith." The life of solitude and contemplation, a life in which men listen more intently to the Word of God, immerse themselves in meditation of the Bible, sing the praise of God in liturgy, and devote themselves to work, study and silent prayer, is not a life remote from contemporary reality. Nor is the contemplative exempt from the problems and difficulties of contemporary man. The life of Christian contemplation is not a life of willful concentration upon a few clear and comforting ideas but a life of inner struggle in which the monk, like Christ himself in the desert, is tested. In a certain sense the monk, alone with God, fully aware of his own poverty, fallibility and blindness, suffers the same trial of faith as other Christians and suffers it in a more acute and penetrating way. It can be said that the contemplative is often less a "professional of vision" than a professional of crisis and of intellectual suffering. What he learns is not a clearer idea of God but a deeper trust, a purer love and a more complete abandonment to One he knows to be beyond all understanding. Yet in his silence, his simple life, his cloistered peace, the contemplative certainly has access to values which modern life tends more and more to forget, to underestimate or to ignore. He wishes to share his experience of these values with other men who are weary of the pressure, the confusion, the agitation of modern life. He recognizes his duty to his fellow man: a duty to preserve for him an area which is most threatened in the stormy existence of a world in a crisis of growth and transformation. The following thoughts can be considered in some sense an extension of the "Message of Contemplatives" delivered to the Synod of Bishops.

We contemplatives are fully aware not only of the general problems confronted by the Christian believer, but also more especially of the particular problem of the contemplative life itself. Many Christians, including priests and even perhaps some bishops, perturbed by the great needs of the Church in the world today, wonder how the contemplatives can continue to remain apparently aloof from the active conflicts in which the Church is engaged. Should not contemplatives abandon their silence and solitude in order to be enlisted in the busy army of apostolic workers?

We contemplatives feel that this question is, for us as well as for the rest of the Church, only another aspect of the general crisis of faith. We know this because we have often searched our own hearts and sought to resolve this question for ourselves, fearing that perhaps our call to desert solitude might be an illusion and dreading that we might be making our silence a pretext for refusing to others a necessary service. Indeed we do realize that we cannot be content with a purely negative rejection of the world. We cannot simply turn our backs on contemporary man. That is not our intention. We must on the contrary share with others something of the benefits of our own life of prayer.

Nevertheless, it is clear to us that our greatest and most unique service to the Church is precisely our life of contemplation itself. Our silence and solitude are not mere luxuries and privileges which we have acquired at the Church's expense: they are necessary gifts of God to the Church in and through us. They are that part of the precious inheritance of Christian truth and experience which God has confided to us to hold in trust, in order that the spirit of prayer and contemplation may continue to exist in the whole Church and in the world of our time.

The laity and clergy who are absorbed in many active concerns are unable to give themselves to meditation and to a deeper study of divine and human things. We feel it is our first duty to preserve for them the reality of a life of deep prayer, silence, and experience of the things of God so that they may not themselves despair but may be encouraged to continue in their own way to seek intimacy with God in loving faith. We also feel it our obligation, at least where circumstances permit, to allow them to share in the peace and silence of our retreats. Some of us may be called to direct or instruct others in the way of prayer, whether by the written word or by oral direction. Some of us, finally, may be called to enter into fruitful dialogue with intellectuals, Christian or otherwise, and perhaps particularly with contemplatives and philosophers of the non-Christian religious traditions. Ideally speaking, the contemplative monastery should present a perfect setting for dialogue and study concerning prayer and spiritual experience.

However, we may be permitted to suggest that it would be to the greatest possible disadvantage for the Church if contemplatives were to be uprooted from their silent and prayerful way of life and precipitated into active works for which they are neither qualified nor prepared and which they can only do badly. At the same time we realize more and more that the contemplative life itself urgently needs inner renewal in order that this experience of mystical love, which has unfortunately grown cold, this contemplative apprehension of divine things, which has become weak and vague, may recover their vital power.

In order to do this, it is necessary for us to maintain the purity of monastic common life in which the freedom of fraternal love in Christ, the discipline of monastic formation, and total obedience of one and all to the Holy Spirit keep alive an atmosphere of prayer in which the authentic purity of Christian contemplation can be handed on from spiritual father to spiritual sons. We recognize especially the importance of silence, solitude, poverty, labor, humility, chastity, fasting and all the traditional forms of monastic ascesis, to keep ourselves open and attentive to the Spirit of the Living God. We also recognize that, as contemplatives grow in their experience of intimacy with God, they will need special opportunities to develop their own personal gifts in their own ways, some of them perhaps living for this purpose in eremitical solitude. In a word, we not only bear witness to the living actuality of the monastic experience that has been handed down to us from the earliest days of Egyptian and Syrian monasticism, but we solemnly pledge ourselves to preserve that heritage and to develop it in ways that are relevant to our own time.

The contemplative life is questioned not only in the active and dynamic West but in the meditative East. In a certain sense the duty to bear witness to contemplative values and to a higher experience is a matter of universal concern, common not only to the Cistercian monk but to the Zen Buddhist and the student of Yoga. We find that many who do not share our religious belief, men of the great Asian religions or even modern Westerners without faith, tend to have a better appreciation of our life than some Catholics. These men often deeply value the advantages of solitude, silence and meditation. The appeals of such men urge us to persevere in our aim of seeking new depths of awareness and meaning in human existence. They also encourage us to study the ways in which the religious experience of the great mystical traditions, both Christian and non-Christian, can continue in dialogue with a world that has ceased to understand the classic language of religious experience. They encourage us to approach closer to the mystery of God in that desert solitude which is the place par excellence of revelation, inspiration and renewal.

In this connection we observe that a Marxist thinker prominent in the Marxist-Christian dialogue has, while clearly stating that to him the language of Christian theology seemed irrelevant, admitted that he found the mystical experience and witness of a St. Teresa of Avila both meaningful and challenging. On the basis of such statements as these, we do not feel that we contemplatives are losing our time if we devote our lives to exploring areas which other more active Catholics consider a mere no man's land.

Like the rest of the Catholic Church, the contemplative orders seek a renewal of their life in accordance with the needs of modern man. The maturity and personal fulfillment sought by one called to the contemplative life are to be found in contemplation itself and not elsewhere. But the discipline of contemplative attention and awareness has to be adapted to the needs of modern consciousness. Contemplative formation today will include a study of the structures of modern consciousness and its new ways of experiencing itself in relation to other men, to the world, and to God.

It should be remarked that in the contemplative life, while study and intellectual development are of great importance, there is something else more important still: the realm of personal experience which penetrates beyond the limits of speculative thought to "taste" the ultimate realities and to penetrate the inner meaning of what is believed and yet remains obscure. For the contemplative, then, what matters is not speculative discussion of the "problem of God," still less the effort to demonstrate the existence of God in ways that often raise more problems than they solve for modern man. The contemplative is not one who has to do battle with militant atheism, and he is thus perhaps in a position to gain a clearer understanding of the confusions now surrounding the whole question of "atheism" and the "problem of God" in the world of our time.

The Christian contemplative is aware that in the mystical tradition both of the Eastern and Western Churches there is a strong element of what has been called "apophatic theology." This "apophatic" tradition concerns itself with the most fundamental datum of all faith—and one which is too often forgotten: the God who has revealed himself to us in his Word has revealed himself as unknown in his intimate essence, for he is beyond all merely human vision. "You cannot see my face: no man shall see me and live" (Exodus 33:20). "No man has ever seen God: the only-begotten, who is in the heart of the Father, he has related it" (John 1:18).

The heart of the Christian mystical experience is that it experiences the ineffable reality of what is beyond experience. It "knows" the presence of God, not in clear vision but "as unknown" (*tamquam ignotium*). Christian faith, too, while of course concerning itself with certain truths that have been revealed by God, does not terminate in the conceptual formulation of those truths. It goes beyond words and ideas and attains to God himself. But the God who in a certain sense is "known" in the articles of faith is "known as unknown" beyond those articles. One might even say, with some of the Fathers of the Church, that while our concepts may tell us that "God is," our knowledge of God beyond those concepts is a knowledge of him "as though he were not" since his Being is not accessible to us in direct experience. We are persuaded that many who consider themselves atheists are in fact persons who are discontented with a naive idea of God which makes him appear to be an "object" or a "thing," or a person in a merely finite and human sense. Such people are perhaps weary of the complications of language which now surround the "problem of God" and find all discussions of that problem fruitless: yet they are likely to be very intrigued by the direct and existential testimony of contemplative experience.

Now, while the Christian contemplative must certainly develop, by study, the theological understanding of concepts about God, he is called mainly to penetrate the wordless darkness and apophatic light of an experience beyond concepts, and here he gradually becomes familiar with a God who is "absent," and as it were "nonexistent," to all human experience. The apophatic experience of God does, to some extent, verify the atheist's intuition that God is not an object of limited and precise knowledge and consequently cannot be apprehended as "a thing" to be studied by delimitation. As St. John of the Cross dared to say in mystical language, the term of the ascent of the mount of contemplation is "Nothing"—*Y en el monte Nada.* But the difference between the apophatic contemplative and the atheist is that, where the experience of the atheist may be purely negative, that of the contemplative is so to speak negatively positive. Relinquishing every attempt to grasp God in limited human concepts, the contemplative's act of submission and faith attains to his presence as the ground of every human experience and to his reality as the ground of being itself. The "absence" of the transcendent God is also, paradoxically, his presence as immanent. Here obviously we enter a realm of apparent contradictions which eludes clear explanation, so that the contemplative prefers not to talk about it at all. Indeed, in the past, serious mistakes have been made and deadly confusions have arisen from inadequate attempts to explain this mystery. The job of the contemplative today is not to avoid this area out of fear—this is the authentic field of his exploration and the place of his own promised and desired fulfillment—he must enter into it humbly and resolutely, following the call of God and obedient to the divine Spirit, like Moses approaching the burning bush, removing the "shoes" of opinion and rationalization.

There is however a new atheism which has arisen even among Christians in their anxiety to share every dimension of modern man's experience. These "Christian atheists" have asked themselves, in all sincerity, if one could be a truly modern man and not be in some sense an atheist. In other words, is religious belief so essentially alien to the experience and consciousness of modern man that modern man cannot believe in God without a psychological and cultural regression to modes of thought appropriate to former ages but estranged from our own? Since this "Christian atheism" or "religion without God" has had the benefit of a typically sensationalist treatment in the mass media, and since those who have proposed it differ greatly among themselves and do not always mean the same thing, there has been great confusion in the minds of many people. Sometimes the doctrine of the so-called "death of God," popular in American Christian circles, is reduced to a mere sensational absurdity. But at other times an attempt is made to raise a serious question in this paradoxical form. The "problem of God," it is said, has new dimensions today because one can no longer take for one's point of departure the same assumptions as in the past. For instance, in the past it was more generally taken for granted that every man had a basic natural way of looking at reality, and this spontaneous, pre-conscious outlook included in it the need for a Supreme Being and at least some kind of tacit assumption of a First Cause. Men who denied the Supreme Being and the First Cause did so at the price of resisting this natural outlook. But now it is asserted that man's outlook has radically changed. It is no longer "natural" for him to assume, as St. Anselm once assumed, that if there are any beings at all there must be a Supreme Being. On the contrary, it is now said that modern man's consciousness is one which no longer needs God and no longer assumes his existence, influence and presence as the basis for a meaningful view of life. What could be said with truth in the past, that the human soul was "naturally Christian," is no longer to be taken for granted: on the contrary, the consciousness of modern man is, according to this theory, naturally atheistic. Therefore it is contended that, as far as the experience of modern man is concerned, "God is dead"—he is not present spontaneously as the basis for meaning in human existence. On the contrary, if "God" once becomes present in the consciousness of modern man, so the argument continues, his presence does violence to that modern consciousness in its modernity—hence in its truth. The act of faith by which modern man adheres, in spite of himself, to the idea of God is an act in which he is untrue to himself, is dictated by fear or some other base motive, and is therefore unauthentic. Faith, for the modern man, must then be by definition "bad faith" in the sense given to this term by J.-P. Sartre.

We have exposed this argument in some detail because it has rather ironical consequences in the lives of those who are most concerned with being "adult" Christians in the world of today. Obviously one of the first indications of the adult is that he is securely assured of his own identity, and his judgments concerning his own experiences are based on his own awareness of what takes place within himself. The truly modern adult person will surely not allow himself to be treated as an alienated and helpless individual whose inner experience is dictated to him by another and imposed upon him from the outside. It is the surest sign of immaturity to be imposed on entirely by the ideas and ideals of others and to substitute these for one's own true personal experience and judgment of life. The faith of the Christian is an inner adherence to a truth which is not imposed from the outside. It is a free personal adherence of love "in the Spirit," and it gives power to resist all external compulsion in the realm of thought as well as of life. In this sense, too, faith overcomes the world. This truth makes one truly and authentically free (John 8:32). The adult Christian is perfectly capable of discovering for himself whether or not a modern man can believe in God and experience him without being untrue to himself. There is a difference between being true to oneself and being à la mode. After all, St. Paul has cautioned us against confusing the wisdom and the experience of God with the slogans of current intellectual fashion (I Cor. 2:6–9).

In actual fact, the gift of supernatural faith does not in any way depend on whether or not man is naturally disposed to accept easily a congenial concept of God. It is after all quite common for us in dechristianized cultures to encounter persons who have never had a serious thought of God, one way or the other, and who have suddenly been struck, in the most unaccountable manner, by the light of faith. It is customary among pious people to imagine that this is always a beautiful and consoling experience. It is sometimes frightening. You fortunate believer! You do not know the confusion, the bewilderment and the suffering of an atheist who has suddenly, without any apparent human intervention, been literally overwhelmed by the reality of God and who does not know what to do. Surrounded by friends who can only mock him if he reveals his trouble, unable to pray, unable to trust himself to the Church of which he is highly suspicious, he is in a state of heartbreaking anguish. Perhaps it may be true that he is not a "naturally Christian soul." God does not present himself to him in a clear and comforting concept but as a completely disconcerting and inexplicable reality, making a demand for total commitment and trust. His anguish is all the greater, but his faith is no less real. And he turns, instinctively, to the contemplatives who, he believes, are men of prayer and know the ways of God. But when he comes to us, in profound distress, we become aware of our own insufficiency, and we carefully weigh any words we may say, knowing that they must not be sentimental or complacent or merely formal. The writer of these lines has recently had one of many such experiences; he knows that it is utterly false to claim that "modern man is incapable of feeling the need for God or responding to his presence."

We are inclined to ask here whether these facile assumptions about modern man and his psychology are not totally gratuitous. That would be a matter for psychology, sociology and historical scholarship to decide in terms of the evidence. But once again, those who are familiar with the apophatic tradition in theology and mysticism are fully aware that the temporary or permanent inability to imagine God or to "experience" him as present, or even to find him credible, is not something discovered by modern man or confined to our own age. This view of religion and of the religious consciousness is too narrow and foreshortened, for it once more assumes that the naive conception of God as "object" is somehow claimed as natural to man and essential to Christianity.

Without entering into a polemic with this new school of thought, we can at least recognize that it is doubtless time for the Christian consciousness of God to be expressed in contemporary language. The conceptual knowledge of God is inevitably associated with a certain cultural matrix. The medieval ideas of God were naturally in accord with medieval thought about the cosmos, about the earth, about physics, and about the biological and psychological structure of man. These ideas have been revolutionized. But the reality of experience beyond concepts (though it may call for a different approach in accord with the new psychological and cultural development of modern man) is not itself modified by changes of culture. The contemplative once again has a certain advantage due to the fact that he is less involved than others in changing conceptual structures and less dependent on the complexities of language.

Far from being a merely mental and conceptual approach to God, far from being the fruit of intellectual speculation which seeks to apprehend God as a most rarefied abstraction, the contemplative approach is highly concrete and existential. Where abstract thought and concrete existence enter into conflict, the mark of the true contemplative is that he is on the side of concrete existence. Our God is the living God who has manifested himself with supreme concreteness to man, not only in words and deeds by which he intervened in human history for our salvation, but above all in his Son whom the apostles "heard and saw and touched with their hands and recognized to be the Word of Life" (see I John 1:1). The Christian contemplative is not content to explore the depths of the human psyche and to expand the capacities of natural consciousness. The heart of Christian contemplation is the revelation of the invisible God. The

Christian contemplative seeks the fullest and most living participation in the experience which has come down from those who walked with Christ on earth, who knew him and saw him as risen and received from him the Gift of the Spirit.

The Christian contemplative life bears witness above all to the deepest and most central truth of all Christian revelation, that of the Holy Trinity. At first sight, nothing could be seemingly more remote from the modern consciousness and more alien to it than the mysterious notion of One God in Three Persons. The modern consciousness is impatient of mystery and impervious to technical theology. One would expect that the danger of abstractness and technicality would make modern contemplatives turn more spontaneously to God in his unity and simplicity rather than to this mystery of God as triune. But on the contrary, the special character of Christian contemplation cannot be grasped unless due importance is given to the revelation of the Father in the Son by the Holy Spirit. We have obviously no intention of entering into a technical discussion of the theology of the Trinity, but only of pointing out why this theology is important both in itself and in special relation to our own time.

Since, as we have said above, God is, in his intimate essence, beyond all our human concepts, the revelation of God as Father, Son and Spirit is in fact a revelation of him as totally other than any being which we can conceive of as existing. In God's revelation of himself we nowhere find him giving a definition of himself. He simply reveals that he *is* (Exodus 3:14). Or rather he reveals that he is who he is: that is to say, he reveals himself not as a thing but as a presence, an active living and personal identity. And this identity, this "Who," is at once Father, Son or Logos, and Spirit or Pneuma. This revelation of God as who he is (not as what) is therefore a revelation of him as living, personal presence, as utterance of himself, as communication of himself, as love, as mercy, as gift, as life. The self-revelation of God as the Father in the Son through the Spirit is the self-revelation of infinite giving and dynamic personal communication. We say with St. John that "God is love" (I John 4:16), and we recognize with the Apostle that the God who is love is known to no one except to him who loves. God is Father who gives himself in love as Son; he is Son who gives himself as love in Spirit; he is Spirit who communicates to us the immense love which we believe to be Father and Son, so that we ourselves, in the Spirit, become sons and give ourselves in love to the Father. This is the self-manifestation of God as the infinite personal ground of all love and all being, of God as loving Creator of all things, not only infinitely transcendent but also present within the metaphysical depths and goodness of being itself. God thus reveals himself not simply as the power to cause all effects but as the Act and Living Presence of Love from whom all beings receive the loving and gratuitous gift to be real.

It is very important to grasp the significance of the fact that God is not conceived by Christian theology as numerically three. The three divine persons are not three countable things or three beings or three natures or three objects lined up, so to speak, side by side: they are (and here the inadequacy of human speech makes itself felt, since we have to use the plural) the inner communication and dynamism of love in which God is present to himself in Being, Vision and Love or, perhaps we might say, in Reality, in Realization and in Ecstatic Delight.

Christian contemplation does not, of course, imply a clear vision or a rational understanding of the processions of the divine persons on a technical theological level. What we mean to emphasize here is something quite different: that Christian contemplation gives a certain intuitive appreciation or savor of the divine inner life insofar as it is a personal participation, by grace, in that life itself. Thus the Christian contemplative experiences in himself, in the love which is granted to him by the gift of the Spirit, something of the dynamism of love that the unknown God has revealed as his actuality, his presence, his identity, his personal and intimate self-communication. The loving knowledge of God is then not something to be acquired by objective study but by subjective (personal) identification (which traditional theology has called "connaturality"). St. Paul makes this clear when he compares a man's consciousness of his own identity to the Spirit "which looks into the depths of God" (I Cor. 2:10). Now we have received the Spirit of God, and hence the Spirit in us gazes into the abyss of the unknown and unseen Father. We recognize the unseen Father insofar as we are sons, in and with Christ. The Spirit utters in us the cry of recognition that we are sons in the Son (Romans 8:15). This cry of admiration, of love, of praise, of everlasting joy is at once a cry of glad self-annihilation on the part of our transient human ego and an exultant shout of victory of the New Man raised from the dead in Christ by the Spirit who raised Christ himself from the dead. Christian contemplation, in one vivid blaze of love and illumination, apprehends at once the reality of God as the totally other and the unknown, as a dynamism of reality, realization and ecstasy, as incarnate in Jesus Christ, as given to us entirely in the Spirit, as taking us entirely to himself in the death and resurrection of Christ. But Christian contemplation is not merely lost in God. It also includes in its vision an eschatological understanding of the world redeemed in Christ. It sees the world transformed in the divine light, it sees all things recapitulated in Christ (Eph. 1:10). It is aware of the victory of Christ and the reality of his Kingdom in the world even now, in all the confusion, the chaos and the risk of this historical and revolutionary time of crisis which we call the atomic age.

It is by deepening this Christian consciousness and developing the capacity for mystical understanding and love that the Christian contemplative keeps alive in the Church that pure and immediate experience without which theology will always lack one of its most important dimensions. The Second Vatican Council has reminded us of this:

> For there is a growth in the understanding of the realities of the words which have been handed down. This happens through the contemplation and study made by believers, who treasure these things in their hearts (Luke 2:19, 51), through the intimate understanding of spiritual things they experience, and through the preaching of those who have received through episcopal succession the sure gift of truth. (*On Divine Revelation*, ii, 8)

Here the Council makes very clear the importance of contemplatives in the Church. Their special task is not merely to pray for those in the active apostolate, but much more to keep alive and to deepen the "intimate understanding" of and "experience" through which divine revelation is handed down not merely in Christian preaching but as a living and experienced reality.

XI

Ecumenism and Renewal

The highly successful Protestant monastic experiment of Taizé has in a short time come to be seen by many Catholics as a providential sign of the times and even as a paradigm for Catholic monastic renewal. Not that Taizé is the only manifestation of its kind, or that it is unique in Protestantism: it does combine a traditional form of Christian monastic life with a welcome flexibility and with a strong ecumenical emphasis. The combination of these elements is even more significant than the fact that a "Protestant monastery" should exist.

The crisis and collapse of Luther's life under religious vows (Luther was not strictly a "monk" since he was an Augustinian) marked a decisive point in the Reformation. Luther's "monastic" experience was in fact quite central to his whole view of the Church and Christian life, and his repudiation of religious vows was a critical point in his theology of *fides sola*. He challenged the whole medieval ethos, dominated by the monastic order as reformed and incorporated into the cultural and political life of Europe since Charlemagne.

The defensive reaction of the Catholic Church was to reject the challenge and to reaffirm without question the essentials of the medieval monastic structure. The Council of Trent did not consider for a moment any radical change in the traditional monastic institution. Monasticism after Trent sought only to restore discipline and to eliminate abuses by a return, not so much to original sources, as to the Carolingian reform of Benedict of Aniane. It is significant that Taizé is located near the site of Cluny, the capital of medieval Benedictinism and the center of the fervent cultural, liturgical, ascetic and artistic life which set the tone for the early Middle Ages. Though Cluny was attacked and severely criticized for its wealth and power by Cistercian reformers in the twelfth century, we must not take too literally or too seriously their sometimes sweeping condemnation of Cluniac monasticism which, like that of the Cistercians, maintained an authentic life of disciplined fervor and mysticism until well beyond the thirteenth century.

Two main cycles of monastic reform have taken place since Trent, roughly in the seventeenth and in the nineteenth centuries. They did not make any fundamental changes in the traditional monasticism of western Europe though they did begin the work of "return to sources" (both theological and ascetic) which prepared the way for the new movement in monasticism after Vatican II. It must be said that the Second Vatican Council did not start this movement, which was already in existence and which had already initiated important changes in the decade before the Council. But only after the Council has the problem of monastic renewal taken on its full dimensions.

The press has given a certain amount of attention to the superficial aspects of renewal in Catholic religious life. The symbolic question of nuns' habits acquired, perhaps naturally, an exaggerated importance. Nor is it difficult to get a column or two of acceptable copy out of the fact that the sisters have been running around more and doing things that are characteristically "modern." This tends to obscure the real nature of the problem which is more than a mere matter of "updating" and getting around.

The problem of monastic renewal, at the deepest level, is theological, and it is at this point that the monks are finally coming face to face with Luther's challenge. In "returning to sources" they are only doing in a more thorough and systematic way what Luther himself did by reexamining his vocation in the light of the Gospels and the Pauline Epistles. Studying the original monastic sources, seen in their historic and cultural contexts, monks begin to ask themselves more disturbing questions than those which merely bear on meaningful observance.

It is now no longer just a matter of recovering a genuine under-standing of monastic enclosure, silence, worship, fasting and trying to adapt these to a modern situation. The very concept of a vowed and cloistered life, of a life devoted to prayer apart from the world, of silence and asceticism, has to be reexamined. This need is realized as yet only obscurely by the majority of monks, but its nagging, dis-quieting presence is felt. And some of those who are now con-sciously aware of it are thrown into a mild panic, with the result that they are more ready to abandon the ship than they are to examine carefully whether it is about to sink.

Catholics anxious for renewal have perhaps been too grateful for press coverage—any press coverage—which gives an impression that much is happening. And certainly much is happening. But both the happening and the coverage tend to be quite equivocal. The fundamental purpose of all monastic life is (to paraphrase a brilliant page of Claude Lévi-Strauss* about Indian initiations) to deliver the individual and the charismatic community from the massive auto-matic functioning of a social machine that leaves nothing to peculiar talent, to chance, or to grace. The monastic vocation calls a man to desert frontiers, beyond which there are no police, in order to dip into the "ocean of unexploited forces which surrounds a well-ordered society and draw from it a personal provision" of grace and vision. But the historical fate of monasticism is of course that it has become more organized and better policed than secular society it-self, and while continuing to offer promises of charismatic vision and liberty, it has in fact subjected its disciples to all the most banal monotonies of an unimaginative ecclesiastical bureaucracy, all the timidities of monastic businessmen intent upon the security and prestige of their institution, all the refusals of operators interested mainly in the corporate image. But it happens that now the business and institutional aspect of the monastic corporation stands to profit a great deal from a solid merger with the forces of mass society. Not all the managers are fully aware of all the implications of this, but generally speaking, the idea that the monk can recover his charis-

*See Claude Lévi-Strauss, *Tristes Tropiques,* Paris, 1966.

matic liberty by joining forces with "the world" (call it Madison Avenue or Secular City) is perhaps the greatest of illusions.

It is one thing to admit that Luther had come to grips with a real problem and another to conclude that one cannot find any other solution than his. If a ritualistic attachment to archaic observance is, indeed, theologically futile, it does not follow that monastic life cannot be lived on a deeper and more valid level. In other words, the monastic community has other choices than perpetuating an antique formula or going out of existence. Nor is everything "old" necessarily antiquated and obsolete. One of the most hopeful things about Taizé has been, in fact, its ability to welcome and to make use of traditional forms when they are found to have a real validity in the present. But the fact remains that Luther's challenge now has a definite relevance for Catholic monks who are anxious to renew their monastic lives and to test the seriousness and authenticity of that renewal.

Before Vatican II it was still possible for monks to ignore the Reformation with its serious charge that the vowed life of the monk, lived under traditional disciplines and devoted to a complex system of pious works, was in fact an evasion of the basic call to discipleship. Instead of responding to the summons of Christ in faith, placing his entire trust in the word and promises of the Risen Savior, seeking salvation, grace and light in the community of those called to confide entirely in the all-merciful Redeemer, the monk took refuge in vows and rites which (in the context of the late Middle Ages) could seriously be seen as a system of more or less superstitious fictions. In Reformation thought, monastic obedience became an abdication of mature responsibility and an escape from freedom which could, in extreme cases, turn the monk into a blind instrument of the most nefarious kind of power politics. Poverty became a mere hypocritical formality which enabled one to enjoy the goods and comforts of the world without even having to do an honest job of work to get them. Chastity was a fruitless evasion of the duty of marriage, corrupted perhaps by the most shameful kind of failures.

Of course there had always been abuses. The monk had to admit it. But on the other hand, he knew that the Reformation polemic had distorted the true picture. He knew that his own faith and that of his community was sincere. And like all good Catholics he was intent on proving the sincerity of his faith by what he considered to be good works. The best works he could think of were those which had from time immemorial been held in highest respect by his community: the complete renunciation of one's own will in order to live in selfless service of God and man, the giving up of all possessions in order to live "poor with the poor Christ," and the renunciation of all sexual pleasure in order to answer the challenging invitation extended to the few who could "take it" (Matt. 19:11–12).

The tension thus set up between the zeal for monastic reform within traditional structures and the often tendentious attack on monasticism from outside provided plenty of energy and motivation in individuals and communities. The result was a rather inflexible but sincerely devout life. Stern emphasis on "regularity," not to say legalism, was justified by a casuistical and sometimes arbitrary theology. Monastic determination after Trent bore fruit now in a fantastically single-minded intentness on "heroic virtue," now in touching, though bizarre, manifestations of mystical stamp.

Not only among monks, but in all kinds of sectarian milieux, this state of struggle and of tension sustains an illusion of special election and of incorruptible truth. The endemic disease of monasteries and of sects is that people in them do so much to save their souls that they lose them: not in the sense that they are damned for being good, but in the sense that they concentrate on such particular, limited aspects of good that they become perverse and singular. This singularity begets blindness and deafness to Christ. The tense concentration of sect or monastery on some completely peripheral concern can give an impression of heroic faith—but so can the feat of engraving the Lord's Prayer on a pinhead. Fidelity to tedious but predictable rule can become an easy substitute for fidelity, in openness and risk, to the unpredictable word. But the whole point of monastic "desert" life is precisely to equip the monk for risk, for walking with God in the wilderness and wrestling with Satan in vulnerable freedom. The monk should by rights be one who knows that faith is his only true protection against the power of great evil. But the monastic institution has surrounded him with so many other protections that the seed which is called to grow, in pure trust in the desert, is in fact nurtured in a greenhouse. The rationalization is that the greenhouse is really a desert in intention and that God, through kindly representatives, provides a steady supply of water. Instead of wilderness faith and the peril of death by dryness or exhaustion, one accepts faith in another kind of desert: that of protective authoritarian routine.

When one experiences the sterility and unfreedom of an existence which has become self-contradicting, then one can of course completely repudiate it, get out of it, put it behind him. That is what Luther did. His repudiation of a false and formalistic monasticism struck a blow for monastic truth. In doing so he was really being faithful to the grace that had originally called him to the cloister. And it is possible, too, that one might undergo the same kind of experience as Luther and yet remain in the cloister—or rather in the community to which one was originally called—not in order to reform its rules but in order to be renewed in experiencing its common recovery of meaning and hope, its common renewal in the Spirit. However, this renewal has to be something more than a matter of legislation or of reforming expedients. It has to be a kind of miracle of water in the desert.

It is at this precise point that two important lines of development are, one hopes, going to intersect in monasticism: one, the lived theology which is the monastic experience, and, two, the expansion and opening of perspectives which lead to a lived unity, the common sharing of Christian grace in crisis, irrespective of Church divisions. I would also extend this to meet a third line: the common religious aspiration of humankind and its groping for transcendent experience, however you may want to qualify it ("mystical," "prophetic," "contemplative," "metaphysical," "shamanic" . . .).

The crucial need in monastic renewal is then something quite different from a simple recovery of pristine disciplines or a deeper penetration of their meaning. The ecumenical opening of the monastery is going to have to mean more than just admitting Baptist or Methodist seminarians to view a living diorama in Church history. Nor will it be enough for monks who still meditate (a few do) to get together and compare notes (or swap *mondo*) with a Zen *roshi*. In a word, if the monastic life is to be validly renewed, it must retain or recover a threefold relevance. First, the monastic life must have an authentic relevance in its own right as a focus of Christian experience with a monastic orientation. The monastic orientation is eschatological: "out of this world to the Father." The monastic community— like Faulkner's Dilsey at the Negro church—is convoked not merely to listen to polite religious discourse but to hear the living word and to open up to it as a flower opens to the sun. The result will be, in one way or another, "vision" or "contemplation" (admittedly a bad word), prophetic and eschatological awareness: the awareness of Dilsey who wept at Rev. Shegog's Easter sermon because it made her "see the beginning and the end." Second, the monastic life must preserve or acquire an ecumenical relevance, in the form of an openness which is not only ready and able to discuss creedal or sectarian differences with polite detachment, but which is able to share on the deepest level the risks and agonies of Christian crisis. And this, certainly, will mean something more than sharing gripes about the stupidities of one's ecclesiastical establishment. Third, the monastic life must prove itself able to be relevant even to the unbeliever who is nevertheless concerned with a self-transcending experience, the unpredictable and unexplained illumination that flashes out of the ground of one's own being.

The monk should not be concerned merely with what is transient and accidental—certainly not with what is merely fashionable— in contemporary Christianity. His renunciation, his simple life in dedicated community, is supposed to clear his view of secondary obstructions and enable him to gaze steadily at the whole truth of Christ. He sees and experiences the Kingdom of Promise as already fulfilled. The monastic life is at once a recovery of paradisal simplicity, of wilderness obedience and trust, and an anticipated completion in blessed light. Monastic "contemplation" is not merely reposeful consideration of eternal verities but a grasp of the whole content of revelation, albeit obscurely, in the deep experience of a fully lived faith. As Luther said: *Ideo habens verba per fidem habet omnia.* This is the exact root of monastic experience, and the "works" of the monk, far from meaning to justify him, should help him to celebrate and articulate the witness of faith.

There are some monks who are so diffident about their charism that they try to make their lives relevant to the rest of the world by systematically emptying them of everything monastic: that is to say, by repudiating all that is eschatological, contemplative, other-worldly, everything that has to do with the desert, with asceticism, with hope and with prayer. There is certainly every reason for an incarnational and worldly Christian witness, especially in the Christian apostolate. But just as in the past there has been a one-sided emphasis on the eschatological, so today we tend to see only the incarnational side and to forget the necessary dialectic between eschatology and incarnation. The reality with which the monk lives is not a deduction of God from the mystery of creation, still less a pure divine immanence at work in the technological world of man: the monastic life is centered on Christ as alpha and omega, as the final revelation of God the Father, in whom one day the meaning of all the rest will be made finally plain—not by man's zeal or ingenuity but by the pure grace of the Spirit. In any case, the monk not only retains the eschatological privilege and duty of smashing idols—worldly, ecclesiastical, secular and even monastic—but he also has the incarnational privilege and duty of having his feet on God's ground and his hands in the fruitful dirt.

The monk should not be too quick to repudiate his admittedly un-profitable task as a farmer (or perhaps forester, conservationist, fire guard in a national park, game warden . . .). There is both incarnation and eschatology in the monastic praying community which is daily aware of the presence of the *kyrios* in the word and the breaking of the bread and celebrates that awareness for those who are less attuned to it. Is it too romantic still to suppose the monk can bake the bread he will eat at table and consecrate on the altar—and bake it well? His work is part of his witness, both to the goodness of God's world and to its transience.

It might be mentioned in passing that the purest kind of monastic witness in this area of work has been given, in America, not by Catholic monks but by the Shaker communities, where an extraordinary integrity of eschatological faith bore fruit in work of consummate perfection. The craftsmanship of the Shakers is the most authentic, tangible and impressive fruit of the monastic and mystical spirit in America. It is also completely *American*, and remains as a model of what the native American spirit can achieve in the monastic sphere. The Shaker spirit is entirely monastic in its celibacy, its poverty, its humility, simplicity, faith, pacifism, gentleness and in its combination of otherworldliness with a profound respect for materials and for their proper use in everyday human existence.

Whether in the city or in the mountains, the monk works for his living and his work is "worldly," not churchly: he is (at least ideally) more directly in contact with matter than other religious and clerics. His should be the least abstract of vocations. The instinct that pushes modern monastic experiments toward salaried employment in industry is sure and authentic, though it raises special problems of its own.

The wholeness that is, or should be, the hallmark of monastic experience is able to resolve the apparent contradiction of sacred and secular not in theorizing but in the proper use of work as a means of livelihood and as a way of prayer.

Monastic work remains, however, eschatological. It resolves the apparent contradiction, sacred-secular, in terms of "the beginning and the end," of creation fulfilled in eschatology, rather than in striving for unambiguous joy over the world as such. The monk does not have to prove that technology is good—or bad—it is enough for him that God is good. Everything else has its use in the light of God's good purpose, and the important thing is to recognize and apply Augustine's distinction between "use and fruition" (*uti et frui*) or his other distinction between "science" and "wisdom" (*scientia et sapientia*). A more modern approach to the same thing has been made by Heinrich Ott,* contrasting the *emeth* of the Bible

*Heinrich Ott, "Hermeneutique et eschatologie," in *Ermeneutica e Tradizione,* ed. by Enrico Castelli, Rome, 1963, p. 28.

with the *aletheia* of the Greeks and Heidegger's *Unverborgenheit*. The definitive truth is that which is unshakably secure, assured by the fidelity of God, but hidden in faith. Provisional truth is that which is "clear" and nonhidden, *unverborgen,* but attained only in the changing historical context of developing science. Wisdom embraces and includes science by attaining to the ultimate, hidden and definitive truth which is believed rather than known and which is the ground of provisional and changing certitudes. Behind all that is unveiled and "discovered," wisdom touches that which is still veiled and covered. As Heidegger (quoted by Ott) says: *In aller Entbergung wartet die Verbergung.*

It is important that the monk retain his fundamental sense of identity and vocation by affirming in his life and work this orientation to the definitive (eschatological) truth, which is God himself. It is in this fidelity to the truth of his own vocation that he renders service to the activist and the scientist who need his witness to the hidden definitive ground of their own visible and provisional certitudes. "Faith, insofar as it is faith," says Heinrich Ott,* "maintains its direction to the last truth, the definitive and irrevocable truth." But the great temptation is to substitute the provisional, the penultimate (Bonhoeffer) for the ultimate, to claim that one has reached the end when one has not begun, to announce that one is going to the North Pole and then take a walk around the block (Kierkegaard).

This brings us to the crucial question. Is it possible that the whole nature of the vows needs to be theologically reexamined? Does the very idea of a vow imply the foreclosure of vital future possibilities, the selection of some provisional certitude that seems ultimate at the moment for the final and definitive truth? Does the vow, instead of surrendering our liberty to the unpredictable liberty of God, on the contrary seek to bind God's hands and confine him to the plans we have determined for our own lives—or, worse still, to the myopic plans that others, who are not guaranteed to be either prophetic or wise, may impose in his name? Does the very nature of a vow put

* *Loc. cit.,* p. 109.

one in a position where he may be forced to choose for his vow in opposition to God himself? Or is it possible that the true concept of a vow is precisely that of a freedom committed to risk and to the unpredictable, to the refusal of all bonds to the provisional, to an open-ended newness of life that peels off the "old man" like a snake-skin which was new last year but is no longer alive and sensitive? Can it be that Luther was mistaken in thinking that the monastic vows and a legalistic existence were necessarily one and the same? Can there be a monastic life without vows? Is a monastic life with vows necessarily better and more authentic than one without vows? Is the rigid juridical structure of the dedicated life an obstacle to real renewal? Does the monastic life have to be organized as it is, in such a way that by his vows the monk is incorporated into a complex institutional machine in which his life is subject to very narrow limitations, his movements are all largely predetermined, his capacity for choice and initiative is sometimes at an absolute minimum so that, in practice, the orders with the strictest rules and most stringent obligations, in which everything is regulated for the monk in advance, have been regarded as "the most perfect"?

In the earliest days of desert monasticism there were no vows, no written rules, and institutional structure was kept at a minimum. The monastic commitment was taken with extreme and passionate seriousness, but this commitment was not protected by juridical sanctions or by institutional control. There was strict obedience on the part of the novice who sought to reproduce in his own life all the actions and thoughts of his spiritual master or "spiritual father." But the spiritual father had been chosen freely because of his own experience and his evident charisma of renunciation and vision. Once mature and able to live on his own, the novice became capable of living under the direct guidance of God.

Today the enormous number of professed religious seeking dispensation from their vows—and of others who leave the vowed life without any permission at all—makes the question of vows inescapable. It is certainly true that all community life demands a definite organization, an element of discipline and of rule, of administration and of control. A community cannot exist without its

188 CONTEMPLATION IN A WORLD OF ACTION

members being reasonably sure of what they can expect of one another from one day to the next. This supposes a certain amount of
codification and a formal commitment to elementary obedience.

However, it is possible that the taking of vows might be reserved
for a minority of monks, and solemn profession might become
something analogous to the taking of the "great habit" in Greek
monasticism. Why could there not be monasteries, with a nucleus
of permanently dedicated monks, to which others come temporarily
for two or three years, for periods of training or for retreat (as for
instance in Zen Buddhist monasticism)? Why could not married
people participate temporarily, in some way, in monastic life?

The monastic community is a covenant community whose gaze, as
we have said, is fixed on the definitive eschatological truth: the *emeth*
of God, the unfailing promise that is obscurely apprehended by faith
as already fulfilled. The vows then are intended simply to bear witness to the monk's completely engaged faith in this fulfillment, this
definitive reality made known by God in Christ. They testify that he
will seek no other fulfillment, and they remind the monk himself that
if he does turn aside and seek fulfillment in something less than the
whole, if he abandons the whole in order to put a part in place of it,
then he has fissured and severed his own identity by an act of un-
truth, an infidelity to what he has once experienced as definitive (cf.
Heb. 6:4–8).

On the other hand, the historical development of the vowed life
has more and more institutionalized this radical engagement and has
transformed it into an organizational mystique, so that in effect it is
the institution itself that becomes definitive. The monastic organization is then seen in practice, though not perhaps in theory, as the
incarnation of God's definitive truth, as the practical realization of
the Kingdom, complete with all kinds of built-in charisma (for instance the "grace of state" invested in superiors enabling them to act
in all things as God's representatives and in fact to replace him; every
expression of their will is automatically guaranteed to be "God's
will"). Thus the vows are expressions no longer of an immediate and
direct engagement to the definitive truth of God's *emeth*, but of a

mediate engagement, the institution itself being taken as practically definitive and as the incarnation of *emeth*.

Once the institution itself becomes a completely conservative establishment, the monastic vows become a firm social commitment to ecclesiastical conservatism. Faith in God's *emeth* is reduced in fact to faith in the status quo, and any criticism of the status quo becomes an act of unbelief, the first step toward apostasy and atheism.

The whole question of ecumenism and monastic renewal must be seen in this context. On one hand, if this problem is evaded, then the monastery will be regarded and used as a point of contact in which the "separated brethren" are painlessly exposed to established Catholic orthodoxy incarnated in a well-regulated institution which incidentally knows how to update its machinery and keep its members modern and happy. It lets them be American and express themselves in dialogue, using all the latest clichés and perhaps enjoying a good laugh over the problem of relics and indulgences, now definitely laid to rest.

But on the other hand, if this problem is faced, Luther's experience and his challenge will be seen as a focus of ecumenical relevance for monastic renewal itself. The dialogue of monasticism and the Reformation will not be academic only. The Reformation experience is something badly needed if monasticism is to recover its own identity in the contemporary Church. But at the same time the depth and authenticity of the monastic experience can and should contribute something to the ongoing Reformation which now takes the form of ecumenism. The Reformation can make monasticism conscious of and faithful to its own truth. A renewed monasticism, in its turn, can do something of the same for the Reformation. True ecumenism enables the Catholic to find himself by discovering what the Reformation means to him and for him (not against him), and the Protestant to rediscover in and for himself the relevance that Catholicism has never ceased to have for him. This is something much more than a mere getting closer, a rapprochement. It is a Christian experience of identity in complementarity, a lived theological dialectic which is essential not only if we are to achieve some kind of unity but also if we are to be faithful to ourselves. The definitive truth of God's *emeth* is not fully grasped without a complementary experience of mercy and reconciliation.

The theological direction taken by the vows since the Middle Ages has led to an affirmation of the part (the monastic institution) over the whole (Christ, Christian unity, the *emeth* of God). As long as the vowed life is seen exclusively in this distorted perspective, it will remain a cause of separation and disunity. It will simply enable the monk to affirm himself coldly as a separate kind of human being and his community as a little, exclusive, perfectly pure and illuminated church. His fidelity to his vows will confirm him in this illusion of separateness and exclusive perfection. In so doing it will short-circuit the personal sincerity of his well-meant faith and close his Christian love in upon itself in a cloistered ghetto of pious fantasies.

In reality the vows are meant to open wide the life of faith and love, not to close it in upon itself. The original expression of the Benedictine vows, "conversion of life" (*conversatio morum*) implies a complete *metanoia,* a total conversion of all one's hopes and aspirations to the unfailing promise of God to send his Spirit and give joy and meaning to the ascetic life of the monk by unifying it in the wholeness of love. The vows then should deliver the monk from fixation upon the partial, the limited, the provisional. They should unify his life in engagement to the definitive, the "one thing necessary," God present in his word and in his promise. They orient his life entirely to a wholeness and fulfillment, realized here and now in the darkness of faith. Whether or not vows can still mean this to modern man I will not attempt to decide here. For my own part, I still think they can, or I would not keep mine. But at the same time I am convinced that a monastic life without vows is quite possible and perhaps very desirable. It might have many advantages. (There are in fact some members of monastic communities—oblates—who live like the other monks but without vows.)

A greater flexibility in the monastic structure would permit the development of ecumenical monastic communities. There is no reason why non-Catholics and even unbelievers should not be admitted to a serious participation—at least temporary—in monastic community life. Obviously the details would have to be worked out, but there is nothing in the monastic life itself which makes this impossible.

However, if this is to be really fruitful for all concerned, it would have to take place in communities that would be well on the way to a renewed sense of identity, a recovery of the authentic and, I believe, primitive Christian monastic outlook. In such communities the support of a strong authoritarian framework would have to be replaced by something else, less tangible and more hazardous: the authority of genuine Christian experience in a really qualified monastic leader (a charismatic guide or starets, perhaps) and in a well-tested, thoroughly formed monastic community. Monasticism cannot possibly retain any seriousness or any meaning without real discipline and spiritual depth. Monastic renewal is certainly not going to be the result of instant charisma and bright ideas in communities which have no more cohesion than a picnic—and which last until the sun clouds over or people get tired of the ants.

In conclusion: the monastic life is seeking authentic renewal. The Reformation experience, the discovery of a more immediate and radical commitment to God's unfailing promises in faith, called into question the highly institutionalized and mediate structure of monastic dedication which came down from the Middle Ages. But on the other hand, tradition has a crucial importance of its own. Return to sources, itself essential for real Christian renewal in every area, is not a mere matter of books and *monumenta*. Monasticism should recover contact with its primitive founts not only through study but through living participation in the theological and contemplative experience of hope which has come down more or less unbroken in the monastic orders, through decadence and reform, despite all temporary aberrations and distortions of perspective. The hope of transcendent and final truth is something that is definitely not dead or dying in the modern world. On the contrary, we see on all sides evidences of an almost desperate need for spiritual depth and authentic hope. It is this very need which results in so much justified contempt for superficiality in popular religion. The monastic spirit is alive today, seeking new ways to express its eschatological hope and to become vitally aware of its own latent potentialities. That is why, on one hand, Protestantism itself is contributing to the monastic renewal and why, on the other, monasteries are promising to become centers not only of ecumenical discussion but of deeply lived and participated ecumenical experience.

The unique and precious dimension that the monastic life can contribute to ecumenical experience is the deepening of unity that comes not only from talking together but from being silent together. The monastic life (when it is true to its own charism) is pervaded with the sense of the definitive that comes to those who, in silence, refrain from the futility of articulation. Yet also what must be grasped are the provisional needs to be articulated in honest and undogmatic speech. The two go together. The monastic dialectic of silence and language underlines the deeper dialectic of eschatology and incarnation.

There is today a glib tendency to treat this division quite undialectically and to dismiss it as "schizoid." This vice is common both to integralists, who cling blindly to their own (institutional) brand of eschatology, and to progressives, who think that by putting all their eggs in one basket (secularity) and dismissing all other baskets they can arrive easily and instantly at the unity which only the patient labor of dialectic can finally attain. Heinrich Ott* points out how the silences of Hemingway and the allusiveness of Antonioni are valid artistic apprehensions of a reality whose wholeness has to include the unspoken. Asian art, especially the "one-cornered" style inspired by Zen, has long known this, and the duty of the monk consists in maintaining this perspective not only by academic clarification but by illumination and silence. Both the words and the silence, which complete each other in deeply validating Christian experience, are rooted in the ultimate presence and reality of love.

*Loc. cit., p. 114.

XII
The Need For a New Education

It is quite evident that the theological formation given to priests in the active apostolate is not entirely suitable for monks. To begin with, though all monks require some theological training, they will not all be ordained to the priesthood. The monastic life, whether in community or in solitude, is primarily a life of prayer and witness, not of teaching, administration or pastoral care. Theological formation for such a life cannot of course be superficial or merely elementary. On the contrary, the prayer life of the monk, liturgically in community and in the solitude of his own heart, implies a deep understanding of the Mystery of Christ and must indeed develop to the point of becoming a "lived theology"—a living experience of Christian truth.

The monastic community is something more than a group of pious men or women who are merely intent on meritorious works for the salvation of their own souls. Nor do they merely seek to win grace for a world which they are otherwise content to ignore. Monks are intent on exploring the inner meaning of the Mystery of Christ in the world of our time, and this requires some understanding of the world and of themselves as modern people, as well as a realization of and witness to the presence of Christ in the world.

This means that monks must be prepared to share something of their own solitude and their own awareness of the Mystery of Christ with those who come to their monasteries. To say that the "world needs solitude, prayer, silence" is to say more than that worldly people need monks to pray for them: it means also that they need places where they can find a little silence and peace and immerse themselves in the atmosphere of authentic prayer. But this means that the monastic experience needs to be communicable in terms which are not utterly foreign to modern man. The monastery must therefore have in it not only genuine men of prayer but also men who can communicate something of their understanding and experience to others.

The monastic life is not only contemplative but prophetic. That is to say, it bears witness not only to a contemplative mystique of silence, enclosure and the renunciation of active works, but it is alive with the eschatological mystery of the Kingdom already shared and realized in the lives of those who have heard the Word of God and have surrendered unconditionally to its demands in a vocation that (even when communal) has a distinctly "desert" quality. This suggests that there is something of a charism in every monastic vocation and in the monastic witness itself. But this does not preclude study and theological understanding. On the contrary, it presupposes a thirst for the Word of God, a willingness to immerse oneself in meditation of the Bible, in a fruitful life of prayer and celebration which is not mechanical and punctilious but full of spontaneity and intuitive understanding. Christian wisdom and understanding must grow and deepen from day to day in the life of the monk. The whole life of the monk is a pilgrimage to the sources of Christian truth. None of this is possible if the monk does not have the proper theological formation.

But the understanding and experience which gradually bring the monk to contemplative and prophetic maturity (which may above all be maturity in sacrifice) should also in some cases open out to communication with others. There must be some monks qualified to share their experience in dialogue with contemplatives from other religious traditions (Buddhists, Hindus, Sufis, etc.). And above all there must be some who will be able to speak to those modern intellectuals, whether religious or irreligious, who are intrigued by the mysterious personal dimensions of inner and spiritual experience—artists, philosophers, poets, psychiatrists, students of anthropology, comparative religion, etc. There are many such men who are curious about the monastic life and who would be very interested in discovering its real existential values in intelligent dialogue with trained minds. Though they might respect the sincerity of a closed, alien type of piety which could not speak their language, they might ultimately be disillusioned or repelled by it. They need to recognize in monks professionals like themselves who have deliberately chosen a different road and a different kind of experience and can give some account of their choice and of its fruits.

Obviously we must not expect everyone in each monastic community to be a specialist in ecumenical or intercultural dialogue. But there may be some who are more qualified for this than others, and with the proper theological and humanistic training they can develop an understanding that will not only open them to others in a valid type of contemplative apostolate but will also enable them to live a more fruitful inner life themselves. Needless to say, they will have much more to share with their own monastic community. The theological training of monks should be especially oriented toward the formation of men of prayer who can give an intelligible account of contemplative experience to others either in spiritual guidance or in teaching, or in dialogue. But on the other hand, to preserve the authentic monastic quality of this theology of prayer, the emphasis should be on prayer itself and on the mysteries of faith, rather than on skills of communication. We will have to remember, however, that to understand prayer today we need to understand man, and we need to understand him in his present historical situation.

Monastic theology will be above all biblical. The Bible should have first place in the formation and education of the monk from the earliest days of his postulancy. His liturgical and patristic studies will be also biblical. The study of monastic history, of early monastic rules and ascetic literature should be seen in the relation of all such documents to their biblical sources. It should never be forgotten that the monastic life is a special way of living the gospel and that the monk's dedication to God by his vows (especially the vow to convert and transform his whole life in response to the Word of God) is to be understood in the light of God's promises, the eschatological Kingdom, and the recapitulation of all things in Christ.

In the light of this knowledge, the monk will also need to acquire by learning and by discipline a mature ability to cope with the forces that seek to stifle the seed of the word that has been planted in his heart. That is to say: the formation of the monk demands some training in the use of traditional ascetic means of perfecting the Christian life of prayer. This will enable him to respond more fully and effectively to his call to understand the Word of God, which does not reveal its meaning fully where there is no sacrifice.

However, while not neglecting traditional ascesis—understood in the light of new needs and of the new situation—the monk must seek to develop the special human capacities which will enable him to experience the deepest values of the contemplative life. These values are not accessible to merely abstract and logical investigation. They imply a certain aesthetic and intuitive awareness, a "taste" and connaturality or a capacity to savor (in an experience that cannot easily be formulated) the deepest truths of the Christian life. In other words, monastic education should, without neglecting scientific theology, open the way to a truly *sapiential* contemplation of the Christian mystery. Monastic theology is not "anti-intellectual," but it does nevertheless aspire to a kind of understanding rooted in love. *Amor ipse intellectus.* In plain words, monastic theology has a mystical orientation.

We have to recognize that today many candidates come to our monasteries without adequate training in the humanities. And we must not make the mistake of thinking that "training in the humanities" means simply a "classical education"—or a knowledge of Latin. Something has to be done for those who are deficient in a rudimentary appreciation of literature, art, and other humane studies. These have a definite relevance for the spiritual life of the monk.

The philosophical training of the monk should not only be a preparation for contemplative theology: it should also help the monk understand those non-Christian traditions of deeply metaphysical contemplation which have flourished especially in Asia. Together with technical philosophical disciplines, the monk should learn something of anthropology, comparative religion, and of depth psychology insofar as it opens out on the regions of primitive mythology and archaic culture. This will be useful not only in possible dialogue with contemplatives of other traditions, but will also enable the monk to understand better the classics of non-Christian religions. Again, the philosophical training of the monk should be "sapientially" oriented, not a mere objective and apologetic catalogue of "non-Christian errors" but a judicious appreciation of the value of such traditions even for Christian monks. In his philosophical training the monk might learn, for instance, to grasp the characteristic differences between Greek, Hebrew, Indian and Chinese-Japanese modes of thought.

The monk should be thoroughly familiar with the mystical literature of Christianity, both Eastern and Western, from the patristic period down to the present day. And once again, the psychological dimension should not be ignored. The insights of modern psychiatry should be useful in helping the monk develop practical judgment in understanding problems and conflicts in the ascetic and mystical life.

The spiritual and theological formation of the monk cannot make sense if it is unrelated to the world of our time. This means that the monk must not only know something of history, in order to understand the roots of present problems, but he should be exposed to those mystiques of history which are of decisive importance in our time (Hegel, Marx, Croce, etc.). He should clearly understand and evaluate their implications for our own Christian eschatology (which must not be allowed to degenerate into a mystique either of history or of evolution).

The monk must be able to understand the crucial problems of our time and see his own monastic vocation in the light of these problems: race, war, genocide, starvation, injustice, revolution. Both the individual monk and the monastic community may have to face crucial decisions affecting their own future, decisions which will not be made intelligently and realistically if there is not sufficient understanding of the wider context of social conflict. In this matter great care and discrimination are necessary. Openness to the "world" must not come to mean a merely uncritical and superficial acceptance of everything that is said in the mass media of one's particular country.

A monastic community can entirely lose its prophetic sense and witness when it identifies itself with some particular party or nation.

Finally, it is most important to relate the sapiential theology of the monk to the technological culture of our century. The monk cannot one-sidedly accept or reject the scientific world of the twentieth century. He must understand the problems and possibilities of that world, and without being dominated by slogans or clichés, he should be able to contribute something of his own to a worldview that is highly expert in science but perhaps deficient in wisdom. (Here let us note however that some of the truly wise—*sapientes*—of our time have been among the atomic physicists and most advanced explorers in the world of matter. Bohr, Schrödinger, et al., are there to back up this statement.)

A contemplative monastery should ideally be able to play a significant part in the development of scientific culture. The qualitative, experiential and personal values developed in monastic life should complement the objective, quantitative and experimental discoveries of science and their exploitation by technology and business. The monastery should by no means be merely an enclave of eccentric and apparently archaic human beings who have rebelled against the world of science and turned their backs on it with a curse.

The purpose of monastic formation is not primarily to produce a community of academic specialists capable of intellectual and mystical dialogue on a high level with everybody from Zen monks to nuclear physicists. That would be utopian. We need to form monks of the twentieth century who are capable of embracing in their contemplative awareness not only the theological dimensions of the Mystery of Christ but also the possibilities of new understanding offered by non-Christian traditions and by the modern world of science and revolution. There will obviously be different levels of training and understanding. Obviously, we will still produce mostly the "simple monk," but of a more sophisticated type nevertheless than the one who used to be content with his beads (admirable though that might be). On the other hand, the monastery should be capable of being a place of dialogue, nontechnical and nonexpert, no doubt, but a place where men of our time would feel they could encounter and somehow "touch" a deep and existential experience of the Mystery of Christ as lived and revealed in a community of men who really measure up to the challenges and promises of a contemplative vocation.

In an age of easy communication, such a monastery would be frequently visited by specialists of all sorts, and in all fields, who would be willing to give conferences and to have discussions with some of the monks. These opportunities would not be neglected, and the monks should be well enough trained to make such dialogue fruitful on a deep level for all concerned.

We must not fear to confront such possibilities as a limited and well-ordered use of modern media, even *educational* TV, while at the same time excluding the addiction to frothy entertainment.

We must also resolutely face the fact that the monastery is not a ghetto and will not profit by being kept as one. An interpretation of enclosure that is merely rigid and formal and which admits of no exceptions (beyond those which involve sickness or profitable business enterprises) will not help monastic renewal.

XIII

Final Integration

Toward a "Monastic Therapy"

A considerable amount of uneasiness and ambivalence in the monastic life today is due perhaps to the fact that, though we possess clear conceptual formulas to explain what our "contemplative life" is all about, and though those formulas may well accord with what we would like to do, it seems they do not help us much with what we are actually doing. Thus we find ourselves with several different sets of problems which, however, we do not manage to distinguish. We have defined our ends in certain terms (a life of prayer and penance, apart from the world but not alien to it; seeking God alone, but in community and fraternal love; purifying our hearts by renunciation in order to pray more intently and simply, eventually attaining to contemplative experience; thus, our community is a living sign of God's presence, etc.). But meanwhile, before we can get around to doing these things, we have to wrestle with a multitude of other problems: how to make our own living efficiently and yet remain "monastic"; how to keep our atmosphere of silence and yet communicate more spontaneously with one another; how to arrange the office, time for work, study, etc.; above all, how to cope with the contradictions in a system which at the same moment—but from different quarters—urges us to go forward and forbids us to move.

Thus, though we may be fairly clear about what we want to do, we are so confused about the way to do it that our ends become almost entirely theoretical and our energies become involved in a rather different form of life from the one we claim to be living. This naturally

causes a lot of anxiety, ambivalence, tension, not to say discouragement and even despair. Then we summon psychiatry to the rescue—
and create still further problems: for the kind of adjustment that
ordinary psychotherapy calls for is a realistic acceptance of our social
situation, an acquiescence in fulfilling a moderately useful role and
in being more or less the sort of person our society would like us to
be. And yet the monastic role defined by the ideal to which we hold
is one thing, and the role as defined by the actual situation of our
community and of ourselves in it, quite another. This difficulty becomes all the greater and more confusing when sociology gets into
the act, for then we are summoned to live at the same time by an
unworldly ideal and by a worldly one: or to be monks according to
norms and standards based on statistics which have nothing to do
with our kind of life.

To put it quite simply: many people come to the monastery with
a strong, if inchoate, sense that they are called to make something
out of their lives. But after a few years of struggle they find that
this "thing" they are supposed to do is not clarified, and though
they may have become acquainted with formulas which explain the
monastic life and justify it, they still do not feel that they are able
to do anything about them. In addition, they begin to question the
relevance of such formulas to modern man. The most difficult kind
of vocation crisis is that in which a monk with genuine monastic
aspirations comes to feel that such aspirations cannot be fulfilled in
a monastery. Which means that they probably cannot be fulfilled
anywhere.

The idea of "rebirth" and of life as a "new man in Christ, in the
Spirit," of a "risen life" in the Mystery of Christ or in the Kingdom
of God, is fundamental to Christian theology and practice—it is,
after all, the whole meaning of baptism. All the more so is this idea
central to that peculiar refinement of the theology of baptism which
is the monastic *conversatio*—the vocation to a life especially dedicated to self-renewal, liberation from all sin, and the transformation
of one's entire mentality "in Christ."

The notion of "rebirth" is not peculiar to Christianity. In Sufism,
Zen Buddhism and in many other religious or spiritual traditions,

202 CONTEMPLATION IN A WORLD OF ACTION

emphasis is placed on the call to fulfill certain obscure yet urgent potentialities in the ground of one's being, to "become someone" that one already (potentially) is, the person one is truly meant to be. Zen calls this awakening a recognition of "your original face before you were born."

In Asian traditions as well as in Christian monasticism, there has been considerable stress on the need for a guide or spiritual father, an experienced elder who knows how to bring the less experienced to a decisive point of breakthrough where this "new being" is attained. Strictly speaking, Christian monasticism is less dependent on the aid of a guide than some of the other traditions. In Sufism and Zen the spiritual master is as essential as the analyst in psychoanalysis. In Christian monasticism, a fervent community, a living and "spiritual" (*pneumatikos*) celebration of the liturgical mysteries and of the office might compensate, to some extent, for the lack of an experienced and charismatic teacher. But if there is no sense at all of the urgency of inner development, no aspiration to growth and "rebirth," or if it is blandly assumed that all this is automatically taken care of by a correct and lively communal celebration, something essential is missing.

The monastic life is not justified simply by a sort of contractual fulfillment of a "work" on behalf of the Church—even if it be the spiritual work of the *opus Dei,* the official public celebration of divine praise, or, for that matter, the cultivation of meditative prayer in silence, strict enclosure, in an austere regime. The monastic community does not effectively act as a sign of God's presence and of his Kingdom merely by the fulfillment of certain symbolic functions. For instance, it is not enough to keep the monks strictly enclosed and remote from all external activity—this does not by itself constitute a sign of the eschatological Kingdom. On the contrary, very often this limitation constitutes a serious impoverishment of the personalities of the monks and at the same time serves to prevent that impoverishment from becoming public! It is of course perfectly true that solitude and silence are essential to the monastic way of life, and discipline does contribute very much to the ends for which monastic communities exist. But the fact remains that people are called to the monastic life so that they may grow and be transformed, "reborn" to a new and more complete identity and to a more profoundly fruitful existence in peace, in wisdom, in creativity, in love. When rigidity and limitation become ends in themselves they no longer favor growth; they stifle it.

Sometimes it may be very useful for us to discover new and unfamiliar ways in which the human task of maturation and self-discovery is defined. The book of a Persian psychoanalyst, Dr. Reza Arasteh, who practices and teaches in America, might prove very valuable in this respect.*

Dr. Arasteh has developed and deepened ideas suggested by the humanistic psychoanalysis of Erich Fromm, by existential psychotherapy and by the logotherapy of Viktor Frankl. But—and this is what is most interesting—he has also incorporated into his theories material from the mystical tradition of Persian Sufism. The *Final Integration* which is the object of his research is not just the "cure" of neurosis by adaptation to society. On the contrary, it presupposes that any psychoanalytic theory that is content merely with this is bound to be inadequate. Dr. Arasteh is interested not only in the partial and limited "health" which results from contented acceptance of a useful role in society, but in the final and complete maturing of the human psyche on a transcultural level. This requires a little clarification.

Contrary to the accepted theory and practice of most psychotherapy derived from Freud and popular in America today, Dr. Arasteh holds that adaptation to society at best helps a man "to live with his illness rather than cure it," particularly if the general atmosphere of the society is unhealthy because of its overemphasis on cerebral, competitive, acquisitive forms of ego-affirmation. Such an atmosphere may favor an apparently very active and productive mode of life, but in reality it stifles true growth, leaves people lost, alienated, frustrated and bored without any way of knowing what is wrong with them. In fact, in many cases psychoanalysis has become a technique for making people conform to a society that prevents them

*Reza Arasteh, *Final Integration in the Adult Personality*, Leiden, E. J. Brill, 1965.

from growing and developing as they should. Quoting E. Knight's book *The Objective Society*, Arasteh says:

> The Western individual, while opposing the integration of the Russian and Chinese models, not only accepts the herd values of his society but he has invented psychoanalysis to prevent him from straying from them. . . . The stresses that modern life often produces in sensitive and intelligent people are no longer considered to call for a change in society; it is the individual who is wrong and he consequently becomes a neurotic, not a revolutionary. No more remarkable device than psychoanalysis has ever been devised by a society for preventing its superior citizens from giving it pain.

This interesting passage, quoted out of context, might give undue comfort to those who assume that, because they enjoy their masochism, they are superior. Nevertheless it does show to what extent psychotherapy and other techniques have been frankly drafted into the service of a massive, affluent organization that is dedicated to "freedom" and yet tolerates less and less dissent. The masochism, the anxiety, the alienation which are almost universal in such a society are forms of organized evasion. The energies that might otherwise go into productive or even revolutionary change are driven into stagnant backwaters of frustration and self-pity. People are not only made ill, but they *prefer* to be ill rather than face the risk of real dissent. (Note the important distinction between real and pseudo-dissent, the latter being merely a token and a symbol expressing and justifying an underlying neurosis.) We know well enough that this pattern, so familiar in "the world," is even more familiar in "the cloister."

Nevertheless there is an important distinction between mere neurotic anxiety, which comes from a commitment to defeat, and existential anxiety, which is the healthy pain caused by the blocking of vital energies that still remain available for radical change. This is one of the main points made by Dr. Arasteh's book: the importance of existential anxiety seen not as a symptom of something wrong, but as a summons to growth and to painful development.

Carefully distinguishing existential anxiety from the petulant self-defeating sorrows of the neurotic, Dr. Arasteh shows how this anxiety is a sign of health and generates the necessary strength for psychic rebirth into a new transcultural identity. This new being is entirely personal, original, creative, unique, and it transcends the limits imposed by social convention and prejudice. Birth on this higher level is an imperative necessity for man.

The infant who lives immersed in a symbiotic relationship with the rest of nature—immersed, that is, in his own narcissism—must be "born" out of this sensual self-centeredness and acquire an identity as a responsible member of society. Ordinary psychotherapy is fully aware of this. But once one has grown up, acquired an education, and assumed a useful role as a worker and provider, there is still another birth to be undergone. Dr. Arasteh studies this birth to final integration in three exceptional individuals: Rumi, the Persian mystic and poet; Goethe; and a young modern Turk who was one of Arasteh's patients.

In the past, final integration was generally a matter only for unusually gifted people. We shall return to this point later. Even today, though the need for final integration makes itself more and more widely felt, the majority not only do not try to attain it, but society, as we have seen, provides them with ways to evade the summons. Clearly, in many cases, that summons takes the form of a monastic, religious or priestly vocation. Clearly, too, there are many who leave the monastery because they feel that the way the monastic life is structured, or the way they themselves are fitted into the structure, makes a genuine response to the summons impossible.

All of us who have had to work through vocation problems with professed monks can, on reflection, easily distinguish obvious neurotics from men whose monastic crisis has taken the form of existential anxiety: this is a crisis of authentic growth which cannot be resolved in the situation in which they find themselves, and the situation cannot be changed. (Very often, in similar situations, it is the mildly neurotic who manage to stay and make some sort of compromise adjustment, nestling fearfully in the protection of the monastery with the obscure sense that further painful growth will not be demanded!)

Since his investigation is purely psychological, not theological, the question of "sanctity" or holiness does not really arise from Dr. Arasteh. But let us make clear that ordinarily a full spiritual development and a supernatural, even charismatic, maturity, evidenced in the "saint," normally includes the idea of complete psychological integration. Doubtless many saints have been neurotics, but they have used their neurosis in the interests of growth instead of capitulating and succumbing to its dubious comforts.

Final integration is a state of transcultural maturity far beyond mere social adjustment, which always implies partiality and compromise. The man who is "fully born" has an entirely "inner experience of life." He apprehends his life fully and wholly from an inner ground that is at once more universal than the empirical ego and yet entirely his own. He is in a certain sense "cosmic" and "universal man." He has attained a deeper, fuller identity than that of his limited ego-self which is only a fragment of his being. He is in a certain sense identified with everybody: or in the familiar language of the New Testament (which Arasteh evidently has not studied) he is "all things to all men." He is able to experience their joys and sufferings as his own, without however becoming dominated by them. He has attained to a deep inner freedom—the freedom of the Spirit we read of in the New Testament. He is guided not just by will and reason, but by "spontaneous behavior subject to dynamic insight." Now, this calls to mind the theology of St. Thomas on the gifts of the Holy Spirit which move a man to act "in a superhuman mode." Though Dr. Arasteh takes no account of specifically supernatural agencies, it is clear that such considerations might become relevant here. But of course they cannot be investigated by experimental science.

Again, the state of insight which is final integration implies an openness, an "emptiness," a "poverty" similar to those described in such detail not only by the Rhenish mystics, by St. John of the Cross, by the early Franciscans, but also by the Sufis, the early Taoist masters and Zen Buddhists. Final integration implies the void, poverty and nonaction which leave one entirely docile to the "Spirit" and, hence, a potential instrument for unusual creativity.

The man who has attained final integration is no longer limited by the culture in which he has grown up. "He has embraced *all of life*. . . . He has experienced qualities of every type of life": ordinary human existence, intellectual life, artistic creation, human love, religious life. He passes beyond all these limiting forms, while retaining all that is best and most universal in them, "finally giving birth to a fully comprehensive self." He accepts not only his own community, his own society, his own friends, his own culture, but all mankind. He does not remain bound to one limited set of values in such a way that he opposes them aggressively or defensively to others. He is fully "Catholic" in the best sense of the word. He has a unified vision and experience of the one truth shining out in all its various manifestations, some clearer than others, some more definite and more certain than others. He does not set these partial views up in opposition to each other but unifies them in a dialectic or an insight of complementarity. With this view of life he is able to bring perspective, liberty and spontaneity into the lives of others. The finally integrated man is a peacemaker, and that is why there is such a desperate need for our leaders to become such men of insight.

It will be seen at once that this kind of maturity is exactly what the monastic life should produce. The monastic ideal is precisely this sort of freedom in the spirit, this liberation from the limits of all that is merely partial and fragmentary in a given culture. Monasticism calls for a breadth and universality of vision that sees everything in the light of the One Truth, as St. Benedict beheld all creation embraced "in one ray of the sun." This too is suggested at the end of Chapter 7 of the Rule where St. Benedict speaks of the new identity, the new mode of being of the monk who no longer practices the various degrees of humility with concentrated and studied effort but with dynamic spontaneity "in the Spirit." It is suggested also in the "degrees of truth" and the "degrees of love" in St. Bernard's tracts on humility and on the love of God.

Unfortunately, we can see at once that if too many people developed in this way, if entire communities were all at once to reach final integration, the effect on the community structure itself might be revolutionary. Hence, in fact, our community life is unconsciously organized to make sure that any such development will be subject to human control. We will not let the Holy Spirit get out of hand! And yet with all its shortcomings and deficiencies, the monastic life is charismatic, and the Spirit does work in our midst. But in monastic communities as well as in the Church at large we are conscious of the obscure and difficult struggle between charism and institution in which the overwhelming need to channel and control the energies of the Spirit (and of course to distinguish them clearly from other more destructive energies) has led to a kind of neutralization of Spirit by organization. This institutional straitjacketing does not prevent individuals from breaking through in their own way and achieving an integration that is perhaps warped and singular but nevertheless authentic (sometimes in amusing ways). But the community itself cannot be truly charismatic, except in a very subdued and harmless way. The penalty paid for this is a prevalence of neurosis, of masochism, of obsessions and compulsions, of fanaticism, intolerance, narrow-mindedness, and various petty forms of destructive cruelty which have proved so ruinous in the past. The present changes and relaxations have been first-aid measures to relieve these tensions at any price: but merely opening the windows is not enough. We must still be ready to face anxieties and realize the difference between those that are fruitless and those that offer a promise of fruitful development. Sometimes the latter are even more painful and seemingly more dangerous than the former. After all, the rebirth which precedes final integration involves a crisis which is extremely severe—something like the Dark Night described by St. John of the Cross. And it is evident that anyone who chanced to fall into the Dark Night of the soul today would (if discovered) soon find himself getting shock treatments, which would effectively take care of any further disturbing developments!

Dr. Arasteh describes the breakthrough into final integration in the language of Sufism. The consecrated term in Sufism is *Fana,* annihilation or disintegration, a loss of self, a real spiritual death. But mere annihilation and death are not enough: they must be followed by reintegration and new life on a totally different level. This reintegration is what the Sufis call *Baqa*. The process of disintegration and reintegration is one that involves a terrible interior solitude and an "existential moratorium," a crisis and an anguish which cannot be analyzed or intellectualized. It also requires a solitary fortitude far beyond the ordinary, "an act of courage related to the root of all existence." It would be utterly futile to try to "cure" this anguish by bringing the "patient" as quickly and as completely as possible into the warm bosom of togetherness. Jung, with whom Arasteh has much in common, says this:

> [The development of the person to full ripeness] is at once a charisma and a curse because its first fruit is the conscious and unavoidable segregation of the individual from the undifferentiated and unconscious herd. This means isolation, and there is no more comforting word for it. Neither family nor society nor position can save him from the fate, nor yet the most successful adaptation to his environment. . . . (quoted by Arasteh)

Seen from the viewpoint of monastic tradition, the pattern of disintegration, existential moratorium and reintegration on a higher, universal level is precisely what the monastic life is meant to provide. In the strictly limited, authoritarian, caste societies of medieval Europe, of India, of China, of Japan, the individual lived within extreme restriction in a framework that denied him social mobility. But the unusual person, from any caste, could become a monk. If he were able to live as an authentic beggar and pilgrim, accept the sacrifices, the insecurities, the risks, the challenges of the solitary adventure, he was freed from social limitations. He was on his own, on the road, in the jungle or in the desert, and he was entitled to develop in his own way, indeed to devote himself with passionate dedication to a freedom even from the limits of his contingency as a creature: he could get lost in the light of eternity, provided he found the way!

In the modern world, things have somehow become reversed. We live in an extremely mobile society in which, though we may not be nearly as free as we think we are, limits are still very flexible and sometimes do not exist at all. To enter a monastery is to enter into the most restricted form of life there is. This restriction has a purpose: it is imposed in order to liberate us from attachments and from self-will. But the big question is: Does it? Yes and no.

The ascesis of communal service and obedience cannot be dismissed as totally irrelevant, antiquated, repressive and sterile. It is necessary and salutary for people who have had little or no discipline at all. But on the other hand it does definitely operate in such a way that while it initiates a certain growth, it goes only so far. It frustrates and stifles growth beyond a median level. It makes no provision for anything but formal adaptation to a rather narrow and limited communal pattern. Within that pattern it tolerates "safe," moderate growth and blesses lack of growth. In fact, it is in practice more tolerant of those who do not grow.

The crisis, the challenge and the demands that Arasteh describes in terms of final integration would seldom be really acceptable in a monastery. They would be too disturbing, too exceptional, too "irregular." They would open up possibilities that would be regarded as altogether too hazardous. The result is that for many authentic vocations today the monastery has become merely a way station. To stay in the cloister for life would be to renounce their full development. And yet there is no guarantee that by leaving it they will develop any better.

Dr. Arasteh has nothing direct to say about the monastic life, but obviously those who have sufficient background and understanding will be able to apply his principles very fruitfully to our general predicament today. He will help us recover some sense of the real aim of that monastic *conversatio* which we have not only mentally approved but actually vowed. We have dedicated ourselves to rebirth, to growth, to final maturity and integration. Monastic renewal means a reshaping of structures so that they will not only permit such growth but favor and encourage it in everyone.

However, as Christian monks, we cannot properly understand the full meaning of "final integration" if we see it only in the terms of psychology. For a Christian, a transcultural integration is eschatological. The rebirth of man and of society on a transcultural level is a rebirth into the transformed and redeemed time, the time of the

Kingdom, the time of the Spirit, the time of "the end." It means a disintegration of the social and cultural self, the product of merely human history, and the reintegration of that self in Christ, in salvation history, in the mystery of redemption, in the Pentecostal "new creation." But this means entering into the full mystery of the eschatological Church.

Now, as Dr. Arasteh points out, whereas final psychological integration was, in the past, the privilege of a few, it is now becoming a need and aspiration of mankind as a whole. The whole world is in an existential crisis to which there are various reactions, some of them negative, tragic, destructive, demonic, others proffering a human hope which is yet not fully clear.

The destructive and tragic solutions are not solutions at all: they simply marshal the immense resources of military, economic and political power to block real development and to maintain established patterns—in the interest of those who know best how to profit from them, and at the expense of everybody else.

The humanly optimistic answers foresee radical changes of a purely secular sort which will initiate a kind of hippie kingdom of love in a cybernated and peace-loving megacity (presumably with free LSD for everybody). Many Christians feel that the Spirit is really summoning us to renounce our sense of spiritual privilege and enter into a fully turned-on solidarity with these secular hopes. Others, of course, and perhaps the majority, have lined up on the side of the armies and the "powers" under the mistaken idea that Christ is fully identified with the capitalist Western establishment which still refers to itself (when convenient) as "Christian."

At this point, the best one can do is hazard a personal guess that neither of these solutions is truly Christian and neither offers a hope of final, eschatological integration to the individual Christian, to the Church, or to the monastic community. Both of these are reducible to identification with one form or other of culture, one form or other of "given" society. They are historical decisions that are merely historical and not eschatological. (Though of course they may contribute in a disastrous way to the ironies of eschatological judgment upon the organizational Church.)

Where are we to look for the true solutions? Precisely from the Spirit who will speak clearly at the right time through a renewed ecclesiastical and monastic community. The path to final integration for the individual and for the community lies, in any case, beyond the dictates and programs of any culture ("Christian culture" included).

TWO

Contemplative Life

Is the Contemplative Life Finished?*

"Contemplative" is a bad word. When we talk about ourselves, monks, as contemplatives, we come face to face with the problem that we are not more than contemplatives. We are not prophets. We are failing in the prophetic aspect of our vocation. Why? Perhaps because we belong to a Christianity so deeply implicated in a society which has outlived its spiritual vitality and yet is groping for a new expression of life in crisis. Our monasteries are not fulfilling any kind of prophetic vocation in the modern world. Whether we should be able to do that or not is another matter. The prophetic charism is a gift of God, not a duty of man.

But on the other hand, if the gift has not been given perhaps we who had the call have not prepared ourselves. It seems to me that contemplatives should be able to say to modern man something about God that answers the profoundly important and significant accusation of Marx against religion. Marx said religion inevitably leads to the alienation of man. It is not fulfillment but opium. Man in his worship of God divests himself of his own powers and of his own dignity and attributes these to an invisible and remote God and then begs God to grant them, give them back to him bit by bit, in retail packages. But that is not the case. We are learning more and more that the denial of God is really the denial of man. Yet, on the other hand, the affirmation of God is the true affirmation of man. Barth somewhere said:

*Notes from taped conferences.

"Merely to talk about man in a loud voice is not to talk about God." Unless we really affirm God, we do not affirm man. Unless we affirm God as he who calls man into existence and to freedom and to love, which is the fulfillment of that freedom—unless we affirm this God, we fail to affirm that without which man's life has no meaning.

Monks ought to be able to reassure the modern world that in the struggle between thought and existence we are on the side of existence, not on the side of abstraction. But can we honestly affirm this? I don't know.

A great deal of monastic life and "contemplative spirituality" is not necessarily abstract in a philosophical sense, but it is an artificial behavior in which thought, embodied in ritual forms, opposes itself to the concrete facts of existence. Do we make a fetish out of subjecting the realities of human existence to ritual forms and legalisms to convince ourselves that in so doing we are leading spiritual and contemplative lives?

We monks should be able to reassure modern man that God is the source and the guarantee of our freedom and not simply a force standing over us to limit our freedom.

In the conflict between law and freedom, God is on the side of freedom. That is a scandalous statement! But it is the New Testament! How are we going to affirm to the modern world the scandal of the New Testament? It is here that we confront the seriousness of our *prophetic* as distinct from our *contemplative* calling.

Surely this is the "message" the monk should give the world. But to what extent can monks express this? We are, so it would seem, as committed to law as anybody. More than others! We multiply laws. We live a highly mediated existence in which at any moment rule and rite can substitute for authentic experience and encounter.

Our encounter with God should be, at the same time, the discovery of our own deepest freedom. If we never encounter him, our freedom never fully develops. It develops only in the existential encounter between the Christian and God, or between *man* and God—because not only Christians encounter God. Every man at some point in his life encounters God, and many who are not Christians have responded to God better than Christians. Our encounter with him, our response to his Word, is the drawing forth and calling out of our deepest freedom, our true identity.

Prayer

To properly understand prayer, we have to see in it this encounter of our freedom emerging from the depths of nothingness and undevelopment, at the call of God. Prayer is freedom and affirmation growing out of nothingness into love. Prayer is the flowering of our inmost freedom, in response to the Word of God. Prayer is not only dialogue with God: it is the communion of our freedom with his ultimate freedom, his infinite spirit. It is the elevation of our limited freedom into the infinite freedom of the divine spirit, and of the divine love. Prayer is the encounter of our freedom with the all-embracing charity which knows no limit and knows no obstacle. Prayer is an emergence into this area of infinite freedom. Prayer then is not an abject procedure although sometimes it may spring from our abjection.

Of course, we have to face the existential reality of our wretchedness, nothingness and abjection because it is there that our prayer begins. It is out of this nothingness that we are called into freedom. It is out of this darkness that we are called into light. Therefore, we need to recognize this as our true starting point. Otherwise our prayer is not authentic. But we are called *out* of this nothingness, darkness and alienation and frustration, into communion and intimacy with God, in his freedom. That is the meaning of prayer. Prayer therefore is not just simply a matter of thrusting ourselves down into a position of abjection and groveling in servile submission, asking God for things which are already our own. That is the picture that Marx in his idea of religious alienation gives us. Prayer is not something that is meant to maintain us in servility and helplessness. We take stock of our own wretchedness at the beginning of prayer in order to rise beyond it and above it to infinite freedom and infinite creative love in God.

Prayer infallibly does this if we believe it and if we understand its true dimensions. The great problem of prayer arises from the fact that if we take the alienated view we remain fixed in our own ego, and we are no longer able to go out from ourselves into freedom. If we remain in our ego, clenched upon ourselves, trying to draw down to ourselves gifts which we then incorporate in our own limited selfish life, then prayer does remain servile. Servility has its root in self-serving. Servility, in a strange way, really consists in trying to make God serve our own needs. We have to try to say to modern man something about the fact that authentic prayer enables us to emerge from our servility into freedom in God because it no longer strives to manipulate him by superstitious "deals."

Good Souls

Suppose, for a moment, that the term "contemplative" has a value and can be retained: in what sense are we contemplatives? In what sense are there real contemplatives in our monasteries? Obviously there are, especially among the older generation, a lot of people who have been and are authentic men of prayer. Yet so few, so very few seem really to be deeply *contemplative*. They are more what you would call "good souls." They are worthy products of the religious system that has prevailed up to now, good regular people who have been faithful to their obligations. They have put their obligations before everything else and come to choir on time. They have been rewarded with satisfaction and peace. They have a kind of solid interior life going. Over the years they have acquired a certain experience and a deep love of God—no question about that. What they have apparently failed to develop is real depth of insight and a real fullness of *life*. Few have a real depth of spiritual consciousness and a real depth of interior experience. If they have, it is something that they are absolutely unable to articulate, something they are not even aware of. And of course, that is as it should be. But are they *contemplatives*? Or *should* they be?

You expect to find simple and deep people in the contemplative life. The true contemplative should not necessarily have much to say about his contemplative life. The business of articulating it can be a charism or it can be a delusion. But the fact remains that there is something to the articulation of this deep experience. One should be able to teach it to others, to make others understand what it is, and help them to attain it. That is the question that is raised by this message of contemplatives of the modern world. Do we have any depth of experience that we can communicate to the modern world in its own terms? Or should we just assume that the modern world is so far out that it does not deserve any message from us?

Is the contemplative merely there to create a sense of stability, devoutness, piety and peace? Is his the message of confidence that what has been is still going on and will continue to go on? He may indeed comfort you with such a message, but when he stops talking and when you start reflecting on all he has said, you realize that what has been is not going to go on. What has been has ended. We hope certainly that some of the qualities of that kind of interior life will continue. We would hate to lose the qualities of simplicity and devotion and piety and all that. But the message of our venerable and ancient system is not good enough. Its emphasis is almost always on something secondary. The emphasis is not on the deep realities of life. You may say our contemplative speaks of the cross and so forth—well, the cross is certainly not secondary. But it is too often seen from the point of view of the secondary. So much is taken for granted, so much is assumed. When the cross is spoken of in the context of what one might call milieu Catholicism (that is to say, in which a Catholic milieu is taken for granted), then we assume that all the big things are taken care of by the milieu, and we are only responsible for minor details. The basic problems of life are taken for granted as having been solved years ago, and nobody even raises them any more. In that context the cross, instead of being a deep mystery which shakes the very depths of man's being in death and resurrection, becomes a matter of not blowing your top when somebody is late. The cross is a matter of being patient when you have to wait outside the abbot's office.

The "contemplative life" is then reduced to little things like: learning to become a man of interior prayer by making good use of the moments when you just have to kick your heels waiting for something to happen—or for someone to provide something you need (and will maybe never get)—or for someone in authority to notice you are there and pat you on the head and say you are a good boy. The cross is emptied of all seriousness by this kind of fiddling around, even though from a certain point of view it's not fiddling around. It can only appear serious within the context of a well-established, stable society, a Christian bourgeois society which is firmly built on its foundation which shall never be shaken. But that has ended. The foundations are thoroughly shaken. That kind of society no longer exists. We're living in a world in revolution. The foundations of everything familiar are menaced, and if in the midst of this the mystery of the cross means practicing patience and offering it up, and so forth, when you're sitting in front of a man's office in order to get permission to do something that you ought to have sense enough to do for yourself, it becomes ludicrous in the eyes of the modern world. Therefore if the message of contemplatives to the modern world springs from something as trivial as this— even though it may be using big words like cross, death, resurrection, prayer, contemplation, vision—it's going to be ridiculous! It's not going to touch anybody. They don't want any part of it. If this is contemplation, then we might as well pick up our marbles and go home.

The Sacrifice of Security

Let us now face the question of how badly we need renewal and how little the renewal is really taking place. We don't even know where to begin this renewal. It has to be our renewal, not just simply a renewal which introduces the active life into the cloister. We cannot seek the same kind of renewal as is sought in the active orders because we have a different job to do in the Church. True, we're all going back to the gospel; but nowhere in the gospel are we told that the mystery of the Cross and the mystery of the Resurrection and so forth are reduced to the little formalities to which we have reduced them. Nor is renewal simply a question of broadening out within the enclosure wall and just fitting a more liberal and more relaxed spirituality into the framework of offices and duties. Nor is it a matter of unending dialogue about those same offices and duties. Renewal means much more than that. You who are interested enough in this matter to be reading and I who am trying to develop these ideas are all involved together in a very crucial search for the realities of renewal. We are trying to see what demands are really going to be made on us. We want to estimate those demands properly and objectively. We want to be ready to pay the price—and the price here is not going to be just a matter of gritting our teeth and following orders that we instinctively realize to be beside the point!

It may be the price of sacrificing our security, *sacrificing the psychological stability we have built on foundations that we do not dare to examine.* We have to examine those foundations even though it will mean unrest, even though it will mean loss of peace, even though it will mean disturbance and anguish, even though it may mean the radical shaking of structures.

Certain structures need to be shaken, certain structures have to fall. We need not be revolutionaries within our institutions. Nowadays one sees too much of the neurotic rebel in the cloister, the neurotic who is interminably complaining about everything and has absolutely no intention of substituting anything positive for all this negation, the person who is always discontented and automatically throwing the blame for everything on somebody else—we don't need that. But on the other hand we don't want to go to the other extreme and just simply be ostriches, refusing to see that these institutions are in many respects outdated and that perhaps renewal may mean the collapse of some institutional structures and starting over again with a whole new form.

There have perhaps been some unwise attempts at experimental foundations. In a few months they have proved to be pathetic: but that does not mean that we must not continue searching for new ways. On the other hand (now I really am rambling), we have to remember that there is an order in these things and that you do not sit down and start writing a new rule first thing of all. The writing of new rules should be the *last* thing of all. What one needs to do is to start a conversion and a new life oneself, insofar as one can. Thus, my new life and my contribution to a renewal in monasticism begin within myself and in my own daily life. My work for renewal takes place strictly in my own situation here, not as a struggle with the institution but in an effort to renew my life of prayer in a whole new context, with a whole new understanding of what the contemplative life means and demands. Creativity has to begin with me and I can't sit here wasting time urging the monastic institution to become creative and prophetic. To begin with there is really not much change to be expected within the framework of the institution. It can change so much and no more. After that the structure won't take any more change. So it is useless lamenting over the fact that it can't be more creative. It's useless lamenting over the fact that the best people continue to leave, and it's useless building hopes on illusory token changes which are after all a little petty. What each one of us has to do, what I have to do, is to buckle down and really start investigating new possibilities in our own life; and if the new possibilities mean radical changes, all right. Maybe we need radical changes for which we may have to struggle and sweat some blood. Above all we must be more attentive to God's way and God's time, and give everything when it is really demanded.

We, the supposedly "contemplative" monks, need renewal as much as everybody else and we've got to do it ourselves. We have to find out for ourselves what we're supposed to be doing. We cannot sit around waiting for somebody else to tell us. You who read this are yourselves studying possibilities of renewal. Let me encourage you as a brother to forget about other people who are supposed to help you do it. Do it yourself with the help of the Holy Spirit. Find out what you are really looking for in the spiritual life. What did you really come to the cloister for? Why do you want to be a Carmelite, a Trappist, a contemplative? What are you seeking? Are you seeking security or are you seeking God? Are you seeking pleasant experiences or are you seeking the truth?

Are we seeking the truth that is to make us free? Are we seeking the truth of Christ? Are we responding to the Word of God which breaks through all structures of human life and institutions? These are the things which we have to ask ourselves. We can hardly expect others to answer these things for us!

The important thing for us is to clarify our aims and to rethink not only the accidentals but even the essentials of the contemplative life—in the sense of rethinking our aims, our motives and ends. What do we come to the contemplative life for? Each of us may have a different answer. And let us not make the mistake of imagining ourselves rethinking the life in order to *re-legislate* it. In other words, let us not kid ourselves by talking now and living later. If our rethinking is valid it is also a re-living. Don't let's get lost in words. Let's live now. Let us not project ourselves too far ahead. Let us live in the present. Our rethinking of the contemplative life is part of our present contemplation. Our new life will emerge from authenticity *now*. This is not merely an empty moment of transition. We are not in an interval of dynamic reconstruction in which we are simply going to put back together again a static life in which we will rest. Our rest is in the reconstruction itself. Transition is also fullness. We can have a certain personal fullness even when the changing institution is provisional, and we have to learn to be able to be contemplatives in the midst of the dynamic, in the midst of movement.

We can do this without being obsessed by the movement, without being too conscious of ourselves in movement. We can live happily in change, not worrying about change. Change is one of the big facts of all life. If we're not able to be contemplatives in the midst of change, if we insist on being contemplatives in some completely stable situation which we imagine we are going to construct in the future, then we're never going to be contemplatives.

So let's move on in a quiet, confident way and be content. Let us not try to be too conscious of ourselves moving and not demand that everything be secure. Let us first live in Christ, fully open to his Spirit, unconcerned about institutional security, free from all care for ideal structures that will never be built, and content with the Dark Night of faith in which alone we are truly secure because truly free!

Contemplative Life

What do we think the contemplative life is? How do we conceive it? As a life of withdrawal, tranquillity, retirement, silence? Do we keep ourselves apart from action and change in order to learn techniques for entering into a kind of static present reality which is there and which we have to learn how to penetrate? Is contemplation an objective static "thing," like a building, for which there is a key? Do you hunt for this key, find it, then unlock the door and enter? Well, that is a valid image from a certain point of view, but it isn't the only image.

The contemplative life isn't something objective that is "there" and to which, after fumbling around, you finally gain access. The contemplative life is a dimension of our subjective existence. Discovering the contemplative life is a new self-discovery. One might say it is the flowering of a deeper identity on an entirely different plane from a mere psychological discovery, a paradoxical new identity that is found only in loss of self. To find one's self by losing one's self: that is part of "contemplation." Remember the gospel, "He who would save his life must lose it."

The contemplative experience originates from this totally new kind of awareness of the fact that we are most truly ourselves when we lose ourselves. We become ourselves when we find ourselves in Christ. Our contemplative vocation can become perverse and selfish if we are surreptitiously using tricks and bad faith. Bad faith for us consists in trying to play around with this concept of finding ourselves by losing ourselves. Bad faith wants to learn some trick way of losing ourselves so that we find ourselves and we come out on top in the end. This is one source of the self-deception and frustration that are so frequent in the contemplative life. Consequently, one of the basic rules is that it is always a gift of God. It is always something for which we must learn how to wait. But it is also something which we must learn to *expect actively*. The secret of the contemplative life is in this *ability for active awareness,* an active and expectant awareness where the activity is a deep personal response on a level which is, so to speak, beyond the faculties of the soul.

Contemplative prayer is a deep interior activity in the very roots of our being in response to God who has the initiative and yet draws us into certain very subtle forms of obedient initiative on our own side. This combination of initiative and expectant passivity is different in different people. So many things enter into it. In the renewal of the contemplative life we must not narrow down the possibilities for individual development as we have done in the past.

In the past, the contemplative life was proposed in a rather rigid, formal sort of way. You entered the contemplative life by making a list of things which you were going to drop, so to speak. You took the world and all its possibilities and you just crossed everything off the list. You crossed off the joys of human love, you crossed off the joys of art, music, secular literature, enjoyment of beauties of nature, enjoyment of natural recreation, sports, swimming. All these things you just discarded: and when you had crossed everything off the list, then the one great thing was left, the *unum necessarium,* the one thing necessary!

I think we have to radically reevaluate our whole view of this "one thing necessary." The one thing necessary is not that which is left when everything is crossed off, but it is perhaps that which includes and embraces everything else, that which is arrived at when you've added up everything and gone far beyond. I don't want to put it in a quantitative way however. Of course you understand, in reality the crossing-off process was supposed to be an elimination of a quantitative view, in order to get down to a strictly qualitative approach. You were supposed to end up not with what was *most* but with what was *best.* I think we should aim for the most as well as the best but not the most and the best *outside* ourselves. The most and the best *in* ourselves. Here I think we need a great deal of subtlety and flexibility in recognizing the real vital possibilities of each individual in the contemplative life. Contemplative discipline is both hard and flexible. The contemplative life should be a life in which there is austerity. There has to be a real challenge. It's got to be a tough life. This business of just softening up the contemplative life is foolish. In fact it means the end of all contemplation. But the contemplative life has to be tough in such a way that it's also livable. The toughness of the contemplative life should not be that restricting toughness which arbitrarily rules out good possibilities. It should be a toughness that tones us up to meet new possibilities, the unexpected, that for which we have not been previously capable, for which we have not been previously ready.

In other words, the toughness of the contemplative life was to lift us above ourselves, above our capacities. A life of self-transcendence must be hard—hard and rewarding, not hard and frustrating.

This should give us some insight into the new way of asceticism, a rewarding hardness, a hardness that brings you out. The kind of hardness you get in football when you have to really *play*. So a re-evaluation of our aims in the contemplative life should, I think, take this new form of not simply assuming, to begin with, that we have crossed off all kinds of possibilities.

Art comes to mind here. By "art" I don't mean fiddling around, please! There is always a temptation to diddle around in the contemplative life, making itsy-bitsy statues. If this is wanted as a legitimate recreation, as a relaxation, or as occupational therapy, let's be honest and call it occupational therapy.

Yet art in the contemplative life can really open up new capacities and new areas in the person of the contemplative. Everything depends on how it is used. The real key is guidance and direction and selectivity. The contemplative life is extremely selective. One of the things that has ruined the contemplative life has been the leveling process which has eliminated this selective quality, this capacity for creative personal judgment in special cases. The contemplative life has become a kind of assembly line on which everybody is put together according to one pattern. This is utterly deadly, and of course it kills selective judgment.

The lack of qualitative judgment, of taste, of personal discrimination, of openness to new possibilities, is bound up with one great defect—a failure of imagination. Our prayer itself is poor in imagination. The pragmatic and legalistic approach to the religious life in general, and to the contemplative life in particular, has resulted in a dreadful banality. Creativity has not been desired, imagination has been discouraged, and emphasis has been on submission of will, accepting the incomprehensible stupidity of a mechanical existence instead of thinking of a realistic way of improving things. But the solution is not in changing observances and practices, or in changing laws. The solution lies deeper, in the life of prayer. If what goes on inside our minds and hearts is banal, trivial, petty and unimaginative, we cannot be creative in our outer works. So much that is new and experimental is proving to be a frightful letdown because it is so second-rate, so superficial, so imitative. And so much of it is in the worst possible taste—as many of our old pieties were also in the worst taste.

The Imagination

Let us consider now whether the imagination has a place in the contemplative life. The imagination is one of the things we have tended to rule out of the contemplative life, largely in reaction against its formalized use in systematic meditation. Most of us, I suppose, ran into a period of revolt against the formalized use of the imagination in systematic "composition of place" and that sort of thing.

Here we must distinguish. I would say that a deliberate use of imagination in prayer might perhaps be a good thing for people who have weak imaginations, whose imagination has never been developed in any way at all. They might profitably be encouraged to exercise their imagination a little. But they must exercise it, not just follow a book written by someone whose imagination has gone dead.

I spoke a moment ago about ruling out everything in order to arrive at contemplation. Those of us who have read St. John of the Cross remember the chapters of the *Ascent of Mt. Carmel* where he strongly emphasizes the fact that anything that can be imagined or apprehended by the inner or outer senses has nothing to do with God. Whatever can be "seen" cannot be God. Therefore it is better to withdraw from imaginative activity in contemplative prayer, and of course that's true.

On the other hand, imagination has an important part to play in our lives. We all know that when imagination is not constructively used, is not creatively used, it uses itself destructively. It works whether we want it to or not, and one of the places where we all run into imagination is in distractions. Because of the constant struggle with distractions we tend to take an excessively negative view of the imagination.

Some people cannot abide to have distractions. Their imagination works automatically, creating distractions, and then they hate themselves for it. Their whole life is reduced to a despairing struggle with distractions which, of course, makes distractions worse.

Distractions are produced by the imagination, and in many people distractions are worse because their imagination has nothing constructive, nothing creative to work on. For some people the great cross of distraction and imagination is the fact that imagination, when not constructively used, has a tendency to fix itself on what we call "impure" images. Now, perhaps I might mention in passing that this should just be ignored. To begin with, no image is impure. It is neither pure nor impure. There is nothing "wrong" or "dirty" about images. The wrong lies in a disordered affection of the will. A mere image is never impure, it's neutral. The thought of a part of a body is not impure, it just *is,* that's all.

I am speaking about imagination that doesn't have any constructive outlet. It is important for us to find creative outlets and work for the imagination. Imagination has to be sublimated, not necessarily in prayer but certainly elsewhere. Where are some of the fields where we can find work for the imagination! Well, obviously the first thing that suggests itself is in reading the Bible. There is plenty in the Bible that appeals to the imagination, and the psalms are full of imagination. Anything poetic, anything literary, anything creative, in that sense, is full of imagination.

Imagination has the creative task of making symbols, joining things together in such a way that they throw new light on each other and on everything around them. The imagination is a discovering faculty, a faculty for seeing relationships, for seeing meanings that are special and even quite new. The imagination is something which enables us to discover unique present meaning in a given moment of our life. Without imagination the contemplative life can be extremely dull and fruitless.

Remember also that imagination doesn't just create fictions. These are *real* meanings that the imagination discovers, not just delusions. Yet of course they can be delusory, and this is another problem. You see, with imagination you also need judgment. Imagination needs to be corrected with a certain intellectual estimate, first of all on a prudential level and, then, also on an artistic level.

We have to consider the artistic truth of things that are brought together by imagination. This, in fact, is what is wrong very often with a crazy imagination. There can be a beauty in a deliberate grotesque and bizarre effect, but then one must be able to be conscious of this. But when imagination goes haywire in the contemplative life people get slightly nutty. They come to you with grotesque illusions, idiotic and often extremely complicated hang-ups—visions, voices, pseudoprophecies, and take them very seriously in the wrong way. This is work of the imagination, and from a certain point of view you can regard it as creative in a nutty sort of way. But they are drawing wrong conclusions from it. They are rationalizing and verbalizing.

The contemplative life should not lead us just to suppress the imagination in order to get more pure messages from God. We must allow both for a contemplative prayer in which the imagination has little or no part and for a creative, imaginative, genuinely poetic side in our life. Our imagination must be able to click and find correspondences, symbols and meanings. It should point up new meanings. It should create nuclei of meaning around which everything can collect significantly.

So when we talk about using the imagination in this particular way we imply a certain training or discipline of the imagination. This training should not be a matter of exterior compulsion, the domination of imagination by intellect and will. There are times of course when that is necessary. But the imagination should be allowed a certain freedom to browse around, find its own spontaneous material and work with that material. The intelligence and will should go along with it meanwhile—permissively, so to speak.

The training of the imagination implies a certain freedom, and this freedom implies a certain capacity to choose and to find its own appropriate nourishment. Thus in the interior life there should be moments of relaxation, freedom and "browsing." Perhaps the best way to do this is in the midst of nature, but also in literature. Perhaps also a certain amount of art is necessary, and music. Of course we have to remember our time is limited and first things have to come first. We can't spend too much time just listening to music.

You also need a good garden, and you need access to the woods, or to the sea. Get out in those hills and really be in the midst of nature a little bit! That is not only legitimate, it is in a certain way necessary. Don't take your cloister concept too materially. Of course now I may be running into all kinds of problems with constitutions. But the woods and nature should be part of your solitude, and if it's not periodically part of your solitude I think the law should be changed.

Liberating the Imagination

The contemplative life should liberate and purify the imagination which passively absorbs all kinds of things without our realizing it; liberate and purify it from the influence of so much violence done by the bombardment of social images. There is a kind of contagion that affects the imagination unconsciously much more than we realize. It emanates from things like advertisements and from all the spurious fantasies that are thrown at us by our commercial society. These fantasies are deliberately intended to exercise a powerful effect on our conscious and subconscious minds. They are directed right at our instincts and appetites, and there is no question but that they exercise a real transforming power on our whole psychic structure. The contemplative life should liberate us from that kind of pressure, which is really a form of tyranny. It should subject our imagination passively to *natural* influences. There has been in the past a certain danger of unnatural influences and sick fantasies in the cloister itself. So often in cloistered life we have seen people simply imprisoned in an atmosphere of total ugliness, the pious ugliness of sick statuary and sentimental holy cards. There has been a great deal of house cleaning in various religious orders, and in the Church in general, in regard to bad art and bad influences on the imagination. In training the imagination we should work with the inexhaustible supply of images in the Bible, for example. Take a certain passage of the Bible and simply be fully conscious, completely aware of what is addressed to the imagination. *See* it and *grasp* it and *experience* it with the inner senses. Liturgy, too, is a favored means (at least ideally) for this education of all the senses and of the whole man.

Our imagination should be spontaneous, but it should not always be completely unconscious or instinctive. Certainly a contemplative has to be liberated from a completely mechanical imagination. The imagination needs a certain critical reflection, a certain conscious awareness, a certain, let us say, conscious freedom of judgment in its exercise. The healthy imagination is one which can spontaneously move itself to what it likes *better*—consciously aware, not self-consciously. Let's make that distinction! The imagination moves in a state of conscious awareness but not in self-conscious examination of itself, not watching itself act but simply acting in full and joyous consciousness of the fact that it acts.

When reading the Bible your imagination should be distinctly aware of the images, the pictures presented to it. Besides taking account of these separate elements, it should also see how they are fused together in a symbolic unity, in what the Germans call a *Gestalt*, a form made by things converging in a new living unity. Train yourself to see those things when you are reading the Bible.

Don't think that every time you read the Bible you must always be getting the loftiest possible theological sense! In the Bible, theology is embedded in material images, and if you don't see the images you don't get the theological sense completely. The theological sense is not only an intellectual message addressed purely to the mind, a purely speculative meaning. There are meanings in the Bible which are communicated in concrete, living, material imagery, in material elements, fire, water, etc. One has to be sensible, sensitive, sensitized to the material qualities of these things in order to get the divine message.

Catholic Pessimism

The English Benedictine Dom Sebastian Moore, in a book called *God Is a New Language,* frankly discusses what he calls "a Catholic neurosis." He hits some nails pretty squarely on the head. He is talking (among other things) about life in Catholic institutions. He talks about how a layman teaching in a Catholic school may complain quite justly of the fact that he is dealt with in a very dishonest and devious sort of way by the religious who are running the school. They won't meet things squarely. Instead of telling him directly and frankly about something, they try to get it to him through a lot of other people. Then, they think, there won't be any argument!

That happens in monasteries, too. Superiors, not wanting to run into open conflict with subjects, don't tell them directly what they want to tell them. They avoid confrontation and try to get it to the subject indirectly or by hints. You get rumors about what the superior thinks rather than hearing from him personally. And you are somehow expected to act on the rumor. An "obedience" based on this kind of thing is pretty equivocal! But that is not the point. The point that he brings up is of great value for contemplatives because it is one of the curses of our cloistered life.

Sebastian Moore talks about a kind of Catholic pessimism. It is related to the disgust and despair and discouragement we get in the contemplative life. This sense of frustration and hopelessness is due to the conditions of the life. This is something that we've really got to learn how to deal with. He says:

The effect of being continually exposed to the truth which is doing one no good is distressing to the soul. There can even result a kind of unbelief, an exhaustion of the spirit which is all the worse for being partly unconscious.

He relates this to the medieval concept of acedia, a kind of spiritual lassitude approaching despair. This is one of the curses of the contemplative life, and we have not even begun to know how to deal with it. "The effect of being continually exposed to the truth which is doing one no good!"

Now let's make a distinction here. Does he mean continually exposed to an *ideal* which is held up before us and which, we feel, is doing us no good? An occupational disease of contemplatives consists in this unconscious conviction that we are in the presence of wonderful spiritual values which aren't reaching us. Somehow we are failing them; we are never quite measuring up.

One of the ways of reacting is to deny that this is happening at all or to get around it in some equivocal way—by verbalizing or rationalizing. The classic example of this is the old Latin choir in which one doesn't understand what one's saying, and the classic "solution" is to make an act of pure intention. The will to mean it is equivalent to meaning it even though you do not understand. Thus it becomes a sacrifice of praise, the prayer of the Church, etc. There is of course some truth in this: but not enough truth to serve as a solid foundation for one's *whole contemplative life!* Now, the key word here is *alienation.* To be alienated is to be a prisoner in something of which you cannot possibly take an active personal part. This accounts for the kind of choir neurosis that people get into. There is a deep resistance that gradually develops against a thing in which one is participating and yet *not* participating.

This is aggravated by an overemphasis on the ideal and on the wonderful values that are present—that we are missing. The ideal is extolled and magnified until it gets to be so great, so superhuman, that we *can't* participate in it. Besides, it is all presented in a completely abstract sort of way. We see with our mind that these values are there. We're told that these values are there and we believe it. We're constantly reproached for not measuring up, and we believe that too. We become obsessed by it. This is all done in an abstract sort of way so that you have to have a peculiar kind of intellect and a peculiar kind of will to be able to measure up to this inhuman challenge. You have to be able to believe in pure, disembodied, mathematical willpower (helped by an abstract kind of grace!). Hence the sense of awful futility, of being confronted with something that we're not measuring up to. Here is this immense truth and it is not getting through to us!

And yet, on the other hand, there is a great deal of this truth around that *could* get through to us. But we are not paying attention because we've not been trained to pay attention. We would even feel guilty for paying attention to it. We think it is not supernatural enough! Here again we neglect the imaginative content of some of the things that we live with all the time, the Bible for example. The imaginative and human appeal of the Bible and the liturgy is something that we completely bypass. We do not pay attention to it because we suppose that it is something inferior, and we "want only the best." So we bypass a value which we *could* participate in and could experience. Take the joy of singing in choir. Of course that gets knocked out of us because when we sing we are apt to ruin the whole choir! Still, that is what the choir is for. People should be able to enjoy the singing and enjoy what's going on! But perhaps when they enjoy it, they make it intolerable for other people, so there is a problem. We have to face the fact, but we would be able to get to a lot of these values quite easily and quite simply if we would just be natural about them.

But we are told *not* to be natural. If you are taking a *natural* pleasure in something it is not *supernatural,* and that's wrong. I think we should be able to take these natural pleasures and realize that they're not opposed to the supernatural at all. They are a means of entering into contact with the real spiritual values which are given to us. We should not be afraid to make use of them. Then we might better face this situation of frustrating alienation in the religious life, this feeling that we're constantly exposed to an immense truth which is not coming through and is not getting to us. We're not responding to it on levels on which we could respond. We are attempting to respond on impossible levels. This is a highly destructive situation, and when a person lives under this day after day the whole thing gets to be incomparably sick. People saying over and over again what these great values are, etc., and nobody experiencing them at all. For you realize that the person who is giving you this enthusiastic pep talk doesn't experience them either. Better just to smell a flower in the garden, or something like that, than to have an unauthentic experience of a much higher value. Better to honestly enjoy the sunshine or some light reading than to claim to be in contact with something that one is not in contact with at all.

So, therefore, I would say that it is very important in the contemplative life *not to overemphasize the contemplation*. If we constantly overemphasize those things to which access is inevitably quite rare, we overlook the ordinary authentic real experiences of everyday life as real things to enjoy, things to be happy about, things to praise God for. But the ordinary realities of everyday life, the faith and love with which we live our normal human lives, provide the foundation on which we build those higher things. If there is no foundation, then we have nothing at all! How can we relish the higher things of God if we cannot enjoy some simple little thing that comes along as a gift from him! We should enjoy these things and then we will be able to go on to more rare experiences. Take the enjoyment of our daily bread. Bread is true, isn't it? Well, I don't know. Maybe one of the troubles with modern life is that bread is no longer true bread. But around here, in this monastery, we have pretty good bread. Things that are good are good, and if one is responding to that goodness one is in contact with a truth from which one is getting something. The truth is doing us good. The truth of the sunshine, the truth of the rain, the truth of the fresh air, the truth of the wind in the trees, these are *truths*. And they are always accessible! Let us be exposed to these in such a way that they do us good because these are very accessible forms of truth, and if we allow ourselves to be benefited by the forms of truth that are really accessible to us instead of rejecting and disparaging and despising them as "merely natural," we will be in a better position to profit by higher forms of truth when they come our way.

Natural Problems

Another point raised by Sebastian Moore: sometimes our ordinary personal and human problems are treated in terms of the highest kind of ethical or religious crisis. Dom Sebastian points out that if all ordinary difficulties are always faced on the highest religious level as crucial problems, matters of life and death in the realm of faith and morals—if they are always treated as ultimate crises, we are never able to get to grips with them on our own personal level.

Suppose a person has difficulty coming to terms with some truth of faith. If this is immediately treated as a religious crisis of the highest order instead of as a personal and even psychological problem, it may be impossible to solve it. Perhaps it is not a problem at all on that religious level. It may not be a problem of sin, for example. If every problem that comes up is immediately treated in terms of sin and betrayal, our grasp of it may be totally unreal. Of course it *may* be a matter of sin. But let us not confuse a feeling of anxiety or insecurity with a sense of moral guilt. If we automatically assume that every little anxiety is the sign of a moral problem and then try to deal with it as a moral problem we may end up in the most awful confusion—and completely without reason. There is usually no need at all for the moral anguish we create over certain problems.

We ignore an important, psychological, natural element which may really be the thing at issue in this particular case of this particular person. The solution of the problem may well not be in the confessional, not on a moral level, not on a religious level. It may not be a matter of faith and it may not involve one's friendship with God at all. It is quite possibly a psychological, natural, emotional problem, something that could be more easily solved on a simple, human level. Some people just can't stand to have their problems on this lower level—they prefer a full-scale crisis because it makes them feel more "Christian"!

The confessor very often does not realize this. Or he may grasp it intuitively, without knowing how to tell the penitent. We have a penitent who is bothered by this kind of problem that is not really a moral problem and, yet, is an acutely anguishing problem nevertheless. He or she goes to confession with the problem, and the confessor realizes that this is neither a moral nor a religious problem. So he simply dismisses it. Then the person gets extremely worried about this because, for him or for her, it really is a problem. That is to say, it causes an experience of real insecurity and anxiety. Now, what the priest is saying is not that this is no problem, but that it is nothing to worry about in confession. But he may brush it off as completely absurd, so that the penitent now feels guilty about having a problem. What he should really be saying is, "Look, this is not a *religious* problem; this is not a moral problem, and this is not a matter of sin. Your friendship with God is not involved here, and even though you may feel that it is, it isn't. This has nothing to do with your friendship with God."

What we really need to learn is how to face and handle this sort of thing on a *natural* level. This is a *natural* problem, and we have to get in touch with the natural values in ourselves that are the resources with which to meet problems like this—for instance, the resources of growing up. Problems of this kind are often problems of maturity and problems of human experience. The real trouble with many religious is that authentic human experience is sidetracked or short-circuited in the convent. One is not allowed to be an ordinary human being because one is always supposed to be living on the superhuman level. One must always be on an intense level of religious crisis or about to lose one's vocation or one's faith. As a result, some people are driven in sheer desperation to "lose their vocation" and get it over with!

But we always have to remember that all problems are illusory without some basis of natural maturity and a natural human growth. It is very important to stress these natural values. We must constantly emphasize the importance of *growing up*. Needless to say, we must not go to the other extreme and make everything an intense psychological problem. There are real religious problems which are not just psychological problems; but they may be more rare than we realize. Many religious are just not mature enough to have an authentic religious crisis!

To sum up, I would say that it is essential for us contemplatives to really hang on to the essentials of our vocation. We must face the fact that we are called to be contemplatives. If there is a real threat to our contemplative life, we must resist that threat. We must refuse to be involved in useless and foolish substitutes for the contemplative life. At the same time, we cannot possibly hang on to a dead formalistic set of pseudocontemplative routines. The contemplative life has to be renewed, and it has to be renewed *from within*. It has to be renewed by us with the help of the Holy Spirit. This is no time for fooling around, and it is no time for being unduly influenced by the slogans of people who don't know our problems. It is possible that a great deal of the conflict that is going on in the Church today is marked by neurosis. Between the obsessive compulsive formalisms of some conservatives and the adolescent autistic thinking of some progressives, the Church today does at times seem a little bit mad! It's for us to keep our sanity, if we possibly can, and to keep a certain amount of lucidity and a genuine fidelity to God's call. Let us keep alive especially the awareness of what is really authentic within our own experience because we know, we have experienced in moments of prayer, in moments of truth and realization, what God really asks of us and what he really wishes to give us. Let us remain faithful to that truth and to that experience.

What Is Monastic?

Let us now try to clear the ground for a better approach to our problems as contemplatives. The main problem is of course the renewal of the contemplative life. Our first question concerns, precisely, the term "contemplative." Should the term "contemplative religious" be used at all? There seems to be some protest about the term "monastic." I find this in a letter which I am taking as my starting point. Reference is made to a sister who protested against the word "monastic." The sister is quoted as saying: "I think that what I am objecting most to is the monasticism that has been imposed upon us and has become part of our structure."

Since I do not know this sister and do not know exactly in what situation the statement was made, I cannot quite comment on it. This letter comes from a Franciscan milieu, and the complaint against monasticism being "imposed" upon others, which is very common and in many cases a justified complaint today, usually arises in the active life and in priestly life, and even in lay life where a monastic form of spirituality has historically tended to prevail since the Middle Ages. As if sanctity for a lay person or for a secular priest consisted in living somewhat like a monk. I think perhaps it would be worthwhile to discuss a little what we mean by the monastic life and also, by implication, the contemplative life.

What is the best way to approach this whole question? There is no point in just giving a definition of the essence of a monk and the essence of a contemplative and so forth. Let us rather approach it from a kind of phenomenological viewpoint. This is a more modern way of looking at it. Let us consider the different kinds of aspiration and vocation which draw people to the particular life that we are leading. What induces them to seek among us something that they particularly want? What brings them here to do, together with us, something that they particularly need to do? What is it that they feel will give their life its true meaning as their personal response to God's call? In other words, let us consider the kind of thing people have traditionally wanted to do in a cloistered life, a life apart from the world, separated from the world.

In all religious life the postulant gets into a special relationship with civil society: a kind of relationship of *opposition* in some way or other with the rest of the world. This is central in all traditional forms of "dedicated life," but it's most central in the so-called contemplative and cloistered orders. After all, when you talk about "cloistered life" you are defining a life (perhaps very unsatisfactorily) in terms of "separation from the world." Of course, this whole idea of separation from the world is a big problem of our time. We have to be not only separated *from* the world but also *open* to it. Let us take for granted that when we talk about separation from the world we are not talking about a fanatical hatred of the world or anything like that.

The whole question of defining our precise relation to the world is another problem which will have to be treated somewhere else. But no matter how we look at it, when we talk about the kind of life that we have in fact embraced we are talking about a life which involves leaving the ordinary life that we knew before in order to do something else which we consider to be better because it is free from certain obstacles and hindrances. We have left our homes and families and civil life and our jobs (if we had them). We have left the university or wherever else we were. We have left our former kind of life and taken on the kind of life that we have now. Doubtless every single one of us has at one time or other stopped to consider whether this was really worthwhile. Certainly one of the great problems in the religious life today is this question: Has it been worthwhile in terms of authenticity, reality, integrity, and so forth, for me to leave that other kind of life and embrace *this* kind of life? Is this really more real? Is this more authentic?

Very often you find people solving this question, or trying to solve it, by going from a more active kind of religious life to what we provisionally call a more contemplative life, a more cloistered and hidden kind of religious life. This assumes that one can create certain conditions which are "better," because the experience of generations has shown them to work in a certain way. We assume we can create this set of conditions and get into this new situation ourselves and thereby arrive at something very special to which we are called by God. And so in our cloistered life we try to set up conditions which make it easier and more effective to do something quite special. And what is this that we want to do? Why do we set up these conditions and do these things, and what is it that we are after?

To begin with, I think that you can't say that everybody in the cloister is simply trying to do the same thing. The monastic vocation really allows quite a lot of scope for individual differences; at least it *should* allow quite a lot of scope for the individual to follow a personal call, to follow something that he feels is especially relevant to him.

Historically, in the beginning of the monastic life, you find people called to a kind of special individual union with God which they are supposed to find out about and work out for themselves after an initial period of training. The earliest model for the monastic life is that of the ascetics and virgins who lived apart from their fellow citizens in the towns of the Roman Empire, or outside the towns. These more experienced ascetics would follow their own manner of life, praying and denying themselves and following a hidden quiet way of prayer and worship. They would receive young people who thought they were called to the same kind of thing, give them a rudimentary and individual training, and then turn them loose to carry on for themselves.

Monastic communities came only later. And these early monastic vocations were people who felt that they had an individual call to a particular kind of life. They would go off in the desert to live in a cave or somewhere, or they would take to the road and live as pilgrims and beggars.

The Franciscan way came into the Middle Ages as a salutary revolt against the highly institutionalized monastic system. St. Francis made possible once again an open-ended kind of existence in which there wasn't very much predetermined for you. You were pretty free to do this or that or anything. You could be a pilgrim, you could be a hermit, and you could be a pilgrim for a while and a hermit for a while and then a scholar for a while. Then you could go to the Muslims in North Africa and get yourself martyred if you had the grace! And so forth.

The Franciscan ideal could really be regarded as a return to the authentic freedom of early monasticism. I would venture as a kind of personal guess at this point that actually the ideal of St. Francis was more purely *monastic* in the true original primitive sense than the life lived by the big Benedictine and Cistercian communities of the thirteenth century where everything was so highly organized behind walls.

A Life of Charismatic Freedom

One of the essential elements of the monastic life is a kind of charismatic freedom. This seems to me to be right at the heart of this monastic vocation; and this creates a problem, of course, precisely because the monastic life as we have it is so highly organized. To what extent does this organized and disciplined and systematic life enable a person to attain a certain level of freedom interiorly in order to do what God has called him to do? To say "a life of charismatic freedom" is to speak of a life in which a person is free from certain routine cares and responsibilities and claims and demands which are regarded as less fruitful, as somewhat deadening. The monastic charism seeks to be free from these in order to be more constantly awake, alert, alive, sensitive to areas of experience which are not easily opened up in the midst of the routines which we shall call "worldly routines." On the other hand, of course, we must not develop a sort of magic idea of the contemplative life and say that when a person puts on a certain kind of habit and goes into a certain kind of cloister and lives a certain kind of rule, automatically a deep inner kind of contemplative life follows. This is not necessarily so and the problem of substituting cloister routines for worldly routines can really be an evasion and a falsification of this call to authentic inner freedom. But the point is that the contemplative or monastic life is supposed to liberate a man or a woman from certain routines which are fruitless for them, although perhaps fruitful for other people, in order to let them do something else that they feel they are called to do.

I suppose here we had better say something about freedom. Here we realize that we are in trouble! We cannot possibly take these big words for granted. They call for a great deal of study, a great deal of reflection from all of us collectively and individually. It is definitely not enough to pick up some of the echoes and resonances and emotional implications of a word like freedom as it is bandied around in the religious life. These are loaded words, and they are being used in a way that can be very fruitful and very helpful, but can also be very destructive.

Freedom is also a fighting word, and we have to reflect on the reasons why. Freedom is a fighting word in the religious life today, just as it is in civil life, simply because it has been denied people so consistently and with so many fraudulent excuses. Religious have been abused in this matter like everyone else. Authority has not always been honest in its exercise. "Obedience" has been used to justify almost anything. The time has come to rectify that abuse. But as I say, we have to consider and study what freedom means, especially for us in the contemplative life.

Asceticism

Freedom for what? Obviously the traditional idea, although this has to be examined too, still holds. Traditionally in the monastic life, in the contemplative life and in the ascetic life as a whole, there's a question of asceticism. It is understood that the freedom we seek is a freedom which is purchased at the price of renouncing another kind of freedom. The freedom that we are talking about in the contemplative life and in the monastic life is the freedom which is bought by the renunciation of license or the simple capacity to follow any legitimate desire in any legitimate direction. Besides renouncing illegitimate freedom we also give up a certain lawful autonomy, so that we come face to face right away with the fact that the freedom we look for is bound up with restrictions. Of course, if we're going to consider contemplative freedom intelligently we must go back to the real sources in the New Testament and especially in St. Paul and St. John. I am not going to do that here. The freedom we seek in the contemplative life is to be understood in the light of St. John's statement that the truth shall make you free and St. Paul's statement that we have the freedom of the children of God and the freedom of the Spirit. It is also the freedom which is not under the law. Monastic freedom does not place its hope in the fulfillment of legal routine observances. Therefore it is very important indeed to understand the contemplative life or the monastic life, or whatever form of life you want to call it, in such a way that it does not become a life dominated by law or a life defined by the hope of salvation through good works. We have to take into account the fact that Luther was a religious. They speak of him as a "monk." He was not a monk—the Augustinians are not monks. But Luther was a religious reacting against a decadent religious system and returning to St. Paul. Luther wanted to "return to sources."

Whether we agree with Luther or not is another matter, but Luther is historically important for the religious life of the Catholic Church and for our monastic renewal. Obviously the reforms of the Council of Trent were aimed against Luther, but now we clearly understand also that one of the main points of Vatican II has been an implicit recognition that we are now beyond the Council of Trent. The need for the defensive measures taken at Trent no longer exists. We are in a totally different situation. Without abandoning the historic continuity which links us with the medieval past through Trent, we have to remember that the defensive attitude taken by Trent cannot be what governs and guides us in our religious renewal today.

To return to my point: in the contemplative and monastic life we have sought out a certain kind of solitude and separation from the world for the sake of *freedom*.

Martha and Mary

One of the ways in which the freedom of the contemplative life is expressed is perhaps not very popular today. Still, let us consider this example. We find it in the gospel of Martha and Mary: Martha working to provide the meal which our Lord is to eat and Mary sitting at the feet of the Lord listening to what he has to say. Martha complains that Mary does not help her, and Jesus defends Mary, saying: "Martha, you are solicitous, you are disturbed with many things! Mary has chosen the best part and it shall not be taken from her."

Traditionally this has been explained by the Fathers of the Church, in a way that we all well know, to justify a certain renunciation of good, productive, healthy social activity in order simply to listen to the words of Christ, to be silent and listen to God. Of course this really doesn't solve any problems, yet the use of this text as a justification of the contemplative life does rest on a solid psychological basis, on a basis of real experience which can be verified in the lives of those who have tried to put it into practice and know what it means.

When someone has an authentic call to the contemplative life or to the monastic life, that call can be understood in terms of this gospel text and experienced in the way that is suggested by it. Our vocation can be understood as the resolution of a conflict which is expressed in this story, a conflict in ourselves. Now the important thing is that the conflict is *in ourselves* rather than projected outward into *institutions.* It is one thing to experience in our own lives the difference between the action of Martha and the listening of Mary— but quite another to "prove" that Trappists are "better" than Dominicans!

The fact that this conflict between Martha and Mary became an institutional matter in the thirteenth century does not concern us here; it simply obscures the issue. Ever since that time, there has been a great deal of argument about the respective value of active orders and contemplative orders. This is no longer to the point. Where the conflict resolves itself is in our own hearts as individual persons or small groups, called to this particular life of quiet, of *freedom to listen* to the Word of God in our hearts. We experience in ourselves a new and special kind of truth when we imitate Mary. We who have this particular call recognize that when we are agitated by all kinds of external concerns which do not touch us deeply at all we are less authentic, less real, less ourselves, less what we are supposed to be. We feel less faithful to the will of God than when we remain simply in an attitude of freedom and attentiveness to his word, his love and his will. This gospel text illustrates our experience that we are summoned by the Holy Spirit to make *an act of preference.* We are called to prefer the apparent uselessness, the apparent unproductiveness, the apparent inactivity of simply sitting at the feet of Jesus and listening to him. We are called to prefer this over an apparently more productive, more active, more busy life. We quietly affirm that there is something more important than "getting things done."

Together with this is another implied assumption: that this preference goes against the ideas of the majority of our fellow human beings at any given moment and especially today in the twentieth century. Our act of preference for "quiet" is at the same time an implicit protest and defiance, a protest against and a defiance of the counter-opinion of those who are absolutely convinced that our life is useless and who reproach us for it.

Here we find another piece in the jigsaw puzzle that we are putting together. A very important piece is this element of preferring to be at the feet of Jesus and to listen to him in secret, even though we can't fully explain it to other people. Other people are not going to understand it. Other *good* people are not going to understand it, other Christians and other Catholics. We realize all this and we make our choice anyhow. In this contemplative life of ours, in our monastic existence, we are going against the stream.

The Discipline of Listening

This puts us in a very uncomfortable position. We realize that if we get excited about those who criticize us and devote too much effort to answering them, we become solicitous and troubled about many things and get into a kind of useless activity which conflicts with a deep inner silence and peace which we are called to cultivate as a special kind of discipline. This brings us to another point in this Martha-Mary picture that we are considering. It is an obscure realization which is never emphasized enough. Just remaining quietly in the presence of God, listening to him, being attentive to him, requires a lot of courage and know-how. This discipline of listening and of attention is a very high form of ascetic discipline, a rather difficult one to maintain. In fact, there are lots of people who do not have the strength nor the grace to maintain this kind of discipline for very long. Doubtless when a person is clearly not able to do this, maybe he shouldn't try. Our asceticism will consist in discovering to what extent each one of us can simply remain quiet in passive attention to God and to what extent we do need some activity, some work that does not completely interfere with this but which relaxes us and takes us away from mere concentration. We all need a certain amount of activity that enables us to participate healthily in the life of our community. We need work that keeps us in tune physically and psychologically so that we are able to listen fruitfully instead of just going stale and turning off completely. There is such a thing as overdoing interior prayer and overdoing concentration and overdoing recollection. This can be harmful. It only deadens our capacity to listen and to attend to God.

This we all know. But let us emphasize the fact that our attention to Jesus alone, our listening to his word, our attitude of interior conviction, is something we come to experience as the highest value in our life. Contemplatives are people who experience this. This is in itself a most effective discipline and a most purifying form of ascetic training and formation. In this tranquil, empty, peaceful solitude a person receives quietly, hiddenly and secretly from God a great deal of benefit, simply by listening and quiet attention.

In this connection let me refer to a passage by St. John of the Cross. Speaking of solitude and the benefits of solitude on the soul, and the tranquil listening to God which he calls the "tranquillity of solitude in which the soul is moved and guided to find things by the spirit of God," he says that in this solitude, in this listening, in this tranquil attention to God, God acts directly upon the one who prays, doing it by himself, communicating himself to the soul without other means, without passing through angels, men, images or forms. He adds that in this solitude God and the beloved are together in great intimacy.

> The solitude wherein the soul lives before time was the desire to be without all the blessings of the world for the sake of love.

Now, that is a good definition, or a good indication of something of that choice that I was speaking of—a desire, an active desire to forgo the benefits, privileges, blessings, advantages which are characteristic of a worldly life or an active life. Characteristic, incidentally, of a good worldly life. We do not deny the goodness of all these things, but we renounce their goodness for something else which we see to be better for us, but which does not appear evident at all to anybody else.

Even at the very beginning of a contemplative life, when a person has received this call from God, he does realize obscurely that for him the supreme value of life is going to consist in a surrender directly to God, in the hope and confidence and belief that God will act directly upon him without the intermediary of ordinary active human ideas or agencies. Of course it may be normal and may be fruitful and sanctifying for most people to reach God through the medium of married love and by bringing up children in an active life, and many may find God better in an active apostolic life fully mixed up with the things of time and of the world. This may be a perfectly normal and perhaps in some respects a better way. Certainly it is a way that the rest of the human race appreciates more. Nevertheless, there is for us this mysterious call to a life of direct communion with and dependence upon and guidance by and formation by and purification by God in silence, in prayer, in solitude, in detachment, in freedom.

It is here that we have to seek the real meaning of freedom in the contemplative life. We renounce other forms of freedom in order to have *this* kind of freedom. Therefore it becomes necessary to accept restrictions, restraints, self-denial, sacrifice and so forth, as we have always heard and always known. But it is much deeper than we have always heard. Restriction and sacrifice have to be accepted in order that this inner freedom may grow. Therefore in the contemplative life, in the monastic life, there is necessarily an element of renouncing advantages, renouncing even certain fruitful activities which sanctify people in other vocations, in order to find our expansion and development and rest and peace in a totally different dimension. For a great deal of the time this solitude and listening are painful, difficult, full of hardship and very demanding. The contemplative life is especially demanding because we are alone and unable to explain ourselves to other people. Admittedly this is very hazardous. So many people are not able to handle this isolation, as we know from experience. They crack up! Perhaps we can say that in our life there are many people who do have an authentic appreciation of what this *might be* for them, and yet they are not able to attain to it. We must not blame them. We must not say that it is their fault. We must not say that they have not been generous enough. It is just a fact that few people are able to live in this solitary "desert" for a lifetime. Those of us who recognize ourselves really called to this should be very happy—much more happy than we usually are about it. We should be very grateful to God that he called us to this life and that he has called us to this particular kind of peace in this particular kind of fulfillment, which in so many respects is an unfulfillment and which is almost scandalous to people of our time so intent upon human fulfillment. Yet even they, when they come in contact with people who have lived in a solitary or cloistered life, recognize that there is a special kind of happiness in this life.

Contemplative and Mystic

Let us finally consider the question of using the word "contemplative" for all this. This word, contemplative, is another one that calls for a great deal of reflection and study on our part. There are many problems. First of all, the term "contemplative" is ambiguous. In the debates that were carried on rather hotly in the nineteen-twenties between the Jesuits and the Dominicans in France about the mystical life, mystical graces and contemplative life, the term "contemplative" tended to be used as it had been used for several centuries before with overtones of *mysticism*. Indeed, very often you find that the word "contemplative" is a safer, vaguer, broader and more discreet word for "mystic." Mystic seems to be a more scary word than contemplative. People hesitate to use it. Also mystic tends to suggest women with stigmata and people having visions, or people who have manifestly attained to mystical union in an extraordinary way. As I understand it from having read a lot of the literature on the subject, the word "contemplative" has been rather widely used as a discreet term for persons enjoying a certain low grade of mystical grace which has nothing to do with visions and has nothing to do with anything very special but corresponds to a kind of quiet, unitive and passive absorption in God. This is definitely a special grace of God, which is much more widespread than is usually realized. It is really accessible to lots of people. Doubtless many who receive it cannot stay with it for very long, but nevertheless it is a sort of borderline mystical state.

Now, this use of "contemplation" can be very misleading because if you say we are a "contemplative order," we are a "contemplative community," this is a "contemplative cloister," are you intimating that everybody in the cloister is a mystic of this particular kind? Or that everybody in the cloister *should be* a mystic of this particular kind? The answer is obviously "No!" Nor is anyone asserting that contemplatives in this sense are found only in cloisters. They are found rather widely outside cloisters. There are plenty of housewives with noisy children and all kinds of duties who are leading a contemplative life in this sense. And there are plenty of people teaching in universities or engaged in intellectual life in one form or other who are or can be contemplatives in this sense without very much difficulty.

It is not even necessarily true that life in a contemplative cloister is more propitious to this unitive way of prayer than any other kind of life. It should be, it's designed for that. We have to admit this when we speak of Carmelite cloisters. Obviously St. Teresa meant Carmel to be a place where this kind of contemplative prayer, quasi-mystical prayer, near-mystical prayer, should be not unusual. Nevertheless, we all know from experience that there are lots of people in monasteries and cloisters who do not respond to this kind of thing at all, who are mystified by it or scared by it or upset by it or disturbed by it, and who nevertheless can do very well indeed in a life of service, charity and devotion. This brings us to the important point that the essential of our life is not precisely or chiefly that it disposes us for contemplation in the sense that I have just described but that it produces *a community in which the Spirit can speak to us all in different ways*. The longing for a real evangelical community life is certainly as strong today, above all in the young people who are coming to religious life.

Christian Community

There's nothing wrong whatever in dropping the use of this word "contemplation" completely if we want to look at the whole thing from a different point of view and use a different language—the language of the last chapters of St. John's Gospel, for example. Here the mystical theology, so to speak, of the New Testament is fully exposed in the context of the Last Supper, that is to say, in the ideal, perfect expression of Christian community. And so suppose that the term "contemplation" is unsatisfactory—suppose there are lots of people who are mystified and put off when we express the idea of union with God and direct communion with him in the language of "contemplation." If this insistence on "contemplation" becomes scandalous and difficult for them let us reformulate it in terms of the New Testament. Let us think of it in terms of knowing Jesus, being one of his disciples, being a member of the loving community which is called together in his merciful love, called to share his body and his blood together around the table of the Eucharistic banquet, called to realize in our love for one another and in our love for Jesus his presence in us. Let us consider the fourteenth chapter of St. John, for example, as an expression of the experience of Jesus present to us in our communal life, in the quiet of that cenacle which we have chosen and which is our cloister.

> Do not let your hearts be troubled. Trust in God still and trust in me. There are many rooms in my Father's house. If there were not, I should have told you. I am going now to prepare a place for you and after I have gone and prepared you a place, I shall return to take you with me. So that where I am, you may be too. You know the way and the place where I am going. Thomas said, "Lord, we do not know where you are going, so how can we know the way?" Jesus said, I am the way, the truth, and the life. No one can come to the Father except through me. If you know me, you know my Father too. From this moment, you know him and have seen him. (John 14:1–7)

Our life in our cloistered community is a life in which we should have access to many mansions. Let us always remember that. That should be a kind of Magna Carta of the monastic life. "There are many mansions in my Father's house." Here is a place where we are gathered together, called out of the world in the sense that the disciples were called there to the cenacle with Jesus. Like the disciples we are waiting for him to come and bring us to the place that he has prepared for us. This is the language of the New Testament. This may appeal more to some than the language of "contemplation," but it comes basically down to the same thing, the same experience, Mary's love and total trust in the Lord who promises to manifest his glory to us and in us through the Church.

In this life of waiting and of trusting, of attending entirely to Jesus' will for us and to his love for us, living in simplicity with the brothers and the sisters in the breaking of bread and in mutual love, we learn gradually to experience a new dimension of our Christian life. We come to see not only that we are going somewhere but that we have already arrived and that Jesus is both the way and the truth and the life. He is the beginning and the end, to live in him is to be not only on the way but at the end, to have arrived.

Our life in Christ is all-sufficient. What we have been calling the "contemplative life" is a life of awareness that one thing is necessary, that Jesus is alone necessary and that to live for him and in him is all-sufficient. To live in him pacifies everything. To live in him takes care of everything. To live in him answers all questions even though we don't quite understand or hear the answers.

So when Philip says to him, as we do, "Show us the Father," Jesus replies (and this is our life), "To have seen me is to have seen the Father, so how can you say, let us see the Father? Do you not believe that I am in the Father and that the Father is in me? It is the Father living in me who is doing this work" (John 14:8–10).

This we have to believe in our own life. If we are living in Christ we are, so to speak, face to face with the Father, but we do not know it, and we cannot see him. We have to be content to be face to face with him in a way that we cannot understand or see. But we must realize that Jesus, working in us, is carrying out the Father's work and manifesting the Father to us. "It is to the glory of my Father that you should bear much fruit, and then you will be my disciples. As the Father has loved me, so I have loved you. Remain in my love. If you keep my commandments you will remain in my love, just as I have kept my Father's commandments and remained in his love. I have told you this so that my joy may be in you and your joy may be complete. This is my commandment, love one another as I have loved you. A man can have no greater love than to lay down his life for his friend. I call you friends because I have made known to you everything I have learned from my Father. You did not choose me. No, I chose you and I commissioned you to go out and bear fruit, fruit that will last, and then the Father will give you anything that you ask him in my name. What I command you is to love one another" (John 15:8–17).

Built into all this passage of St. John is the basic idea that if we live by Christ's love in the Christian community, we will experience, obscurely, in some way, what it means that Christ is sent to us from the Father and dwells in us by his Spirit, fulfilling in us the will of the Father, so that what we experience in our communal Christian life is what it means to be united to God in Christ and to be children of God in his Spirit.

We have now considered two aspects of our life, one more personal and solitary, the other more communal. We have emphasized the fact that these are two aspects of the same thing. We do not need to know which one of these is right because they are both right. What we really have to discover for ourselves and for our communities is how to reach the right kind of combination of these two elements so that each one of us will be able to live fully the kind of vocation to which he or she has been called.

Active Service

The word "contemplative" is used both juridically and mystically, and this creates confusion. The term "contemplative life" has become a kind of juridical term synonymous with "cloistered life," and yet it also has mystical overtones. Now, you cannot really have such a thing as a *contemplative institution.* Contemplation simply cannot be institutionalized. In fact you can create a cloistered life with certain laws and regulations, and inside this cloistered life there may be some people who are really called to be contemplatives in the sense of mystics of a very simple kind. There may be other people, perhaps the majority, whose whole life is centered on a kind of simple active service and worship within the cloister, without a thought of mystical prayer. And this is a very special, very real kind of vocation. It emphatically does not want to become involved in active, outside, external concerns and does want, simply, to lead a quiet, well-ordered life in the cloister, centered principally on liturgical worship, on manual work, simple service, and communal life and fraternal charity.

What we have to do at this present point in our study is to realize that when the law talks of the contemplative life it is really thinking of this second class of people, interested more in active service in the cloister than in simple contemplative prayer. Now, it would be a great mistake to oppose these two to each other because, in fact, a person who is called to be a contemplative in the cloister is going to be greatly helped toward that end by living the simple life of service we have been talking about. Also those who live a life of cloistered service and liturgical prayer, with a certain amount of meditation with reading, will come very close to a kind of simple contemplative peace in their hearts which, however, they will experience in a slightly different way. It may be a sense of peace from having done their duty—the peace that comes from living an ordered life, a quiet industrious life of devotion and consecration. Perhaps this simple and active, dutiful and devout peace is what most cloistered religious seek.

The opposition between the two kinds of approach can be exaggerated and cause an unfortunate split in the community. To some extent this is due, I think, to the fact that the active service people lack imagination. They seem to feel that we who have emphasized solitude and contemplation are somehow running them down. There is a kind of "chip on the shoulder" attitude on the part of the active service types—they resent the claims of the more contemplative members of the community, as if on the one hand we claim superiority and on the other are trying to get out of work. So we notice a kind of defensive attitude on the part of some in our monasteries who are good people and work hard. They get a lot of satisfaction out of work, which is fine, but they feel that the "Marys" are shirking their responsibility and are not realistic. They seem to think the "contemplatives" are deceiving themselves and just sitting around twiddling their thumbs in a state of quietism and inertia. There has been a certain amount of tension between the two groups on this account.

And so contemplation, even in the so-called contemplative monasteries, tends always to be in disrepute. Even so-called contemplatives can look upon contemplation as something unrealistic, as if the real point of monastic life were only active cloistered service. Perhaps it is—I'm not coming to any conclusions on this now. I am just sorting out the different manifestations of these two tendencies. Many so-called contemplatives are simply called to a kind of cloistered service, and it is therefore unfortunate that the life should be officially called contemplative because the use of the term is ambiguous for these people and causes a lot of doubt and confusion. In practice they solve it by saying that liturgy is contemplation, and he who is zealous about going to choir on time is a "true contemplative."

Attentiveness to God

I am now talking more particularly to those who really seek a deeper experience of God, a deeper expansion of the religious consciousness, a deeper understanding and knowledge of the things of God through love. A moment ago we described two approaches to the life of Mary, the life of sitting at the feet of Christ. The life of Mary can be seen as a life of solitary listening, solitary attentiveness, interior purification, interior disposability, openness, readiness to be spoken to, an interior sensitivity, an interior awareness, all of which we cultivate in prayer. A person called to this kind of contemplation will quite spontaneously seek more time to be alone, quiet, simply listening to God.

Of course where people go wrong is that they fail to realize that this simple prayer can go on even though one may be at work. This state of attention to God certainly can coexist with a simple kind of action, and the fact that one is not aware of attending to God is perhaps better. It is not necessarily the best and most healthy thing for a person to be sitting quietly, intensely aware of himself as passive. It is better for a person to be somewhat active and not to be aware that anything special is going on, provided that there is no absorption in anything else.

Take the activity of sweeping the floor or washing dishes or chopping wood or cutting grass or something like that: these activities are not distracting. We do not become absorbed in them, and it is quite possible to engage in them without any sense that we are praying or that we are doing anything other than simply doing what we do in such a way that we remain quietly close to God. Now, the point I am trying to get to is this: what this attentiveness to God really means is not just a particular psychological state or a peculiar kind of recollection, but it is part and parcel of the experience of love in everyday life. Consequently love is the thing that really creates unity in the apparent division between the Marthas and the Marys of the cloister. It also creates unity in ourselves—and unites us with *reality*. Maybe the Marthas obscurely realize that when they are giving their bodies and their senses something neutral to do they are at peace and somehow or another united with God, without realizing it or experiencing anything special. They may find that when they sit down and do nothing and simply try to attend to God in a recollected state they become tense and confused, too aware of themselves. The other people, the contemplatives and the Marys, so to speak, are able to do this and enjoy listening to God, and they think perhaps they are better off that way. In actual fact, what happens is that the Marys also enter into great dryness and do not necessarily enjoy or get much sweetness out of this attentiveness to God. But they have to go on with it anyway because they cannot help themselves.

They are called and drawn to this in such a way that they realize that the greatest benefit in their life is going to come from this simple peaceful attentiveness to God even though it is arid and quiet and dry. And they too will learn, as I said, to combine it with simple tasks and manual work. It is also a good thing to be involved in some work that takes your mind off prayer completely, that rests the mind and gives it a change. The mind is not rested by falling into complete inactivity but by varying its activity. This variety is important.

The essential thing in our life is this fact that it be centered on love as sufficient unto itself. Love alone is enough, regardless of whether it produces anything. It is better for love not to be especially oriented to results, to a work to be done, a class to be taught, people to be taken care of in the hospital, or anything like that. In the active life, love is channeled into something that gets results. In the so-called contemplative life, love is sufficient unto itself. It does of course work, it does do things, but in our life the emphasis is on love above everything else, on faith above everything else. Especially on faith above works! The characteristic of our life is that it makes us realize more deeply how much we depend directly on God by faith, how much we depend directly on the mercy of God, how much we depend upon receiving everything directly from him and not through the mediation of our own activity. While we continue to act, we act in such a way that this consciousness of dependence on God is greater, more continual, more all-embracing and more satisfactory than it is in the active life. It is in this that we find our peace. It is in this that we find our whole meaning for existence. What is called the contemplative life is really a life arranged in such a way that a person can more easily and more simply and more naturally live in an awareness of direct dependence on God—almost with the sense of realizing consciously, at every moment, how much we depend on him; and receive from him directly everything that comes to us as a pure gift; and experience, taste in our hearts, the love of God in this gift, the delicacy and the personal attention of God to us in his merciful love, which St. Thérèse of Lisieux brought out so beautifully.

This is of course true to some extent of all religious life. But in other forms of religious life the emphasis tends to be outgoing, centered on what we are doing and on the results we are getting and on the relationships we are setting up with other people; whereas in our life, the so-called contemplative life, the emphasis is on our direct relationship to God and our experience with that relationship, that experience of spiritual childhood, sonship in the spirit. We cultivate a sense of direct dependence on God and look to God in order to receive all from him at every moment.

And this life takes two forms, as I say. Some see it more in terms of a simple service in the cloister, liturgical prayer, and active work around the house. Others see it more in terms of solitary meditation and direct listening. The contrast between these two should not be exaggerated; they're really doing pretty much the same thing, and they should feel that they are sisters to one another, like Martha and Mary. For the medieval writers always ended up by saying that Martha and Mary complete each other and that no community would be a full monastic community if there were not Marthas and Marys together. They are both needed, and the real community is a synthesis of these two aspects of the one monastic life.

Deviations

At this point it might be well to pause and consider the fact that in both these approaches to the hidden life of prayer, the cloistered life, there can be and often are, as we know by experience, deviations and wrong directions. Many people misunderstand both these ways of approaching our life with God, the way of cloistered service and the way of solitary meditative absorption and prayer and listening. Now, the problem is in each case to insure a genuine, living, healthy occupation with God which is based on faith, on real living faith and also on common sense. We must cultivate a realistic and healthy view of human life. It is easy to live *inhumanly* in a cloister, to cultivate a sort of fanatical and compulsive addiction to the practices of cloistered life. Instead of living one's life in a healthy, productive, normal, humble, quiet, matter-of-fact sort of way, on a basis of deep faith, one may get tense and overpreoccupied, overanxious, almost superstitious and fanatical about the things that he or she is doing. The more active people whose life is centered on cloistered service tend to develop a kind of scrupulosity, a kind of obsession with doing everything the right way—they become obsessed with the idea that there is only *one* right way to do it and that's the way it's going to be done by everybody! They are obsessed with what they are doing and in seeing that it is recognized as right by others. In other words, they develop an excessive preoccupation with themselves.

The same thing happens in a different way with the person who tends to prefer a silent, solitary, meditative approach. By way of brief and shorthand identification, I would say that what we are concerned with is people who become unconsciously centered on themselves rather than on God. We find that they develop a kind of cult of themselves, a cult of their own works, their own personality and their own activities. They are engrossed in their own prayers and their own feelings and their own experiences, instead of the cult of God. They're not worshipping God, really. They become, as it were, hypnotized by themselves. And they can do this sometimes with the best will in the world. They can rationalize all this very cleverly as service of God, and it can become really a complicated business, this sort of fanatical involvement in oneself, justified by rationalization in which everything is theoretically ordered to God.

So there are people who are intensely involved in themselves, all tied up in themselves, and rather unpleasant to live with because of this. They take it out in various subtle ways on other people. They justify all this by appealing to God, to faith and to religion. Sometimes passive meditating people are extremely aware of every little thing that disturbs them and become extremely critical of anything that interferes with their absorption in the experience of sweetness that they are having. This is, generally speaking, a sign that there is something wrong somewhere, that the contemplative thing isn't quite as authentic as it appears to be. It is more centered on one's own self than it is on God.

In all cases, we have to remember the basic importance of a good, common-sense, realistic, human view of life; and where this common-sense, human realism is not found it must be cultivated. If it cannot be cultivated, then there is something definitely wrong with that person's vocation. But of course there will always be people who have been to some extent wounded, twisted, and injured by the inhumanity of an abstract kind of life. They will be semi-neurotics who nevertheless get along in the cloister. They can remain in the cloister.

They can be lived with and helped. They can even be of real positive value to the community in spite of their shortcomings. I suppose we could say that in a certain way we are all slightly nuts. We are all a little bit crazy and we all have to get along with one another in spite of our little eccentricities and quirks of character. There is evidently a little bit of the neurotic in almost everybody today. This has to be understood and accepted. Anyway, the great thing is to maintain a healthy atmosphere.

The basic requirement of the contemplative and cloistered life today is this: before all else, before we indulge in asceticism or go on to quiet contemplative absorption in God, we must recognize the need to maintain a healthy human atmosphere and a normal human relationship to one another and to reality in our communities.

This, of course, goes without saying, but it cannot be overemphasized; it's so easily forgotten. People become so tied up in abstract ascetic or contemplative projects, things that they think they ought to do, that they forget the basic reality of living as human beings first of all. We have to be, first of all, healthy, mature, honest, objective, humble men and women before we can go on to be ascetics and mystics and contemplatives. This must never be forgotten, and it has to be continually returned to because it is the foundation on which all the rest is built.

Penance

Now let us take up another very important aspect of the contemplative life. Insofar as it is a life of freedom it has to be a life of penance. This may sound contradictory to those who only take a superficial view of freedom, but when we realize the true depth of the Christian idea of freedom we realize that it is essentially bound up with penance. What our life is supposed to do for us is to guarantee us a certain freedom of spirit. The true freedom of spirit that St. Paul and St. John speak of is the truth that makes us free. The monastic life seeks to provide a certain kind of truth by a really authentic penance. One of the things necessary today in the renewal of our religious life and our contemplative life is the renewal of the spirit of penance. But it has to be a *renewal*, not a return to a concept of strictness which has prevailed for the last two or three hundred years. True penance is more than legalistic strictness, a fanatical, obsessive and compulsive sort of strictness about keeping small and rather arbitrary rules just for their own sake. Let us face the fact right away that this unsatisfactory concept of penance, while it had a value at a certain time, is much too limited and much too rigid. It has to a great extent lost all meaning to people in our time, whether for better or for worse. I won't go into the discussion of whether this shows that the people of our time are better or worse than people of other times. But the fact remains that the kind of penitential discipline presupposed by a series of formal and rigid little observances has ceased to have any meaning to modern people.

A person who had bought this concept of life felt that in doing all these things he was being a real "penitent" and "denying himself." And yet they were comparatively easy to do. It was to some extent simply an act, playing a penitential role. Of course it was not all that easy. Some of the penitential things were really a hardship. For example, the old rules about clothing when you had to sleep in all your habit even in the hottest nights of summer. There was all the paraphernalia of the old habit with the rather complicated and heavy underwear we used to have. You really were hot in that dormitory cell sleeping in all those clothes! You knew that it was summer! That was a trying and exacting and difficult thing to do and it required a lot of resolution and a lot of prayer! It meant a certain amount of anguish—the business of having prickly heat all summer long with no relief possible from it. You just couldn't get away from prickly heat because you just never stopped sweating and there was no way to be dry for more than ten seconds. You just never dried out.

Well, without going on with this, you can see that this refinement of discipline in matters of petty regulations is no longer adequate as a Christian idea of penance, even though it may be difficult, even though it may be demanding. This is not the right approach. Experience has taught us that this simply no longer really works. We still have in our communities many excellent people who have been formed by this kind of practice, and we admire these people very much; but we also have people who have been broken and twisted and distorted by this kind of practice. We instinctively feel that they did not come to the cloister just to be deformed in this particular kind of way, and therefore this dehumanizing concept of penance is insufficient. It does not come near the demand of the New Testament idea of penance. The distinction is this: the old idea of penance that I've been talking about is a limited one, very demanding within a small area but not really going very deep. It is external and, in a certain sense, it's easier—it's kind of an evasion of the real penance of giving up ourselves. Is it real self-sacrifice or is it only will training? It may be purifying up to a point, but it leaves intact the inmost ego, and a person can be really strict in this kind of penance and remain very proud and harsh and extremely uncharitable. A cruel, aggressive and vindictive kind of person can flourish on this kind of penance. Real penance is aimed at the deep root of pride and the deep root of uncharitableness. Real penance aims at that vindictiveness and that persecuting mentality which so many of these strict people developed in the past.

But we must not go to the other extreme. That we now in the monastic life or the cloistered life or the contemplative life are simply throwing away all these practices and living in a kind of freedom of spirit without any real discipline is fatal. There is no hope of any good coming out of this. It will only destroy monasticism. The freedom that we are looking for must never be considered a kind of mere spontaneous following of natural tendencies, innocent natural feelings, and so forth. This idea of mere personal fulfillment, a more or less natural fulfillment of spontaneous good instincts and desires, is not good enough. If there is real charity present, if you have real honest-to-goodness community relationships in which there is real love, certainly this will do an enormous amount—but you can't have this without real self-denial; and the problem is, of course, to what extent real love is found in these relationships which, perhaps, are sought for and pointed to as the solution. To what extent are they really love and to what extent are they mere gregariousness, vapid togetherness? We cannot be content with a superficial chumminess and euphoria, the kind of cheerfulness which depends on having a good time. We have been at this kind of thing for a couple of years, and I think we are beginning to see the insufficiency of a community life in which there is a great deal of chumminess and a certain amount of openness and also a lot of confusion. Community means more than people propping each other up in a desperate kind of way. It means more than interminable talking and interminable wandering around looking for something that brings joy. This is not going to do the trick.

Basically there is only one Christian freedom, which is the freedom of the cross. It is the freedom that comes for one who has completely given himself with Christ on the cross, has risen with Christ and has his freedom—not simply in ordinary human spontaneity but in the spontaneity of the Spirit of God, who is given to us in exchange for our own spirit when and if we die on the cross with Christ. The pattern of the monastic life is a real death and resurrection, and for us especially there is this element of a real death to the world, to the ordinary life that we would otherwise be living as Christians or as active apostles. Whatever we call our life, cloistered or contemplative or monastic, it does imply a real break and therefore a real liberation, by a kind of death, from the claims and demands of a highly distracted and confused life in the world, although this, of course, may have a few Christian dimensions of its own. It might even be more Christian than our life. In certain circumstances it might be, but the fact remains that in response to the call of God we have made this real break and sought this real liberation from the whole network of needs, servitudes and demands which secular life imposes on people. There is no real freedom in our life without this death and resurrection—without this clean break.

Our freedom is by no means simply a removal of obstacles which permits us to fulfill our best natural aspirations. That has to be perfectly clear. We do not come to the cloister simply to become artists or to become musicians or to make friends with other people. We do not come to the cloister for the expansion of a merely human existence because that can be done much better somewhere else. The real expansion of human existence in that kind of dimension is to be sought in married life. We do not come to the cloister to find the same kind of fulfillment and expansion of our human character and personality as we would find in marriage or in a creative secular existence, a professional career in the world. We come here for a specific and precise aim, which is a special kind of transformation in Christ and a special kind of transformation in the Spirit. The root of our penance is not at all just the embracing of ascetical routine. We come here for transformation, to be transformed not by simple convent discipline or by monastic ascetic practices. We come here to be transformed by the Spirit. We do not bring to the cloister or to the solitude of the monastery or the woods simply our own personality and our own aspirations, plus a set of ascetic tools that we're going to work with to make ourselves more perfect. The idea that one remains essentially oneself and in command of oneself, and simply uses ascetic techniques to become more perfect, is essentially misleading. It leads to a wrong concept of penance, which is really no penance at all. It is mere willful rigidity without any transformation.

We come to the cloister to surrender ourselves to Christ and to his Spirit in a kind of death in order to live again in a life which he gives us. The freedom that we seek in the cloister is the freedom to be open to the new life which comes from Christ, the freedom to follow his Spirit. We seek a virginal freedom to follow the bridegroom wherever he goes, to be attentive to his every inspiration and to listen to the personal message that he has for us. This can come to us from no other source except from him speaking in our hearts. The institution of a certain kind of strict cloistered and solitary life is aimed precisely to protect this inner atmosphere of silence, listening and freedom in which Christ can do in us the work he wishes to do.

The root of our penance is faith. The root of our life of *metanoia* is a real faith in Christ, a real faith in our vocation, a real faith in the transforming power of the cross, a faith in God's promises, a faith that if we give up ourselves and our ambitions, even our spiritual ambitions, if we deliver ourselves utterly and totally into the hands of Christ and to his love, we will indeed be transformed in his time, in his way, by his Spirit. Not in our time, not in our way, and not by our own spirit.

We do not come here to be transformed by our own will and our own spirit. We come here to make this complete surrender in faith. Whether we go by the old way or by the new way, this faith is radically and urgently and critically the most important thing. This is what we have to cultivate and this is what we have, above all, to pray for.

Prayer for Faith

So I would say, the root of renewal for our life implies renewal in the spheres of prayer and of penance. We do not yet know exactly in what this renewal will consist. These are the things that we have to discover collectively and individually by a real cooperative search under the guidance of the Holy Spirit. But the root of it all for all of us is prayer for faith. We must pray to the Lord at every moment to increase our faith because the root of renewal is faith. In proportion as we grow in faith, we keep closer and closer to him who has called us. In proportion as our faith develops, it gives us the vision by which we can see our errors, and we can see the wrong road, instinctively. By our faith we will come to a closer union with Christ, a deeper dependence on him so that he will be able to guide us through the difficulties, the obstacles, the confusions and the errors that we are likely to meet in this way of renewal. So prayer for faith is absolutely the most fundamental thing, and we must not forget how great is the power of God to give us what we need, and in the most surprising ways. For example, I just had a letter from a person who claimed that she had been an atheist for quite some time. She is a young married woman, evidently baptized a Catholic in childhood and brought up perhaps as a Catholic. She could see no logical reason for the existence of God. People had been trying to prove to her the existence of God and it made no impression on her whatever. All this had no meaning whatever to her and she simply could not believe in God. Until all of a sudden one day, instead of arguing with her, some priest said, "Look, God wants your heart, not your mind: God loves you!" All of a sudden this whole thing collapsed and there broke through into her heart the sense of who God really is and what he really meant to her. She saw how desperately she needed this God who loved her, who was calling her to accept his love and to love him in return. The whole reality of the thing just simply burst through, whereas arguments about the existence of God and intellectual discussion of God, and so forth, had meant nothing. So it is with us. We get so involved in all these intellectual and abstract discussions that we forget the basic—this call of God's love to us, urging us to love him in return and to open our hearts to him and to give him our hearts so that he may fill them with love and faith. So let us then do this. Let us pray for faith, let us pray for an increase of faith and give ourselves, totally, completely, and with perfect confidence, to the God who loves us and calls us to his love.

In closing, let me quote a sentence from Clement of Alexandria which I just happened to turn up in some notes here. Comparing the Christian to Ulysses on his ship as he traveled in his journey homeward, he speaks of how Ulysses escaped the lure of the sirens by being tied to the mast of his vessel. This has traditionally been a kind of image of the soul resisting the allurements of what does not really concern it. Clement of Alexandria compares the Christian to Ulysses bound to the mast. It is a good image of our life and its restrictions. He says:

> Bound to the wood of a cross, thou art free from all danger of destruction. God's Logos will steer thy ship and the Holy Pneuma or the Holy Spirit will give thee a safe return to heaven's harbor.

So let us consider our own lives in the light of this image and, trusting God, remain bound to the wood of the cross; so that dying with Christ and rising with him we may be brought to union with him forever in heaven by his Holy Spirit.